Legal Feminism

Legal Feminism

Activism, Lawyering, and Legal Theory

Ann Scales

NEW YORK UNIVERSITY PRESS
New York and London

NEW YORK UNIVERSITY PRESS
New York and London
www.nyupress.org

Library of Congress Cataloging-in-Publication Data
Scales, Ann.
Legal feminism : activism, lawyering, and legal theory / Ann Scales.
p. cm.
Includes bibliographical references and index.
ISBN-13: 978-0-8147-9845-4 (cloth : alk. paper)
ISBN-10: 0-8147-9845-4 (cloth : alk. paper)
1. Feminist jurisprudence. 2. Sex and law. 3. Feminist jurisprudence—United States. 4. Women—Legal status, laws, etc.—United States. I. Title.
K349.S296 2006
340'.115082—dc22 2005037590

New York University Press books are printed on acid-free paper, and their binding materials are chosen for strength and durability.

Manufactured in the United States of America

10 9 8 7 6 5 4 3 2 1

In memory of Elizabeth Randel Scales, 1918–1992

Contents

Acknowledgments

Many people have helped in many ways with this book. Judge Robert Henry of the United States Court of Appeals for the Tenth Circuit instigated the project and encouraged me to reach out to judges. The University of Denver College of Law provided summer research support that made it possible to do this, rather than other work.

Diane Burkhardt and the staff of the University of Denver College of Law library have been wonderfully responsive, thorough, and prompt. The same is true of my research assistants, Matthew Linton, Dara Lum, Lukas Staks, and Keelin Griffin. The students in my Advanced Jurisprudence seminar in the spring of 2005 read an earlier draft, commented extensively, and identified exemplars of the ideas I address. My friend and former colleague Jane Caputi read an earlier draft, and provided invaluable insight about what nonlawyers needed to benefit from this book. My editor, Deborah Gershenowitz, kept me on track and provided cheerful confidence that I could not have mustered on my own. Finally, Laura Spitz has been tirelessly generous in the editing of the text and discussion of the ideas. Thanks to all of you. Errors and misjudgments are my own.

Introduction

Whatever happened to legal feminism? Has it done any good? What is it or was it? It is still around? Does it have a future? Perhaps these questions could be answered in a linear way, but I am better equipped to address them inside out, from the point of view of a founding mother, so to speak.

I started my career as a feminist lawyer in 1978, was a ground-floor participant in what came to be known as "feminist jurisprudence,"[1] and am said by some to have invented the term.[2] I taught law from 1980 until 1998, during which time feminist legal theory took off. It was never a monolithic movement, but it was possible in those early years—more or less—to chart the competing versions of legal feminism, and even possible—more or less—to place specific authors and activists on that chart. Professor Martha Chamallas has provided a reliable history of that time,[3] showing how the liberal feminism of the 1970s was joined in the 1980s by cultural feminism and radical feminism, sometimes called "dominance feminism," a dramatic turn that is indelibly associated with the work of Professor Catharine A. MacKinnon. The 1990s saw the emergence of more versions of feminism and what Professor Chamallas calls "allied intellectual movements," notably Critical Race Theory and queer theory.[4]

As more voices joined the debate, it got pretty raucous. Even though there were sharp disagreements and discomforts, those were heady days. Most of the feminist jurisprudes knew one another, talked with one another, and kept track of one anothers' work. Some of us had been associated with Critical Legal Studies, the most innovative jurisprudential movement of the 1970s, and some of us became prominent Critical Race Theorists. In the 1980s and for part of the 1990s, the Crits, the Fem-Crits, the Race-Crits and the emerging Queer-Crits were almost familial in both our affections and our disputes.

Now, it is not as if we are a broken family. Rather, time has moved on, divisions and disputes have proliferated, and it is just not possible to know everyone as well as we did when I knew who "we" were. Insofar as I became disenchanted with the collective enterprise, it was a result of exhaustion and grief.

I was shattered by the 1991 murder of Professor Mary Joe Frug. That murder in Cambridge, Massachusetts, generated national attention for two reasons. First, it was considered a "classic whodunit," and is still unsolved, even though police searching for a motive went to the trouble of learning about feminist jurisprudence and poring over the transcripts of Mary Joe's former students.[5] Second, after the *Harvard Law Review* published an unfinished, obviously unpolished, and not fully baked article by Mary Joe, some of that law review's editors produced a vicious parody of the article on the anniversary of her death.[6] I happened to be at Harvard for a gathering in Mary Joe's memory the morning after the parody became public. It was a toxic experience. That parody provoked cries for punishment of the editors (which never happened), and became part of another public meltdown at the Harvard Law School. Mary Joe herself became lost in the controversy. I shouldn't have been surprised that Harvard law faculty and students managed to make it *all about them*.[7]

That was awful, but not as awful as losing her. I told Mary Joe that she was like a golden retriever on speed. Not only did she have the salient strawberry-blond big hair; she was *that* loving, *that* engaged, and *that* energetic. Many of her friends and colleagues would agree, I think, that she was the glue for lots of conversations. She got the Crits to listen to the Fem-Crits. She put the Fem-Crits and the Race-Crits in the same room. Famously, she got our friend Professor Drucilla Cornell to sit down and explain, word for word, taking as long as it took, a single paragraph from a postmodernist text. Mary Joe Frug was always the last person awake at a conference, and always the first person to discover a new voice and make it central to the next discussion. When we lost Mary Joe, a lot of the collaborative fun of what had been feminist jurisprudence was also lost, at least for me.

Of course I experienced the fun-leaching only gradually. When I was financially able, in 1998, I took a break from academic life in a big way, by giving up my tenure at the University of New Mexico Law School. Thereafter, I practiced law a bit, lived in Canada for a while, and though I taught a few courses on an adjunct basis, I assiduously did not pay attention to the intellectual agenda of the legal academy. Some academic acquaintances told me later that they thought I was dead, too.

Various familial, financial, and intellectual considerations brought me back into full-time law teaching in 2003. Upon my return to the academy, it seemed to me that much of feminist jurisprudence had gone missing at the same time that I had gone missing. Before my disappearance, I was already a bit grumpy about what I regarded as the encroaching domestication of feminist legal theory, the dulling of some of the sharpest edges.[8] Sure enough, as of my reentry, I discovered that we were in a "postfeminist" age.

For example, in the spring of 2005, I attended a conference built around the topic of Professor Janet Halley's admonition that it is time to "take a break from feminism."[9] I shall have more to say about why that is a bad idea, and much more to say about what it might be—this legal feminism thing that some believe we should take a break from. In the meantime, however, I would underline the assumption in Halley's injunction: taking a break from feminism assumes there is some influential group that has actually embraced something called legal feminism to such an extent that anyone could meaningfully take a breather from it.

The postfeminist imperative stands in stark contrast to official ignorance. In 2002, just as I was considering reentry into the academic realm, the Honorable Robert Henry of the United States Court of Appeals for the Tenth Circuit invited me to speak to a plenary session of that court's judicial conference. The topic assigned to me was "law and feminism," and I had ten whole minutes to address the issue. My comments were intentionally mild and elementary,[10] but the response I got from every other judge at that conference boiled down to this: I was a representative of just another whiny interest group who wanted its subjective preferences enshrined in law.

I could say that the judges of the Tenth Circuit—as well as almost all other judges in the United States—have taken a break from feminism, but that would be an odd way to put it. That which was never fully understood or embraced cannot be abandoned. What I've observed upon returning to law teaching is a disjunction between theory and practice that surpasses anything I had previously experienced. It is that disjunction that provokes me to write this book.

I intend to take the reader back to some feminist basics, via discussion of the problems that make judges identify people like me as representatives of whiny subjectively inclined interest groups. I hope that my reiteration of the problems of jurisprudence and the ways feminism can assist with them will be enlivening. At least one judge thinks so. In discussing the highly exposed "disjunction" between judges and legal academics,[11] Judge Henry opined that decision makers could use a de-jargonized account of why legal theory, and feminist legal theory in particular, should matter to them. All that account needed to be, he said, was graspable, fascinating, and nonthreatening.

So, this is a book about legal theory for theoreticians and nontheoreticians alike. More precisely, this is a book that seeks to steer away from the problems lawyers invite when we imagine that legal theory is separate from what lawyers do. Equally, it is a book that seeks to steer legal theory back toward feminism, focusing particularly on the pragmatic and political promise in doing so. Thus, this is also a book about lawyering—structuring approaches, being a responsible legal actor, and even avoiding malpractice.

Does She Have to Use the T-Word?

Theory is not popular among lawyers and judges. They typically pride themselves on their practicality. Clients must be served, dockets must be moved. In the professionalist view, there is neither time nor patience for academic gobbledygook. If you want to know whether this judicial district allows motions to be filed by fax, your time will not be well spent by looking to Kant's *Critique of Pure Reason.* Usually, lawyers sharply distinguish between experience and theory, celebrate only the former, and are content to let law rest on its own internally generated standards and justifications.

I want to reclaim for feminism the wisdom in that stance, without devolving into complacency. An enterprise is practical if it is appropriately evaluated by its successes and failures in worldly application, rather than by the satisfaction it provides upon quiet contemplation, or even by the votes it secures during a race for tenure. This is also part of what theoreticians mean by referring to an enterprise as "instrumental." Law is the exemplar of an instrumental discipline. Even if it has some value in itself, it is primarily a means to an end or ends. The problems arise, of course, when we seek agreement on what the ends are or should be. Feminism is all about informing that debate.

Even to begin that debate is relatively new in jurisprudence. My students are, understandably from their twenty-first-century point of view, incredulous when I tell them that in the longest part of intellectual history to date, the law was considered a self-contained discipline that proceeded according to fixed, objective rules. The maxim *fiat lex, pereat mundi* (let law exist though the world perish), etched in marble above many a courthouse door, is to them a matter for beery Friday evening amusement and/or another reason not to study Latin.

In the twentieth century, a movement called Legal Realism retired the notion—permanently, one hopes—that the law is a self-contained enterprise. Legal Realism was a complex movement,[12] but it stood at least for the propositions that law is elastic, interdependent with politics, and interdisciplinary by nature. Law is about the rest of society, and works only when tuned to social experiences. So thoroughly absorbed are these lessons that no one can even recall who first said, "We are all Realists now."[13]

Not all lawyers find their intellectual history as inherently fascinating as I do. Indeed, although it is not possible, to paraphrase Professor David Luban, for lawyers simply to stipulate the philosophical implications of their work out of existence,[14] theory is not compulsory study for lawyers. Four reasons to be familiar with legal theory, however, underlie this book. First, when they are lucky enough to have interesting work, lawyers will likely have to make choices that are theory-laden. Becoming conscious about the theoretical context of those choices will make those choices better. Ideas win cases. As Justice Holmes said, "[Theory] is not to be feared as being impractical, for, to the competent, it simply means going to the bottom of a subject. . . . To an imagination of any scope the most far-reaching form of power is not money, it is the command of ideas."[15]

Second and relatedly, philosophical inquiry incites doubt. Doubt causes a person to examine his presuppositions, and that is a good thing, if only as a matter of intellectual hygiene. Theoretical competence, in Judge Richard Posner's phrase, helps us to "clear the underbrush" in analyses of legal problems.[16]

Third, people that I care about really do care about the questions addressed by legal theory. Law students worry about possible connections between law and justice. Lawyers wonder whether their work matters. Judges feel that they walk a fine line of legitimacy, and some agonize about it. It can't hurt any of us to have a sense of where these concerns fit into legal thinking, and to have a vocabulary to address them.

Fourth, I don't believe there is a meaningful split between theory and practice. Concrete and stable legal successes are grounded, consciously or not, on theoretical foundations. If theories don't work in practice, they are not very good theories. The habit of dividing theory from practice eventually impoverishes professional life and the law itself. Moreover, when lawyers cease to think of their enterprise as theoretically grounded, therefore impervious to change from theoretical critique, they systematically harm groups who weren't part of creating legal codes in the first place.

Theoretical pursuits were expanding dramatically right at the time I entered law school. The jurisprudence of Critical Legal Studies was being built by the people who were teaching me contracts and legal history and jurisprudence. As noted earlier, I was blessed to be there to help build what came to be known as feminist jurisprudence. Since then, theoretical contestation among legal academics has become ever more intense.

Having said that, and having happily been around for a great deal of the brouhaha, I would be hard-pressed to identify any dominant intellectual agenda in the legal academy. There is still plenty of talk about postmodernism, law and society, law and economics, and now "the new realism." However, these are diffuse movements, if movements they can be called, and none present anything like a united front. In terms of influence on the profession, Professor Thomas Grey has observed that each of the existing jurisprudential approaches

> challenges others as defective, and partly as a result, they tend to cancel each other out, leaving the effective triumph to the ever-present professional default option: law is law, an autonomous activity with its own self-justifying standards of internal reflection and deliberation—"thinking like a lawyer."[17]

I think the lack of an intellectual agenda is itself dangerous, because it leads to that professional default position, and encourages unexamined self-interest among lawyers and judges.

Does She Have to Use the F-Word?

I am therefore asserting that feminist legal theory can make a difference all over again. Some might think it is an awkward time for me to be doing so, or that I am thoughtlessly rendering myself ineffective. For example, in 2003, after the Tenth Circuit gig, I gave a talk to another group of judges about the application of feminist method to adjudication. I was honored when an eminent state court judge, notably well-read and progressive, stayed after my talk for a discussion. My lecture, she said, admirably addressed how good judges actually approach their most difficult challenges. Why then, she asked, would I contaminate my own message by labeling it as "feminist?" Why be so unnecessarily contentious?

My first thought, I'll admit, was to think of one of my heroes, Will Rogers, who said, "I'm not a member of any organized party—I'm a Democrat."[18] It is true that feminism has a tumultuous history, complex contested meanings, and conflicted constituencies. The judge in the conversation was giving the critics of feminism every benefit of every doubt. I should have engaged her in a different mode: all of the contention and complexity in feminist theory makes it more mature, and more interesting. The bottom line is this: lawyers and judges have lots to learn about law from feminism, their outspoken resistance notwithstanding.[19]

Among the most intriguing lessons of legal feminism is how the mere use of the "f-word" discredits a point of view. Ordinarily I resist the requirement that every feminist on every occasion has to explain feminism again. I'm always tempted to say, "I'm only going to tell you this one more time." But that is what I will do, shortly. The second half of this book engages the specific contributions of feminist legal theory to jurisprudence, particularly in response to the problems that I describe in the first half.

In the meantime, however, at least to postpone contamination, perhaps I should provide an abbreviated map of the field in which I'm operating. At the risk of beginning on a negative note, it is critical to state what, in my view, feminist work is *not.* It not produced only by women or something that all women produce. In law, it is informed by but not confined to issues that are historically and socially of particular concern to women, such as reproduction, rape, prostitution, "domestic violence," pornography, pay equity, sexual harassment, and the legal creation and dissolution of the "family." Finally, though gendered lenses can illuminate new aspects of almost any legal problem, the feminism I practice is not reductionist: I don't believe that all social problems are created by gender inequality or solvable by gender equality.

Starting from the positively descriptive side, feminist work is the study and practice of all that follows from the proposition that women are people. That sounds simple, but it leads to a number of insights that, I believe, provoke the charge that feminism is too contentious. This includes the observation that women have historically been understood as "women" while men were understood as "people." That is why merely to call work "feminist" is to risk dilution of its importance. The historical norm was to identify only half of the world's population with humanity and rationality. This genderization has systematic negative effects on women as women, on men as men, and on the multitudinous aspirations of the human species.

To divide the world that way is to embrace partiality as universality, hence systematically and intentionally to misunderstand how partialities constitute the whole. It degrades every person and every community. Gender literacy is among the most serious pro-life work that anyone can undertake. The charge of contentiousness flows from daring to name gender hierarchy as something other than natural and neutral. To me, this is not "male-bashing"; it is both male- and female-liberating.

Positively, the feminism I know is concrete, antiessentialist, contextual, instrumental, eclectic, and open-minded. It is concrete because it grew from and answers to the real experiences of subordination caused both to women and men by gender hierarchy. It does not depend on any transcendental moral principle, unless a commitment to equality is that. Indeed, the feminism of which I speak is antifoundationalist, a concept developed in chapter 2, because it recognizes that foundationalist explanations usually are excuses for social inequalities. The feminism of which I write is antiessentialist because not only is point-of-view the primary referent for social action but point-of-view is itself an elastic and contextual phenomenon. All of the ways that each of us participates in our various identities are constituted by historical, cultural, and individual practices. The sources of essentialism are beyond feminist control. Existing modes of power attempt to essentialize our identities, the better to capture each and every new incarnation as a market niche. My feminism is built from resistance to that.

This feminism partakes in a great tradition of viewing law as an instrumental enterprise. Law is not a fixed mirror of human rationality but a flawed and fluid means to various human ends. Feminist scholarship and advocacy aim to expand upon legal goals and map paths to their achievement. We have to be eclectic, using ideas derived from many sources. We have to be prepared to revise our beliefs and strategies when necessary because experience is too complex to be captured by any reductionist or rigid approach.

Maybe it is just the "f-word" that puts people off. There are alternatives to the term "feminism." Most likely for me would be "antisubordination theory,"[20] referring to the set of movements that focus on how law constructs and maintains hierarchical power relations on the bases of race, sex, ethnicity, class, sexual orientation, gender status, disability, or, importantly, any synergistic combinations of discriminations, whether experienced at present or arising in the future.

Feminism is certainly part of antisubordination theory or vice versa. I don't think I get any persuasive mileage out of using the term "antisubordination theory," however, because it, too, is oppositional: it leads to the naming of who has power and who doesn't and why that is not neutral and natural. Moreover, it would be a slight misrepresentation of my own credentials, coming as I do from the feminist wing. If there is any truism to emerge from antisubordination theory, it is the necessity to attend to dissimilarities between and among experiences of subordination. Perhaps I should dance with them that brung me, with awareness of the broader implications of antisubordination theory.

Another semantic candidate to substitute for feminism is "gender mainstreaming."[21] It is the term for the commitment by the European Commission and almost every member state of the European Union to go beyond equal treatment guarantees and attention to specific "women's issues" toward a new vision of sex equality. My hat is off to all of the European feminists, race critical scholars, antiviolence specialists, and environmentalists who are pushing and pulling, inch by inch, with astonishing patience to make the European vision real. "Gender mainstreaming" has much to commend it in scope and intention but may be insufficiently oppositional. We shall see whether its proponents will be able to keep the bureaucracy from transforming it into happy-face feminism, a practice devoid of fire, fury, and respect for our foremothers.

For now I will just emphasize that everything I know about practicing law, teaching law, and theorizing about law is what I have learned by studying feminism and participating in the feminist legal project. I cannot believe that mine was a singular intellectual journey, nor that it is a path now unavailable to those who want to understand more about the common enterprise of doing law. Moreover, I believe that the ideas tested and contested in the feminist project have reached a state of maturity and pervasiveness to have already become a solid part of the competent lawyer's intellectual repertoire. The day may not be too far off when no one can remember who first said, "We are all feminists now."

Organization of Book

This book does not jump into feminism right away. Rather, it is organized according to the steps of the journey that a thoughtful student will likely encounter as she attempts to fit the enterprise of law with other considerations of knowledge, ethics, and politics.

In asserting that feminist legal theory provides guidance, I believe that it is important to first set out the problems, and the typically false solutions that lawyers are likely to encounter. No professional dispositions, arguments, or philosophical fashions can simply catapult the law beyond these problems. The most basic issues—including metaphysical ones—keep cropping up. So, before directly introducing the insights of feminist legal theory, I mean to situate the reader among the problems that any jurisprudential approach must assist in solving, or must provide justification for ignoring. Understanding the issues, creating a personal economy to name and deal with them, is fundamental to doing better. These are the questions that make our brew yeasty or flat; acknowledging and grappling with them makes the difference.

Thus, the book begins with the broadest inquiry, what is "the Rule of Law"? We're engaged in a common enterprise that seems to be more than the sum of its parts, more than just the rules and the elements of causes of action that are memorized in the first year of law school. It may be useful to step back and consider what the common enterprise in service of "the Rule of Law" might be. There are many ways of understanding it, some that will be comfortable for most lawyers, and some that will pressure lawyers to think more about the ideal of "justice."

In chapter 2, I turn to the question of doubt, its pervasiveness, and the historical range of responses to it. This very broad inquiry is necessary—and I cannot give this notion enough emphasis—because responsible lawyering and judging are in large part about *doubt tolerance.* Lawyers must constantly calibrate various aspects of uncertainty in our work, for two reasons. First, certainty is impossible. Second, and more important, reckless or habitual claims to certainty are a brutal means of dissolving the fragile bonds of trust that constitute the rule of law.

The next two chapters concern the inadequacies in the default professional position. Chapter 3 insists that, as much as lawyers may resist it, law is a metaphysical enterprise. In particular, that chapter is an extended reflection upon the metaphysical implications—and delusions—generated by claims to legal "facts." Nature doesn't disclose facts once and for all. Rather, language users establish what counts as a "fact" by contextual and purposive means. Chapter 4 explains the philosophical context—classical Liberalism—that has for so long made it OK for lawyers not to have to think beyond the immediate interests of themselves and their clients. In that chapter, I introduce feminist notions in contrast to habitual modes of liberalism.

Stated differently, the first four chapters locate typical intellectual and emotional refuges from the responsibilities imposed by engagement with the law. Some take refuge in institutional constraints (The Rule of Law). Some take refuge in radical skepticism (Certainty and Doubt). Some take refuge in "the facts," particularly as "proven" by "science" (Intractable Questions). Law school teaches that there is refuge in radical individualistic proceduralism (The Limits of Liberalism). I hope to show that we can run to, but cannot hide behind, these shadows.

In the second half of the book, I turn to the theoretical and methodological contributions of legal feminism, those precepts and practices that I believe have already found their ways into successful lawyering and judging of all manner of legal problems. Chapters 5 and 6 are substantially recast versions of articles I have previously published.[22] Chapter 5 is theoretical in the sense that it asks the reader to suspend his point of view, and to try specific different ways of thinking about legal problems. Chapter 6 attempts to locate exact junctures in judgment that can be self-defeating, and to suggest specific different ways of analyzing those critical junctures. Chapters 5 and 6 concern bad habits of legal reasoning, and attempt to inculcate more productive habits.

Chapter 7 is about delusion, and the ways that varieties of delusion preclude social progress. That chapter is titled "False Consciousness" because that is a specific term that has in past debates—quite unnecessarily—reduced the momentum of legal feminist progress. A general analysis of delusion, I believe, is necessary in a postliberal, postmodern, postfoundationalist world. If individual perceptions and preferences aren't the answer to all social problems, how can that be conveyed, and how can anyone go about describing any alternatives?

Chapter 8 explores the future of legal feminism by engaging poststructuralist/postmodernist/postfeminist challenges to it, in the context of ongoing legal disputes. In that chapter, I list many points of agreement between feminists and postfeminists, in pursuit of finding more productive ways of discussion.

Content of Book

Up front, I need to note four things about the content of this book. First, I use the collective pronoun "we" many times. In most of those usages, I believe that the context illuminates the group referent, such as "we lawyers." In other cases, the "we" refers to the collectivity of author and readers, those of us who are engaging with the words I've put on paper. I have tried not to assume agreement from readers, nor any characteristics of readers that implicitly belittle their points of view. Most controversially, I sometimes use the pronoun "we" to refer to groups of people substantively affected by law because of group status. Those "we's" are the groups with whom I identify: women, lesbians, "outsiders," feminist lawyers working together since the 1970s, children of the 1960s, and political progressives. Those groupings are not to essentialize anyone or any groups of people but to indicate my belief that group statuses are real. Any groups may be constituted only provisionally, but various groups are also treated differently and often cruelly. Nothing that I can say about law or social progress makes sense unless the reader will allow for the social reality of groups and some established linguistic shortcuts to discuss them.

Second, the main focus of my jurisprudential discussion is adjudication, both actual cases decided by courts and the criteria by which courts go about making such decisions and maintaining at least the appearance of legitimacy in doing so. Though this focus on adjudication is very much in the mainstream of Anglo-American jurisprudential literature, I agree with other scholars who say that we tend to weigh adjudication too heavily among legal institutions. At the same time, though I've been a drafter of legislation, a legislative witness, and a participant in a wide array of political actions, my primary field is adjudication. I probably couldn't write a share-purchase agreement to save my life, but

I know how to litigate cases and I enjoy working on those that have a chance of making law better.

Being a child of professors of history and government during the Warren Court era meant that the characters in my bedtime stories were more likely to be named Thurgood than Thumper. Perhaps those happy memories are what lead me to agree with Richard Rorty that, as our executive and legislative branches become "ever more corrupt and frivolous," the judiciary is the only political institution for which we can still "feel something like awe."[23]

Third, this book makes many references to the work of Professor Catharine A. MacKinnon. Some helpers have suggested that those references alone could put readers off. Before critics dismiss the book solely on that ground, I would ask them to consider why they would do so. Even those who vehemently disagree with MacKinnon must acknowledge that much contemporary legal theory is inspired by her work or transpires in (sometimes saliva-sputtering) response to her work. As a purely academic matter, it is distressing to me how MacKinnon has been caricatured. I have observed, again and again, how often MacKinnon's critics have not read her writings, or not read them with care, or have failed to reread those works as circumstances required. I will leave to a later time why MacKinnon inspires as much hatred as admiration. One doesn't have to agree with everything MacKinnon says. Rather, one needs to understand, paraphrasing Alfred North Whitehead's characterization of European philosophy as a series of footnotes to Plato, that much of contemporary United States jurisprudence is connected to MacKinnon. No serious treatment of feminist legal theory can fail to engage her work.

Fourth, although perhaps I write about courts too much, I write too little about what U.S. lawyers, judges, and teachers can learn from other countries. To the rest of the world, the United States appears both insular and imperialistic, and that is true jurisprudentially as well as in more dire and dramatic contexts. Judges in other countries, less directly affected by U.S. military and commercial might than other actors, have the institutional freedom to reject our analyses and calcified assumptions.[24] I have no nationalist stake in being a jurisprudential beacon to the world, but I am embarrassed by both the rate at which the U.S. legal system makes itself irrelevant to the rest of the world and the degree of indifference U.S. lawyers and judges show toward catching up. More important, in our self-absorption we are undoubtedly spinning our wheels, acting both inefficiently and unjustly when there alternative ways of implementing "the Rule of Law." I'm trying to absorb information and inspiration from elsewhere; my next project will be more directly concerned with those lessons.

Some years ago, a Super Shuttle van took me to the San Francisco airport. Airport trips are not anyone's favorite activity. On this one, though, traffic delayed us on Lombard Street, billed as the steepest, windiest road in North America. The stalled van felt as if it were perpendicular to the earth. The otherwise silent driver said, "At least we're doing something interesting."

Law school is a special hell of anxious drudgery. Many lawyers would not wish their fate on their children. I've heard more than one judge wish out loud for a unique case and/or the company of talented counsel. Though part of this system, I feel lucky to be a teacher, to take only the cases I wish to take, and to be genuinely enthralled by the kinds of ideas addressed in this book. I can't promise the reader Lombard Street, but I hope to provide something of interest, and to transmit a bit of my keenness for these topics.

PART I

Places of Stuckness

Roles, Rules, Facts, and the Liberal View of Human Nature

1

The Rule of Law

Conscience is but a word that cowards use,
Devised at first to keep the strong in awe:
Our strong arms be our conscience, swords our law.
March on, join bravely, let us to't pell-mell;
If not to heaven, then hand in hand to hell.

—William Shakespeare, *King Richard III*

There is no concept more central to the American experiment than the "rule of law." We all somehow accept it as the cornerstone of the republic. The rule of law comes to us, seemingly, in mother's milk. Given its centrality, it is interesting how little agreement there is about its meaning.[1]

I've contributed to this conventional lack of examination. For example, during the summer preceding President Nixon's resignation in 1974, I was seated at a shipboard table with an Italian gentleman. At every meal, he pressed me to explain why Americans were so agitated. Government, he said, was all about corruption and scandal and cover-ups and moving on to the next government. Could Americans really be so naive and/or so self-righteous? I had just graduated from college but hadn't learned how exactly to respond to his persistent questioning about the nature and excesses of government. Eventually, however, the magical term leapt to my lips: even the President, I said, had to be subject to the rule of law. I stuck to some version of that utterance for the rest of the voyage. The Nixon saga required no further justification from me. Nixon was not criminally indicted, and didn't need to be impeached because he resigned. It was as if Nixon himself and all the rest of us (including a unanimous Supreme Court)[2] were following a script learned in junior high school. It was as if we all knew what the rule of law was, what it required, and how it might be damaged if Nixon had refused to listen to the Supreme Court.

That worked out relatively smoothly, but I've subsequently realized how often the phrase "rule of law" substitutes for serious discussion of the most basic question of jurisprudence. What does it mean for an utterance to be called "law"? Is it just any old thing that a legislature or king says? Perhaps a simplified spectrum can convey the problem. On one extreme, was Richard III right that law is just the sword of cowards, or those who cannot otherwise win inevitable contests of raw power? On the other end, is law by definition (or only by aspiration) more majestic? Does the ideal of law bring with it—dare I say it—matters of conscience, or morality, or justice? Are there any basic principles conveyed by allegiance to law?

All of the possibilities are implied in contemporary rule of law discourse. Consider three examples. The first is the impeachment and trial of President Clinton, a gavel-to-gavel transcription of what was probably the most extended "rule of law" twaddle in American history. Throughout those proceedings, the term was used more than five hundred times, almost equally by proponents and opponents of impeachment.[3] Among proponents of impeachment, Representative Stephen Buyer (R-Indiana) contrasted the rule of law to the rule of "kings, tyrants, czars, monarchs, emperors, chiefs, sheiks, lords, barons and lords [*sic*] and even nobles." As applied to the case at hand, which rested largely upon the President's alleged perjury in a civil deposition, Representative Buyer stated that the rule of law is absent "[w]hen plain spoken English language is twisted into the vague and ambiguous. . . ."[4] Representative Henry Hyde (R-Illinois), the House Impeachment Manager, intoned that the rule of law "is no pious aspiration from a civics textbook." Rather, it "is like a three-legged stool. One leg is an honest judge, the second leg is an ethical bar, and the third is an enforceable oath."[5]

The President's lawyers, on the other hand, opined that the framers of the Constitution did not intend impeachment to be a means to enforce every conceivable provision of the criminal law. The criminal law could do its business in the ordinary course as necessary, once the President's term expired. In their view, the rule of law argued more forcefully for upholding the results of elections.[6] Crucial to the President's argument was that proportionality is a concept central to the rule of law; to impeach would be a disproportionate response to whatever the President had done.[7] President Clinton was impeached by the House of Representatives, but not convicted on the Articles of Impeachment by the Senate, so was not removed from office. I just wonder whether discussion of the rule of law added anything to the proceedings or to our understanding of the constitutional requirements for removal of a President.

As a second example of recent rule of law rhetoric, consider that the phrase is "enjoying a new run as a rising imperative of the era of globalization."[8] The rule of law is touted as a panacea for a huge range of ills in what commentators used to call "developing nations," but now call "emerging markets." The good news about the rule of law is that "hardly anyone these days will admit to being against [it]."[9] But that very irresistibility may mask a destructive manipulation. Different players are likely to define the rule of law in ways that advance their interests. There is a vast literature about what aspects of the rule of law should be emphasized—and funded—as the United States includes "democracy" among its requirements for foreign policy patronage. It turns out that the export version of the rule of law has more to do with getting other countries to establish courts that will enforce contracts for U.S. investors[10] than it has to do with the equal protection of the laws for citizens of those countries.

Third and finally, the rule of law has recently had exposure both as a reason for war and a reason for lawlessness in war. The original justification for the use of preemptive military force in Iraq in 2003, the elimination of "weapons of mass destruction," has evaporated. That justification may even have been manufactured by latter-day princes of the military-industrial complex. When no weapons of mass destruction were found, the justification for war mutated. The new justification was to bring democracy to the people of Iraq. According to the executive branch, fostering the rule of law is both an essential element of democracy and a means for combating terror.[11]

At the same time, the rule of law seems not to apply to the liberators. On February 7, 2002, President George W. Bush signed a memorandum declaring that the Geneva conventions, the international law of war achieved in 1949, did not apply to the U.S. invasions of Afghanistan and Iraq, or to the treatment of prisoners taken in those conflicts.[12] It has since emerged that United States military personnel committed grievous abuses of war prisoners.[13] A number of service people are now on trial for these abuses, but it remains to be seen whether any executive branch officials will be charged with war crimes. At least some in that branch have been concerned that such charges are possible.[14] What emerges is a picture of executive actors who, only after public discovery of their actions,[15] are rushing to assign legal blame while having laid the groundwork for exempting themselves from responsibility.

This book is not about political shenanigans or U.S. foreign policy. Examples like these can be taken from the front page of the paper on any morning. In light of examples such as these, though, one wonders whether the "rule of law" means anything. Perhaps, as Professor Judith Shklar suggests, the phrase "has become just another of those self-congratulatory rhetorical devices that grace the public utterances of Anglo-American politicians."[16] Perhaps, whenever you hear the phrase, you could delete the first two words. Is there any difference between the Supreme Court's statement that the President's evidentiary privilege "must be considered in light of our historic commitment to the rule of law,"[17] and an edited version, instead stating that a privilege "must be considered in light of our historic commitment to the law"? Does the rule of law indicate only a logical regress, as if we were to say, "rule number one is to obey the rules," and "rule number two is to obey rule number one"? Is there a rule of the rule of law? Or a rule of the rule of the rule of law?

Some have argued that it is time to junk the rhetoric of the rule of law; I am not prepared to do so. If law is just a fool's game, as Richard III argued before his demise, too much energy has been wasted. Those stakes are too high for me. Law seemed the remedy for my first social heartbreak, when I heard as a kid that the city of Jackson, Mississippi, would rather close all its public swimming pools rather than give access to African-American people.[18] The road away from summer misery in my Oklahoma hometown was the road to the public pool. I did not know then about the complexities and inefficiencies of law, but I did know that I would try to thwart similar efforts of mean-minded control freaks.

I suspect that legal aid lawyers, public interest lawyers, and indeed all lawyers and judges who resist the harmful effects of arbitrary power have a story regarding what originally brought them to their careers. I expect that all of these professionals could articulate coherent distinctions between mere "law" and the "rule of law." It is just that we are not asked; we don't often have occasion to think it through.

Let's start at the beginning of one's legal career. It is still the convention in U.S. law schools to make students buy textbooks containing appellate opinions concerning the subject of the course. The books vary primarily on the ratio of "cases" to "materials," that is, on how much statutory and regulatory stuff the authors throw in, and how much explanatory material and questions for discussion they provide. Some classic cases will always be included, but otherwise there will be some differences among cases in each book. The editing of cases will differ as to both length and coherence.

I've always been amazed by how little explanation the textbooks give for inconsistency among cases. Back-to-back entries on the same topic often have diametrically opposed results. Sometimes the reasons for that are simple, such as origination in different jurisdictions having different laws. Sometimes the cases just come from different eras, and we are accustomed to regarding beliefs from the olden days as loopy. But the average textbook gives little information about why thinking changed, or why legal thinking yields different points of view in the same case (as in majority versus dissenting opinions), or, indeed, what counts as sound legal thinking in the first place. Hence the much-commented-upon mystification of the legal system by the legal education establishment. In my experience, legal education most rewards the students who, usually for reasons of their own histories of privilege, just *get it* without too much disclosure or exertion on our parts.[19]

I don't think law school is particularly fair or fun. The traditional curriculum is very difficult to change, an indication of how well it protects those power relations in society. There are many innovations, of course, that individual teachers can bring to individual courses. One thing I constantly urge is that students investigate the assumptions underlying any judicial opinion. I don't mean to consider whether the judicial author is a Republican or a Democrat, or where the judge went to law school. I don't mean to focus on any psychohistory, that is, to investigate whether this judge is notably cranky or mellow, eager or cautious, optimistic or depressed, oblivious to privilege or still angry about his confirmation hearings, or anything like that. Rather, I want students to begin to think about larger questions that are part of decision making, that is, this judge's attitude toward the limits of knowledge, the possibility of doing ethical good works, and the myriad aspects of reliable governance of society. In short, I want them to begin to think about the possible connections among legal-decision making and persistent philosophical questions.

I think students want to believe, as many in the law business believe, that judges are just following rules. But that generally is not so. If a precedent or statute or regulation clearly decided the dispute, the case wouldn't exist. For there to be a reported appellate opinion, there must be litigants who have their own financial resources or insurance company backing, and there must be disagreement about interpretation of a rule or standard for which there are plausible arguments on both sides. This, I tell my students, is where the rubber meets the road. I believe that important cases actually turn on conflicting philosophical assumptions beneath the legal arguments. A competent lawyer is aware of all this going on. A capable judicial system does not shy away from unpacking the assumptions at work.

Many traditional jurisprudence courses are organized around the basic questions I noted above. What is "law"? What makes a system a "legal" system? Can we distinguish between legitimate and illegitimate uses of law? These are not mere abstract musings. The great questions of the day, from the validity of the use of military power to the allocation of authority to decide national elections, are at bottom questions about legal legitimacy.

Some years ago, I wrote that law is "second-rate philosophy backed by the force of the state."[20] There are several aspects of that characterization that deserve further explanation from me. Let's start with "backed by the force of the state." Almost all Western political thought grows from the assumption that a fundamental task of society is to control violence. At the same time, almost all Western political thought assumes that force cannot be completely eliminated.[21] The permanently contested question is when violence will be socially sanctioned. The list of contexts where society allows violence toward people is very short: war, sports, and law.[22]

I left philosophy for law because I wanted the world to be more just, and felt that some changes required coercion. I liked law because it can make itself stick.[23] Police are entitled to use force to keep order and to apprehend suspects. If you don't pay your parking tickets, the cops will come and get you and drag you into court. If I don't give you money as agreed in a contract, you can eventually get the sheriff to come out and take my stuff. If I kill someone, I can be forcibly imprisoned or even put to death. When we have obligations imposed by law, we fail not at our peril. The existence and scope of a legal obligation is therefore always in need of justification.

Both law and philosophy are about debate. Both are discursive enterprises that rise and fall on arguments. The arguments matter more in law, at least in the short term, because law is backed by force and philosophy is not. In order for the social sanctioning of legal force to kick in, law has to give reasons. The reasoning happens in different modes, with different levels of formality and compunction. Policemen have to explain their "probable cause" for arrests. Legislators produce a plethora of reasons to vote for or against bills. When the mayor stands for reelection, she'd better explain what that ugly statue in the park was about. Trial courts sometimes and appellate judges almost always generate highly stylized accounts of their actions. The degree of persuasiveness of the reasons given for any legal decisions correlate with the perceived legitimacy of law.

It turns out that legal arguments are closely akin to familiar philosophical arguments. With few exceptions, Western philosophy has revolved endlessly around three questions: What can we know? How shall we act? How shall we govern ourselves in society? These are the problems of epistemology, ethics, and politics. It is obvious why philosophical debate is endless. On the epistemological front, there is no way finally to be certain what *is* in the universe (quarks? God? perfection?) because there is no ultimate criterion for verification of the information available to us. Getting on the subway is essentially an act of faith.

Regarding ethics, I have a general sense of when people act well and when they act badly, but there is a large and constantly shifting gray area. In any ethical context, there can be extended respectable debate, and there will never be certainty about what is the right thing to do. The same point about politics is elementary. Politics is a perpetual contest among conceptions of a good society and methods for achieving it.

Consider this experiment regarding the correspondence between legal arguments and philosophical problems. Close your eyes and point to any case in any casebook. In it, you'll likely find a dispute about a fact (an epistemological issue), a dispute about the quality of an actor's intention (an ethical issue), and/or a dispute about the authorization for (a category that includes the possible interpretations of) an exercise of legal power (a political issue).

I know that there are differences between law and philosophy. Given the correspondence among categories of issues addressed by the disciplines, however, perhaps we can agree that law is a department of practical philosophy. It is not the bricks-and-mortar parts of law, however, that led me in my perhaps too terse youth to refer to law as "second-rate philosophy." What, in my view makes law an inferior explanatory enterprise is its pretense that it doesn't have to have any opinion regarding hard metaphysical questions.

Of course, each discipline or set of disciplines has its own conventional assumptions and protocols for change.[24] Each discipline has its own institutional reasons for its posture toward uncertainty. Law, for example, can't put away debate for another day. I have a fantasy of being a judge, and when the parties turn to me after six months of a bench trial, I throw up my hands and say, "Beats the hell out of me!" But I couldn't do that. I may make my ruling very narrow, or hope that appellate courts or the legislature will fix my mess, or I may yearn for an opportunity to revisit my decision, but I can't just refuse to decide the matter before me.

In deciding, and in having force at my disposal to enforce a decision, however, I've got to recognize that my enterprise is contingent. Forces of nature aren't the determinants of my task. I'm not challenged to find a cure for HIV/AIDS. Of course I'm not writing on an entirely clean slate, either, but it only diminishes the endeavor for me to pretend that I am not a participant in a wide-ranging ethical debate about the requirements of a good society.

An English barrister once said that "lawyers could no doubt reform their education and training, reform the practice and processes of law, even reform the law itself, if they felt like it. But probably they will not feel like it."[25] Indeed, there is some inherent conservatism in the institution of law; it is structured to resist sudden and constant change. But, in light of lawyers' considerable power to invoke the force of the state, surely we ought constantly to be assessing the necessity and scope of our discipline's conservatism. And surely we ought be taking inventory of the emotional and political habits that make us "not feel like" doing better.

Returning to the big questions of jurisprudence described earlier—beginning with "what makes law law"—let's consider another spectrum, related to the one I proposed earlier that had Richard III at one end and "justice" at the other. This version has lots to do with the dichotomy between certainty and doubt, discussed more broadly in the next chapter. "Natural Law" is at one end of the spectrum (the certainty end) and the legal positivist tradition is at the other (the doubt end). Some in the natural law tradition would insist that "an unjust law is not a law." There is an obligation, both moral and legal, for citizens to resist those unjust commands. In natural law thinking, there is a divine or naturally existing law that supersedes all man-made law, and —here's where the "certainty" aspect comes saliently to bear—we can "discover" what that higher law requires of us. At the other end of the spectrum, legal positivism holds that even if there is such a higher law, there is no way for mere mortals to comprehend in a given situation what it requires. "Positivism" means that we regard as law only that which was positively enacted, made, done, brought into black-and-white being on a sheet of paper by whoever has the earthly power to do so. In that view, civil order requires that in legal matters we look only to what duly constituted authorities tell us. As the legal philosopher John Austin famously wrote in 1832, "The existence of the law is one thing; its merit or demerit is another."[26]

Try saying these statements out loud. "An unjust law is not a law." Now say, "The existence of the law is one thing; its merit or demerit is another." I suspect that you can imagine hearing the first statement on, say, talk radio, but not in a courtroom. The second statement, however, underlies arguments made by judges and lawyers every day. We've been well taught: the "merits of the case" have nothing to do with any larger senses of goodness, conscience, justice, or survival. We are consumed with discerning merely what the law "is."

The bigger and always pending question is how we might evaluate the existing law, with an eye to what the law should be. Is there any way to distinguish between bad law and good law? How can we talk about that? I believe that this distinction—between law and good law—is what we're getting at in talking about respect for the rule of law as opposed to unreasoning, robotic, selfish obedience to the law as it is.

It is not only ivory-towered academics who presently worry about the "rule of law." A discourse authored by United States Supreme Court Justice Stephen Breyer is illustrative. He proposed a series of cases to illustrate his vision of development in the rule of law. In historical order, the first case he notes is *Worcester v. Georgia,*[27] decided in 1837. This particular case, though just a snapshot in the ongoing mistreatment of Native people, is famous as an example of executive branch defiance of judicial authority. The Supreme Court held that the laws of the State of Georgia (which was attempting to drive Indians off their southeastern homelands) could have no effect on the Cherokee Nation. Nonetheless, both the state of Georgia and the United States refused to enforce that holding, eventually allowing federal troops to put the Cherokees and other eastern tribes on the Trail of Tears out of that part of the United States.

My ancestors were on that trail to the Oklahoma territory. The new lands were also eventually stolen from the tribes. Family legend has it that my grandfather was three days old, swaddled in the back of a wagon in 1889, as his parents waited to find a new farm on the morning of the Oklahoma land rush. I do not know whether they retrieved as much land as they had been forced to abandon. Oklahoma is celebrated as the "Sooner State" because so many people went under the wire sooner than they were supposed to and gobbled up a lot of the good land.

In Justice Breyer's list of illustrative cases, next historically is *Cooper v. Aaron*,[28] the 1958 case in which the Court told the Governor of Arkansas that he could not "stand in the schoolhouse door" to prevent racial integration of public schools. After the *Cooper* decision, the President of the United States dispatched federal troops to Little Rock to keep the schoolhouse doors open. In subsequent speeches, Justice Breyer has added to his list the matter of *Bush v. Gore*,[29] the 5-4 decision after the 2000 presidential election that awarded the electoral votes of Florida, and thus the presidency, to George W. Bush.

I believe Justice Breyer wants us to note that in the 1837 example, troops were deployed against the decision of the court; in the 1958 example, troops were deployed to enforce the decision of the court; after the 2000 *Bush* case, although as notorious as any decision of the United States Supreme Court, no troops were deployed on either side, and no para-military-Democrats (though it is a stretch even to imagine them) took to the streets with guns.

I do not think Justice Breyer is telling a simple story, because the story of the rule of law cannot mean only diminishing violence after judicial actions. Surely, *Worcester v. Georgia* was not "not law," just because it couldn't immediately be enforced. Just as surely, *Bush v. Gore* was not "good law" just because it produced no blood in the streets. Justice Breyer does not think that is all there is to it. Instead, our constitutional system "consists of habits, customs, expectations, settled modes of behavior engaged in by lawyers, by judges, and by citizens, all developed gradually over time. It is that system, as actually practiced by millions of Americans, that protects our liberty."[30] But where do these habits, customs, and expectations come from? Perhaps we should worry about how little it takes for the legal system to command so much talent and dedication. Perhaps we have been bamboozled.

Professor Duncan Kennedy has noted several unhappy consequences of blind faith in the rule of law. For one thing, legal discourse maintains the pretense that judges don't fill gaps and ambiguities in law with conscious, half-conscious, or unconscious ideology.[31] We judges and lawyers are obligated to wear our neutrality outfits, but that attire proclaims that law is just, natural, and necessary.[32] However, we all know in our hearts that politics pervade the law. And, according to Kennedy, because that is common knowledge, lawyers and judges are operating in bad faith, "in the Sartrean sense" of allowing ourselves to live in protracted denial.

Most good lawyers know this. When we act as if a judge's decision awaits legal and factual data, while knowing exactly what that particular judge will decide, we are consciously deceptive players on that stage. But I think Kennedy's analysis is somewhat reductive. It doesn't account for the persistent fact that not only do we muddle through but that we do so—at least occasionally—in an aspirational gear. I've known great lawyers and great judges who are smart and sophisticated and making the world a better place. They understand the contradictions in our enterprise. They know how serious it can be, and the degree to which it is and is not in our hands.

If the rule of law is more than a sedative, more than a means to discourage those trained in law from becoming effective political actors, what should it mean? Are there any necessary ingredients to the rule of law? Not surprisingly, we can choose from a large range of recipes. In 1885, English scholar A. V. Dicey brought the term "rule of law" into the vernacular. In Dicey's view, it required three things: the supremacy of law over arbitrary power, the subjection of all classes to law, and judicial determination of legal controversies.[33] More recent versions are variations on these central themes, some requiring only five ingredients,[34] some identifying up to fourteen.[35]

The most famous list of aspects of the rule of law is from Professor Lon L. Fuller. Professor Fuller wrote in the post–World War II period, when most scholars wanted to give a narrow interpretation to the reach of the law. I don't wish to caricature a rich jurisprudential era, but one might say that the question was, what sort of legal system might have resisted the rise of the Third Reich, or might prevent the rise of such a regime in the future?[36] World War II was a powerful motivator for the age of legal positivism and later jurisprudential efforts that focused on procedure as the meaning of justice. The Third Reich's ideological fundamentalism intertwined with a number of "legal" steps in cementing Hitler's power. Most legal scholars on the victors' side therefore advocated a jurisprudence that was "value-free," distant from foundationalist philosophical systems, and thus distant from anything smacking of moral authoritarianism.

I admire Fuller because he was prepared, in that antifoundationalist age, to say that the law had to mean something more than the actions of duly constituted power and/or formal rules of procedure. He used the words "law" and "morality" together, in insisting that at a minimum, to deserve respect as a legal system, a regime had to exhibit the "internal morality of law."[37] It is worth reviewing Fuller's admonitions in that regard because they constitute much of what I mean by the rule of law.

According to Fuller, the internal morality of law has eight attributes. First, the law must be general. The requirement of generality means that both individuals and governmental entities (and, realistically, we should add corporations)[38] must be subject to laws, but also and equally important, that the laws cover classes of conduct, as opposed to one instance of conduct. This latter notion is implicit in the idea of a "rule." When I tell my child to eat his peas, the "rule" at work is not that he shall eat peas, only and always. The rule is that I get to have considerable control over his dietary intake, at least while he is a child.

Second, the law must be made public, its requirements made accessible so that people can know what is expected of them. If the legislature votes that taxes will be due on a date earlier than in the past but keeps this new law secret, the law will simply not work to achieve its intended purposes (whatever they may be).

Third, with very few exceptions, the law must operate only prospectively. I cannot guide my conduct if the legislature is in the habit of enacting retroactive laws. Deciding today that citizens must have licenses for their dogs by yesterday is not a good way to achieve the purpose of animal control.[39]

Fourth, the published law must be expressed with reasonable clarity. Perfect clarity is often unattainable; indeed, laws often and wisely incorporate inexact standards such as a requirement of acting in "good faith." But at a minimum, the law cannot be incoherent. No purpose is achieved by requiring, without further definition, that "all persons seeking to do business in this state must gahootenaire."

Fifth, the laws must be internally consistent. Fuller uses the example of a legislature saying, in one enactment, that automobile license plates must be affixed on January 1st, and in another enactment, that it shall be a crime to perform any physical labor on that day.[40]

Sixth, a law must not be impossible to comply with; it must be practicable to obey. Some laws are logically impossible to obey, such as a requirement that all prospective persons must declare their own legal names before birth. Some laws are only practically impossible. Suppose the legislature says that all children, at their peril, must be capable of long division by the age of twelve. That level of mathematical competence may be a laudable goal, but it cannot be achieved by naked legal command.

Seventh, the law must be relatively stable, not continuously and randomly changing. This concern is conceptually related to the five attributes of a legal system just described: one can't conform one's conduct to law if one cannot discern at a given moment what the law is. Laws change, of course, like everything else. But lawmakers and administrators are rightly if sometimes overly concerned, in doctrines such as *stare decisis,* about not changing the laws too much or too often.

Finally, there has to be congruency between the words of the laws and their actual administration. Fuller notes that this is the most complex requirement of the internal morality of law because so much can go wrong between declaration and implementation, for reasons both innocent and sinister. These are the vital problems of both lawyering and legal theory.[41]

It has become commonplace to dismiss Fuller's list as another example of proceduralist flight from hard questions, as a mere reiteration of what U.S. lawyers understand by the term "due process."[42] I believe, however, that the conventional dismissal misses Fuller's emphasis on the ethical pursuit at the heart of legal systems. In the first place, what lawyers contest as "due process" is a highly ethical enterprise, and it is not completely indeterminate. What we understand as "due process" is not a free-for-all; it has to do with conceptions of fairness that are, may I say, essentially ethical.

In any case, and relatedly, Fuller's internal morality of law corresponds to the conventions of ethical discourse. Acting in good faith, we do have sustained discussion about all sorts of important issues for which there are not and never will be clear, final, uniquely right answers. The rules of discourse are indicia of good faith but are pointless in themselves. When contestants engage, we have to have ways of knowing what we are discoursing and contesting about, around, for, and toward. In one of my favorite quotes, Fuller and a coauthor stated, "We are still all too willing to embrace the conceit that it is possible to manipulate legal concepts without the orientation that comes from this simple inquiry: *toward what end is this activity directed?*"[43]

I ask myself that question many times each day. If it doesn't always lead to guidance, at least it provokes thought on questions ranging from getting out of bed in the morning to sorting the laundry to deciding whether to represent a particular client. This interrogative practice has been therapeutic because I am otherwise disposed to legal thinking of a sort also described by Fuller. He quotes Professor Thomas Reed Powell as saying that if you can think about something that is related to something else without thinking about the thing to which it is related, then you have the legal mind.[44]

I think this has less to do with an inherent quality of law, or a predictable aspect of legal training, than with a destructive habit that U.S. lawyers in particular have become accustomed to: talking about everything except what is really at stake. Consider the example of *Hill v. Colorado*,[45] in which the United States Supreme Court rejected a free speech challenge to a "speech bubble" statute. The state law at issue provided criminal and civil remedies against those who leafleted, protested, or counseled within eight feet of a person entering a health care facility. Upholding the statute hinged on a finding that it was "content neutral" as to expressions restricted. In the majority's words, "the statute applies equally to used car salesmen, animal rights activists, fundraisers, environmentalists, and missionaries."[46]

This sounds like the punch line of a lawyer joke, because the legislative record clearly showed that the Colorado Assembly wanted to protect women seeking abortions.[47] The enactment could not have been more viewpoint specific. The legislature could not have worried less that a used car salesman might increase patient anxiety by selling cars or encouraging wart removal or anything else.

So let us ask, toward what end was that activity directed? The *Hill* decision disgruntled both liberal and conservative commentators, among the former group because it seemed to violate various First Amendment principles, among the latter group because it seemed to restrict efforts of antiabortion protestors.[48] I don't belong to either group. I believe that the result in *Hill* was a good one—to allow for legislative protection of women entering abortion clinics—but was accompanied by a terrible rationale: pretending that abortion protesting is just like any other speech. It isn't. If there were frank exchange about the worthiness of purpose, the United States Supreme Court could have applied a higher level of scrutiny and still upheld the statute because of the magnitude of the female patients' interest in securing an abortion without fear of interference. Our professional conspiracy to avoid full airing of purpose sets up the powerful to reverse reality, as when Justice Antonin Scalia referred to abortion as a "highly favored practice."[49] That kind of rhetoric takes hold, and we allow it to do so when we don't insist upon candid discussion about what law—the bubble law or any other—is really there for.

Teaching in Canada in 1993 changed my life because I saw purposiveness in action. In constitutional cases, Canadian courts to their credit regularly refer to decisions in other countries, most often from those in the United States, and then do or don't follow those examples depending on the Canadian commitment to purposive interpretation. Thus, in a matter similar to *Hill*, a provincial legislature didn't have to fake neutrality, and could actually name its work the "Access to Abortion Services Act." The reviewing court could uphold the legislation, while being blessedly frank about the competing interests at stake. Yes, the act was a modest imposition on free expression but that interest in that particular context had to give way to the interests of women seeking abortion, concretely understood with appreciation of actual harms to women done by the protestors.[50]

In this book, I postulate that all legal actors would be happier if we frankly and perpetually asked, "Toward what end is this activity directed?" Let me put it in starker terms. The law is already necessarily about its ends, if the law is to command any loyalty at all. In the United States, women and slaves were not part of constituting our vaunted rule of law. What happens now that those groups, formerly excluded, and all the other "others," have ostensible voice? Isn't loyalty a two-way street? Nothing less than justice is at stake. What I mean by the "rule of law" includes all of Fuller's ethical commitments, as well as consciousness of former exclusions and the requirements of inclusion now. Without all of that, the rule of law has no compelling meaning.

Naturally, the questions become how to identify groups, ends, and other commitments that might lead to anything that anyone would call justice. Because of that difficulty, I turn in the next chapter to the problem of certainty, and the inevitable affliction of doubt.

2

Certainty and Doubt

[T]here aint any answer, there aint going to be any answer, there never has been an answer, that's the answer.

—Gertrude Stein

In chapter 1, I suggested that something called "justice" was at stake in our relationships to the rule of law. If you have been (or are being) well trained in law school, you are probably wondering where I come off using that word. In response, I would ask you how we acquire the habit of running from justice?

A student hasn't had to read too many opinions in law school before she realizes that the strategy for each judge is to show that his position better reflects what the law "really is." The persuasiveness of opinions depends upon the standard of fidelity to law, measured by indicia of technicality and deductive, impersonal reasoning. That's what makes them "opinions" rather than outbursts. The usual message of any opinion is "the law made me do it." Dissenting judges in appellate cases make parallel arguments. Dissenters score points by arguing that majority opinions are either an incorrect application of existing law, or are not really loyal to some aspect of existing law, or are nothing more than products of that most feared of all evils, judicial subjectivity.

In the United States Supreme Court, this game is played over and over again. The most famous example is Justice Holmes's dissent in *Lochner v. New York*. In a blow for freedom of contract (or for exploitation of labor, depending upon your point of view), a majority of the Court had invalidated a state statute that limited working hours for bakers. Dissenting, Justice Holmes immortally drew the sword of judicial restraint:

> This case is decided upon an economic theory which a large part of the country does not entertain. If it were a question whether I agreed with

> that theory, I should desire to study it further and long before making up my mind. But I do not conceive that to be my duty, because I strongly believe that my agreement or disagreement has nothing to do with the right of a majority to embody their opinions in law. . . . [A] Constitution is not intended to embody a particular economic theory, whether of paternalism and the organic relation of the citizen to the state or of *laissez faire*. It is made for people of fundamentally differing views, and the accident of our finding certain opinions natural and familiar, or novel, and even shocking, ought not to conclude our judgment upon the question whether statutes embodying them conflict with the Constitution of the United States.[1]

More recent cases use testier language. In 2002, a majority of the Court held that execution of mentally retarded criminals is a violation of the Eighth Amendment's prohibition on cruel and unusual punishment.[2] Dissenting, Justice Scalia stated, "Seldom has an opinion of this Court rested so obviously upon nothing but the personal views of its Members. . . . The arrogance of this assumption of power takes one's breath away."[3] Similarly in 2005, a bare majority held that execution of criminals younger than eighteen years of age violated the Eighth Amendment.[4] Justice Scalia was not happy about this either, characterizing the majority opinion as a "mockery" because constitutional meaning should not be determined "by the subjective views of five members of this Court and like-minded foreigners. . . ."[5] Scalia contrasted the majority's "mirror of the passing and changing sentiment of American society regarding penology" with "*real* law, *real* prescriptions democratically adopted by the American people."[6]

Justice Scalia does not exactly pin down what makes his version of the situation *real* law but rests his argument on the majority's dreaded subjectivity. Much has been written about Justice Scalia's style. I won't add to that commentary except to observe how often Scalia's criticisms sound like "you throw like a girl." It isn't just Scalia who sometimes invokes the judgely judge in the sky to shame wayward majority members. These criticisms assume that everybody knows how real judges are supposed to behave and this ain't it. Indeed, the unjudgely behavior is fluffy-headed, slavish to fashion, and selfish, to be resisted just as femininity is to be resisted.[7]

This is a story that is replayed endless times in American law and legal commentary. We are accustomed to seeing the story as a morality play, as the struggle between a judge's "personal ideology" and the angels of his objective better nature.[8] But to retain this characterization is both to concede too much ground to the bullies and to miss the underlying metaphysical struggle, one that resonates in law and life on a daily basis.

It was absolutely crucial for me as a young feminist lawyer to come to grips with these story lines. I learned how unexamined certainty is an invaluable attribute of privilege. Feminist and other progressive thinkers throughout history have underscored how inequitable systems of supremacy sustain themselves by making their critics feel stupid, incompetent, and crazy.[9] The best defense is to appreciate the centuries-old struggle in human thought between certainty and doubt.

The Endless Debate

The endless philosophical debate between certainty and doubt can also be called a debate between foundationalism and skepticism. This tension is represented in the preceding chapter in the description of ranges of answers to the question "What is the rule of law?" There is no choice, in studying or practicing law, but to grapple with the philosophical spectrum. To understand the nature of the arguments is a matter of lawyerly competence, even if one's conclusion is that they are silly and misleading arguments.

Foundationalism refers to philosophical schools that posit some point of reliability (even certainty), some foundation on which we can stand, when attempting to answer questions about knowledge or ethics. These are the ways of understanding that depend upon a "skyhook." The most common foundationalist philosophies are empiricism and rationalism. Empiricism holds that what can be "known" is only that which is available to our senses. We believe it when we see it. Most people are happy with empiricism as a commonsensical explanation of how they live their lives. The obvious problem with empiricism as a philosophical position is that it would conclude that there is nothing beyond what meets the eye. Empiricism would seem to deny the existence of, say, subatomic particles and the dormant commerce clause. That is, when most people think about it, they are willing to admit that at least in some situations, there is more than what meets the eye.

Rationalism refers to the set of philosophies that attempt to identify grids of meaning underlying or accompanying what can be seen. This is called "rationalism" because it depends upon reasons for things. Thus, subatomic particles could be understood as "reasons" for observable objects like roller skates. The doctrine of the dormant commerce clause could be understood as a reason that explains (and is a necessary part of) a more general commitment to unimpeded interstate commerce.

Empiricism and rationalism are not necessarily mutually exclusive. I have noticed, for example, that almost without exception, every time I get on the subway, it goes. From this experience I do not deduce that I cause the subways to run. Nor do I get on the subway car just hoping to end up downtown. Rather, I bring to my empirical experience certain rational powers that allow me to understand the explanation for this transportation system and to manipulate it accordingly. Most people proceed with their lives according to a fairly complex but usually unconscious model of interdependent empiricism and rationalism.

In contrast to foundationalism is skepticism, meaning any philosophical position that favors doubt over certainty. This includes lots of philosophical schools as well as lots of political positions. As a general matter, at least in my lifetime, doubt is hipper than certainty. It is easy for skeptics to make anything other than skepticism look like either gullibility or a power grab. Moreover, it is commonplace to assert the superiority of doubt as a philosophical posture without entertaining any doubt about the fundamentalism of that commitment.

At the logical heart of skepticism is the argument based on the "infinite regress." It is simple to understand. At every alleged "foundational" point in an argument, one can question that foundation. Take the simple statement "Here are my roller skates." The skeptic asks how I know that. I respond empirically, that I see them. The skeptic asks why I'm connecting that alleged optic impression with the alleged presence of my alleged roller skates. I'll be astonished at the question, but I could answer by drawing on my rationalistic habits. I could say that seeing the roller skates has always reliably led to being able to use them. The skeptic asks whether my experiences of both "sighting" and "use" might not just be hallucinations. And so on and so on. I may think this is a goofy conversation, but at some point I don't have "proof" of my answer. Each successive level of justification is subject to doubt *ad infinitum*.

One doesn't have to be too skilled at argumentation to make skeptical mincemeat of allegations of fact or necessity. At some point in the skeptical routine, however, one will begin to look like a bully. At some later point, one will begin to look like a silly person, who is also a bully, and who is not worth listening to. Persuasiveness in argument depends in part on identifying those invisible lines, stopping before arrival at them, and acting as if one were speaking sensibly all along.

No one has to choose once and for all between "certainty" and "doubt." There are many intermediate points along that continuum, and multidimensional tangents that one could creditably take for specific purposes. I've noted above that most people, by whom I mean people in nonprofessional contexts who are counting on gravity to help the rain go down the sewer, rely on a classical combination of empiricism and rationalism.

Another common combination of philosophical positions, and one common to law, is skepticism with empiricism. In a sense, those philosophical big words describe some of the more formalistic decisions of judges. An example is Justice Hugo Black's dissent in *Katz v. United States.*[10] Every other member of the U.S. Supreme Court had agreed that the constitutional prohibition on unreasonable searches and seizures extended to wiretaps of conversations in telephone booths. Justice Black noted that a general right to privacy does not appear in the Constitution, and that the Court could not rewrite the Constitution "in order 'to bring it into harmony with the times.' "[11] Justice Black referred several times to the plain meaning of language, as if "searches" or "seizures" referred to some objects in the universe known to the authors of the Constitution, the existence and dimensions of which were empirically undeniable. Whatever the framers of the Constitution were talking about, they weren't talking about telephone booths. In a famous passage, Justice Black said that for the Court to include telephone booth conversations within the Fourth Amendment prohibition on unreasonable searches and seizures would make the Court "a continuously functioning constitutional convention."[12]

I don't want to provoke yet another debate about originalism in constitutional interpretation. I just note the structure of Black's argument. It is undoubtedly true that the framers of the Constitution never used a telephone booth. It is also undoubtedly true that the framers knew about the ancient practice of eavesdropping, and could have prohibited governmental eavesdropping in the Fourth Amendment if they had wanted to. Given these facts, Justice Black said, it was abusive of language and reality and power for the Court to disagree with him.

Most law students, in my experience, think Justice Black was wrong in *Katz* but have a hard time saying why. I think that is because we don't discuss Justice Black's philosophical assumptions, and more important, don't discuss the majority's rationalism. Theirs is a standard rationalistic argument. There is a grid of reason, or reasons, underlying the words in the text of the Fourth Amendment. What the framers of the Constitution actually had in mind when they wrote the words is important but is not the end of the matter. True they hadn't used telephones; true they knew about eavesdropping. But the wiretap in the telephone booth represents rather a special situation. On balance, it is more akin to confiscating papers in a private home than it is to overhearing a conversation while standing outside an open window. Rather than rewriting the Constitution, according to a rationalist view, this interpretation makes sense of it.

The same analysis applies to the recent death penalty cases discussed earlier in this chapter, where Justice Scalia went ballistic over the majority's decisions that the death penalty could not be applied to mentally retarded defendants and to defendants under the age of eighteen. In his dissents, Scalia was the foundationalist (one might even say, the fundamentalist) parading as the institutionally constrained skeptic. Though accused of being illegitimate foundationalists, the majorities in those cases might be said actually to be rationalists with full awareness of the lurking challenges of skepticism.

The standard skeptical response to judicial rationalism is to invoke the "slippery slope," to wit, if you're going to go around making sense of things as you see them, where does that power end? How is that different from acting as a continuously functioning constitutional convention? And a standard answer to that is, we'll make as much sense of things as we need in order for our experience to fit together. No one knows for all purposes where the line is, or where it will need to be tomorrow.

An example is subatomic particles. When I was in high school, there were supposedly three sorts of them: neutrons, protons, and electrons. Last I looked, there were at least seventeen varieties of subatomic particles, not including the "graviton" (which accounts for gravitational force) and the "Higgs particle" (which gives mass to all other particles), both as yet "unobserved."[13] This system is considerably less tidy than what I learned in tenth grade. Although I suspect that this listing is not the end of the story, I believe that particle physicists are nonetheless helping to make sense, if only temporarily, of a gloriously complex world.

Certainty and doubt are seldom polar opposites in human decision making. Each of us has considerable practice in using different methods of thought, and we'll never know for sure if one of them is "right." What we do know, particularly if we are lawyers, is that we'll be called upon to participate to the best of our ability in contests of persuasion, and that we will find ourselves in the position of persuadability from time to time.

A much-cited and genuinely delightful essay provides a hypothetical scene for the philosophical drama. A philosopher named W. B. Gallie gave the name "essentially contested concepts" to disputes that are by definition not capable of resolution but that are sustained "by perfectly respectable arguments and evidence."[14] I am generally suspicious of sports metaphors, but Gallie illuminates his argument by reference to an imaginary sport. Suppose there is a game where winning is not determined by a score but, rather, by quality of play.[15] Each team has a loyal group of supporters who persist in efforts to convert undecided fans "not through any vulgar wish to be the majority party, but because they believe their favoured team is *playing the game best.*"[16]

The continuous competition is not only for the championship but for acceptance of the proper criteria for championship. In this game there is no possibility for any purely mechanical method of winning, nor any fixed general principle for deciding, nor any ultimate universal agreement about which team has played best.[17] Gallie's point is that the permanent fluidity of the situation does not make it irrational, or mean that particular team loyalists are acting from superstition, or according to their own untethered subjectivities, or because of some biochemical imbalance. It is conceivable that minds can be changed. Particular arguments or pieces of evidence can be recognized as having logical force for some disputants, if not always conclusive force for all disputants. Perhaps most important, recognition of a concept as essentially contested implies recognition of competing uses of it "as of permanent potential critical value to one's own use or interpretation of the concept in question. . . ."[18]

We might usefully think of the contest between certainty and doubt in Gallie's terms. Without any disrespect to the great philosophers, we could of think of this contest as a centuries-old rivalry between two debate teams. On the Foundationalist/Rationalist roster have been some immortal names: Plato, Aristotle, Descartes, Kant, Hegel, and Newton, to name a few. The Skeptics have had their own heavy hitters: Sextus Empiricus (for whom empiricism is named), Zeno, Hume, Berkeley, and Nietzsche among them.

In this great rivalry, each of the All Stars has brought something to the game: a style, perhaps genuine innovation, and sometimes towering —though always temporary—dominance. They have different conceptions of and attitudes toward the criteria for excellence. Some—notably Nietzsche, Wittgenstein, and Derrida—have questioned whether the game is worth playing. Critically, almost none of the greats can be said to have played for the same team, at least not in the same way, throughout their careers.

The only candidate for absolute team loyalty I can think of was the pre-Socratic Greek named Pyrrho. Pyrrho is considered to be the ultimate "radical skeptic," that is, one who denies that we can ever be justified in our beliefs or values. Pyrrho doubted that he could ever "know" anything. He even doubted his own skepticism. He could have been completely mistaken about whether "doubt" was a meaningful concept, or whether the "doubt" that seemed to go on in his head was happening inside a real head, and so forth, per the pattern of the infinite regress. He was supposedly a purist. He never wrote down any of his own thinking.[19] Why bother? What quill? What parchment? What future reader? What conceivable continuity in consciousness, if consciousness exists, on which one's writing could have any coherent bearing?

What we know of Pyrrho comes from those who were his "students," or who otherwise hung around with him. The story goes that they always made sure Pyrrho never set out on his own because, having no reason to believe, for example, in what we call "gravity" (product of those as yet unobserved gravitons), he might just walk off a cliff. It turns out, however, that Pyrrho was not an absolute purist. There is another story that on one occasion, Pyrrho chased his servant down the streets of Athens with a frying pan because the servant had served a poor meal to Pyrrho's guests.[20] So Pyrrho not only had friends who looked out for him but also had a frying pan, a servant, guests, and a standard of hospitality that was vigorously enforced on at least one occasion.

The most recent version of skepticism to capture the academic imagination is postmodernism, or poststructuralism. Most adherents to this skeptical path do not label themselves, and it seems central to the definition of postmodernism that it is incapable of definition. With due respect to the variousness of postmodernist schools, it is perhaps best to focus on the "postness" of them—they claim to break free of the traditional boundaries of dispute. Many describe postmodernism as an unwillingness to be ensnared by traditional questions of philosophy. Among the traps to be avoided are metaphysics, binary divisions of traditional thought, grand theory, metanarratives, and claims to authority of any sort. Postmodernism not only denies that philosophy can provide a useful roadmap but also claims that no map is ever possible. The "real" is a perpetually modified product of discourse, and any discussion about what is real results in a "foregone inconclusion."[21]

There are both mild and wild versions of postmodernism, as there are more and less radical versions of any philosophical mode. The most fundamentalist strands of postmodernism (oxymoronic as that designation may seem) cause consternation among progressive people because they seem to preclude the possibilities of political commitment.

To some extent, however, it was always thus: skepticism discourages activism. Before the postmodernist versions of skepticism, we had (and still have) liberalism, which is depressing enough as a skeptical political stance. The philosophical tradition called liberalism is all about radical individualism, which in turn yields moral relativism, which in turn yields the social paralysis when we (collectively) believe that we are each a person in our own right and entitled, damn it, to our own opinion. What I regard as progressive causes therefore run up against natural limits in liberal thought. Affirmative action causes a big stink because it seems to deprive some people (usually white people and/or male people) of what they regard as the just rewards of their individual industry. Antipornography and anti-racial-hate speech campaigns have come under fire because in a morally relativist regime, they are labeled as thought policing.[22]

With liberalism, however, at least we could band together under the banner of individual dignity, and demand equal treatment for individuals (though often disagreeing on what such treatment might look like). Postmodernism, however, denies the coherence of the concept of the self.[23] Thus, postmodernism can lead to doing nothing[24] even faster than traditional liberalism: if a text has an infinite number of readings, then not only is one man's trash another man's treasure but I am deluding myself when I entertain any belief, a belief that I treasure something or that there is a thing to treasure or that there is an "I" to maintain the sentiment. Even the provisionally agreed upon landmark of individual dignity cannot be maintained with a philosophical straight face.

Charting Middle Roads

It is important to understand the full power of all kinds of skeptical positions. Indeed, to be able to maintain full skeptical powers while still participating in interpretive debate might be said to be the definition of "critical thought." Most people seem consistently to want to know reasons for things, want to know whether there is a point to existence, and want to know how to go about making decisions about how to act. That is at the bottom of Aristotle's definition of man as the rational animal. There may not be final answers, but our species keeps asking the questions.

The name of the jurisprudential game in the twentieth century was to chart some middle ground between rationalism and radical skepticism. The former was called "natural law," a matter whereby the answer to any legal question could be achieved by access to Right Reason. Natural law has its roots in both ancient philosophy and Christian theology. Because it relied on some sort of transcendence or mysticism, natural law became unacceptable in an antifoundationalist age. On the other end of the spectrum is radical skepticism. Again, particularly in this antifoundationalist age, it is an easy philosophical position to defend but is unbecoming to lawyers and judges. By definition, we are forced to take the position that there is some authority somewhere that can be relied upon to provide guidance in a legal dispute. There will be gaps in authority or it will be ambiguous. It will not have any transcendent imprimatur. But there have to be some norms somewhere to which those of us who recognize an obligation to law will regularly point.

I earlier referred to the "professional default position," the notion that experienced lawyers know the sources and limits of authority, and know how legal standards apply. But that is itself a kind of mysticism. Depending simply on professionalism might be justifiable if the legal system reliably worked in most contexts, or could be believed by the public reliably to do what feels like justice. Some of us are bigger supporters of the legal system than others, but I don't know of anyone who feels that it functions efficaciously and without need of perpetual justification. Whether or not law actually does any good, because it is an instrument of socially sanctioned violence, it strikes me as an enterprise that demands a rather precise (though of course fluidly precise) relationship to skepticism.[25]

A skeptical modern jurisprudence is that known as "legal positivism," noted in chapter 1, and advocated in the most nuanced way by Professor H. L. A. Hart.[26] In positivism, the law is that which is positively enacted, there on the page in black and white, duly enacted by duly constituted authorities. Legal positivism has its intellectual roots in British utilitarianism. The great utilitarian Jeremy Bentham had warned that foundationalist legal theories such as natural law presented the "twin evils" of anarchy and conformity. That is, as explained by Professor Hart, if we accept the proposition that an "unjust law is not a law," the danger on one hand is that the authority of law will be decimated by each individual's conception of justice. On the other hand is the danger that existing law (that which we've accepted as "law" because we think it is just) will supplant morality as the final test of exercises of political power, and that vests too much authority in government.[27]

The way to avoid the twin evils is to approach law with clarity and modesty. It is true that decision making is not merely a matter of deduction. Still, according to Hart, legal rules have some settled core meanings about which there is little disagreement. If there is an ordinance that prohibits vehicles in the park, we know the city council didn't want automobiles in there. Other than some obvious core meanings, rules have "penumbras" of meaning that provide guidance, if not absolute certainty, about what the law requires in a given case. Do roller skates constitute a "vehicle" within the meaning of the ordinance? We don't know. We need more context. Fortunately, to supply meaning, to navigate the "open texture" of language and rules built from it, is what language users do. We are really good at it. We shouldn't make things more mysterious than they are.

Moreover, when we mystify law unnecessarily, according to Hart, we give it too much power. We don't need to encourage highfalutin theories about the moral content of law. We need to encourage practical expertise in moral judgment. There is no need to fight about whether an unjust law is a law. Better to say, simply, "The law is the law," and then move to a different discussion about whether a particular law is too evil to be obeyed. To promote clarity in such contexts is the moral benefit of skepticism with respect to the authority of law.

The fact of contemporary life, however, is that legal discussions almost never get to the point of civil disobedience, or even much organized resistance on the progressive side. Particularly in the context of U.S. judicial review, we've come to expect that the law will entertain more than strictly legal, merely positivist arguments. In the U.S. republic, the courts are major contributors to discourse about political values and aspirations. Thus, although Hart's positivism has profoundly influenced judges and lawyers, it has not completely satisfied their normative itch. It is perhaps particularly unsatisfying in U.S. lawyers' experience to provide so little moral and political content in a jurisprudential account, given that even our positivistic rules—particularly the broad guarantees of the federal Constitution—require normative interpretation.

In the United States, mainstream jurisprudence has responded with what can be called institutional coherence theories, that is, approaches that treat the entirety of legal rules and relationships as the product of an implicit rational plan. In this tradition, which has had contributors from several generations, the answer to a legal question is generated by asking what ruling best fits with the institutions and existing practices within the entire system.

Of course, merely to require that a judge's decision cohere with some underlying rational plan, particularly when the plan is unarticulated or difficult to articulate, gives that judge considerably greater leeway than to require that he stick closely to the settled core meanings of rules. As Duncan Kennedy says, every nonlegal argument that enters into decision making is viewed as a potential Trojan house within law's fortress of legitimacy.[28] Some call it "policy" argument. Whatever we call it, there's a fine line between it and political ideology. Once inside the gates, there is a fear that ideology will sack the city.

The task for the institutional theorists is therefore to come up with some limiting principles for its liberated judiciary. Process-based and institutional-competence theories are part of this tradition, but surely the best known institutional theorist is Professor Ronald Dworkin. Dworkin has asserted there are right answers to legal questions. The judge arrives at them by reference to values that inhere in community life. Dworkin famously personified the community in a fictional judge named Hercules.[29] Judge Hercules "deduces" answers from rules when he can, but often that is not enough. Where the road is uncharted, Hercules wants to move toward justice. His personal ideological vision of justice is disciplined by the requirement that his ruling be consistent with the community's traditions and earlier decisions, a matter made considerably easier in a legal regime that establishes "rights" as trumps on other interests. Hercules presides over a rights-based rather than policy-based regime. What critics would call ideology in other judges becomes "political theory" when wielded by Hercules.

The overall Dworkinian project is to make liberal judicial decisions seem legitimate and conservative decisions seem illegitimate, that is, to construct a principled-looking adjudicative ratchet that turns the way liberals want it to turn. That is pretty much, though, what the other side is doing as well, in all that chatter about objectivity and subjectivity described earlier in this chapter. I appreciate that Professor Dworkin and his supporters keep at their task like Energizer Bunnies. Of course, neither side can ever decisively win the contest. That part is fine; I appreciate a perpetual interpretive competition. I'm just not sure it is turf —"our side is more objectively principled than your side"—that is particularly worth defending.

Revisiting American Pragmatism

I think it is time for courts and lawyers explicitly to abandon the debate between objective and subjective points of view. The obvious option is philosophical pragmatism. As noted in the introduction, perhaps the greatest compliment one lawyer can pay another is to call him "pragmatic." A useful movement in legal philosophy has been to enlarge what we might mean by these legal virtues, to embrace philosophical pragmatism within them.[30]

Pragmatism is a school of thought founded by three great American philosophers: Charles Sanders Peirce in the nineteenth century, and William James and John Dewey in the twentieth. To simplify matters, pragmatism is among the philosophical schools urging that it is time to get over philosophy. The "certainty versus doubt" conundrum is a matter of stuckness, of philosophical bad habits, specifically the bad habit of dualistic thinking. Traditional philosophical thinking revolved around a set of presumed opposites: object/subject, mind/body, material/spiritual, public/private, and theory/practice, just to name a few. All of that dualistic thinking followed from the assumption that there is a "reality" out there, if only we could discover a way to know it. This is called the "correspondence theory of truth." An item counts as knowledge only if it corresponds to reality. Skepticism, seemingly irremediable as of the twentieth century, was the inevitable result of the correspondence theory. There is simply no way reliably and permanently to distinguish what is "reality" and what is mere perception of reality, thus no way dispositively to test whether our perceptions correspond to reality.

John Dewey urged that we replace those habits of dualistic thinking with efforts to understand how organisms survive in their environments. We can't discover any ultimate truths; we can't be the end of philosophy or any other sort of inquiry. Culture is a process of creating new habits and institutions in order to enhance human experience. Other philosophers, such as Willard V. O. Quine, denied that items of knowledge have to be copies of whatever are "realities" in the world, what I will later refer to as "the furniture of the universe." Rather, what people count as "knowledge" depends on the difference a given belief would make in an ever-changing world if it were counted as "true."

Truths are instruments we invent to help us cope with circumstances, beliefs that change as necessary to account for experience. What matters is the web of communication and learning that helps us to arrive at hypotheses about reality that work independently and with one another. Every person inherits truths from learning to be a language user. Every language user contributes to the evolution of truth, as she goes about squaring experience with that inheritance, otherwise known as "common sense."

The optimistic mantle of American pragmatism is now borne by Professor Richard Rorty, a man who writes seldom about law but around whom a great deal of contemporary legal scholarship revolves. We can't get over the philosophical dilemmas. The most influential of skeptical philosophers, David Hume, had said in the eighteenth century that skepticism isn't a practical option.[31] Echoing Hume, Rorty says that the skeptical philosophy called postmodernism is philosophically right but politically silly.[32] The rationalist alternative—that long battle waged by Ronald Dworkin and company—is not worth the energy it takes to keep it afloat. Rorty wants us not only to get over philosophy but to throw off the epithets that are particularly debilitating to legal theorists: relativist, subjectivist, result-oriented. All theory that is coherent is already rooted in practice. Theorizing is of use only in service of the projects of diminishing human suffering and increasing human equality, equality being the platform for every person to have a chance at happiness. "It is a goal worth dying for, but it does not require backup from supernatural forces."[33]

As described in the introduction, my closest affiliation is with feminism, but it is a version of feminism that has much in common with contemporary pragmatist thought. Both reject the subject/object split and the metaphysical divide between certainty and doubt. Both are antiessentialist, antireductionist, and explicitly contextual, proceeding from the facts of social life and in resistance to the hierarchical organization of the world. The mere title of Rorty's wonderful book, *Contingency, Irony, and Solidarity,*[34] encapsulates a lot of feminist philosophy and commitment.

In chapter 5, I will have much more to say about what feminist jurisprudence is and how it works to inform legal judgment. We shall see that legal feminism does not discriminate among ideas because of their origin. With W. B. Gallie, feminists of my stripe regard competing arguments as being "of permanent potential critical value to one's own use or interpretation" in a given contest.[35] I think that feminism is enriched by several philosophical traditions. These include pragmatism, Wittgensteinian language philosophy, and an emerging discipline somewhat scarily known as "virtue ethics,"[36] a mode of discourse that gives prominence to human striving and the collective desire that all should be provided every resource in order to flourish.

Before a more sustained discussion of feminism, though, I will devote considerable inquiry to two areas that falsely promise refuge from the strenuous work of implementing feminist, pragmatic, and ethical analyses in the law. Those tempting dead-end paths are, first, the belief in the reliability of determinations of "facts," and second, an overreliance on traditional liberal thought.

3

Intractable Questions

Knowledge . . . is not itself power, although it is the magnetic field of power. Ignorance and opacity collude or compete with knowledge in mobilizing the flows of energy, desire, goods, meanings, persons.

—Eve Kosofsky Sedgwick, *Epistemology of the Closet*

In the prior chapter, I described the tension between certainty and doubt with reference to familiar legal problems. Whether lawyers like it or not, the U.S. Constitution doesn't explain what it means in every controversy by "searches and seizures" or "cruel and unusual punishment." The first set of words is inherently ambiguous: one cannot assert with certainty or finality either what behaviors the Framers of the Constitution intended to be subsumed within the terms "searches" and/or "seizures" or what behaviors *should* be subsumed within those terms. The second set of words—particularly the word "cruel"—is inherently ethical, what is often called a "value judgment." I meant to convey in that chapter that it is simplistic and irresponsible just to retreat into the supposed superiority of "objective" over "subjective" assessments of such words, and even that the divide between "objective" and "subjective" is a smoke screen.

The underlying problem is that, even if there were some objective, fixed, external world beyond what we perceive, there is no way for us to verify when we truly "know" it. That dilemma is among the four that Immanuel Kant described as philosophical antimonies: questions that keep coming up but for which there can be no ultimate resolution. These are the "intractable questions" for which this chapter is named, and there is no getting around them in law.

Another of the metaphysical antimonies is the question of whether we have free will or have all our thoughts and actions (including our perception that we're acting freely) determined by some larger force. On this one, law has decided to pick the side of free will generally but to make exceptions in recognition that many circumstances compromise human choice. Once in a while you get an extraordinary judicial discourse on the broad philosophical outlines of this problem. Look, for example, at *United States v. Moore*,[1] where some of the most distinguished judges ever to sit on the Court of Appeals for the District of Columbia debated whether a drug addict could form the state of mind necessary to be convicted for possessing narcotics.

Of course that court didn't finally *decide* the issue, and no court ever will. The free will problem will present itself forever, in ever-changing contexts, for example, as we learn more about neuroscience[2] and the influence of genetics[3] on behavior. In the meantime, judges cut certain deals for certain subclasses in certain contexts, an ongoing process that is hotly contested, but otherwise the legal system ambles along as if free will were the most obvious thing in the world.

Regarding another of Kant's antimonies—the existence of God—the law just proceeds in perpetual chaos. The legal question is never overtly whether God exists. Rather, government in the United States prefers religion over nonreligion (which it isn't supposed to do) in many contexts, for example, child custody determinations, where a churchgoing parent usually gets a big boost.[4] Doesn't that, at some level, amount to a governmental pronouncement that God exists and that he is good?

Of course, the perpetual font of intractability is the First Amendment. Two cases about public display of the Ten Commandments, decided on the same day in July 2005, exemplify the conceptual whirl. In one case, a five-person majority of the Supreme Court said that the Establishment Clause of the First Amendment to the U.S. Constitution precluded two Kentucky counties from displaying the Ten Commandments on courthouse walls.[5] In the other case, five Justices said that the Establishment Clause did *not* preclude Texas from maintaining a granite monument inscribed with the Ten Commandments on the grounds of the state capitol.[6]

Each case generated seven separate opinions as well as close votes. In most respects, however, the cases were unremarkable—just seventy pages of further wrangling in decades of wrangling about whether to maintain any or all of existing Establishment Clause doctrine. There was one remarkable aspect of the cases, however, illustrating my claim that even garden-variety First Amendment religion cases cannot avoid intractable questions of theology.

In 1952, the Supreme Court majority wrote a much-quoted sentence: "We are a religious people whose institutions presuppose a Supreme Being."[7] Rather than being a blank check for government endorsement of religion, this (historical?) (theological?) premise has allowed that some governmental references to religion, and some governmental subsidization of religious expression, do not violate the Constitution. These include a number of what Justice Breyer might call "borderline cases,"[8] cases that often feel like bickering over matters of barely discernible degree. I had long thought, however, that the basic principles of Establishment Clause jurisprudence were solid: the government may not discriminate among religions, and the government may not favor religion over nonreligion.

In the recent *McCreary County* case, however, three members of the Supreme Court made an astonishing claim. The Establishment Clause, according to Justices Scalia, Rehnquist, and Thomas, allows government to discriminate in favor of *monotheistic religions*. This gang of three was careful to say they endorsed such bias only in a limited context. Government still cannot favor individuals' exercise of monotheistic religious faiths over polytheistic ones; nor can government favor the exercise of some religious faith over no religion; nor can government discriminate in expenditures in favor of monotheisms over polytheisms, or in favor of religious over nonreligious recipients of public funds. When it comes to the government's own expression though—by God—governmental actors can spout all the Christian, Judaic, and/or Islamic beliefs they want, including putting up the Ten Commandments on the taxpayers' walls in McCreary and Pulaski counties, Kentucky.

From this, law review commentators will glean much for their mills. I will not jump into many amazing aspects of the debate (for example, the dispute between Justices Scalia and Stevens regarding how many U.S. believers are monotheistic).[9] I would just note that this discussion proceeds on both sides from a startling level of theological certainty about what constitutes monotheistic religion, polytheistic religion, nontheistic religion, or the absence of religion altogether. Are we sure that we would classify the Founding Fathers—many of whom were Deists—as monotheists?[10] And what about Hinduism? Isn't it profoundly about the illusoriness of the distinction between the many and the one? Might I argue for preferential treatment of Hindus on the grounds that it can be considered monotheism made pure? And though Islam is an ostensibly monotheistic religion, the foreign policy of the United States seems pretty clear that there are theologically correct Muslims and deeply mistaken Muslims.[11] I'm not sure who decides that and on what grounds, or whether Justice Scalia is prepared to distinguish among monotheists. Even if the Supreme Court could successfully avoid the particular questions I have raised, can there really be any end to "this business of judicially examining other people's faiths?"[12]

The spiritual antinomy will arise sharply again should Congress decide to reinstitute the military draft because we would be immersed again in the problem of conscientious objection to military service. As of the time that the draft was discontinued in 1973, the rule of conscientious exemption had been expanded beyond those who held identifiably religious objections to war (such as Quakers, who are "card-carrying members" of a theologically pacifist church group). Exemption was available also to those who held "a sincere and meaningful belief which occupies in the life of its possessor a place parallel to that filled by the God of those admittedly qualifying for the exemption."[13] That standard was notoriously difficult to administer, provoking many to urge that the United States take a broader approach, but that has its problems, too. Europe has done so, providing legal protections beyond military exemption for those holding "any religion, religious belief, or similar philosophical belief" that fits certain criteria such as having "collective worship." Some in the United Kingdom were worried that the 390,000 Britons who listed "Jedi knight" as their religion in the 2001 census would claim a religious holiday upon release of the new Star Wars movie.[14] If *Revenge of the Sith* brought Europe to a screeching halt, I haven't heard about it yet. I can imagine that, should the United States reinstitute the draft and liberalize the exemption rules, the proliferation of Darth Vader outfits at induction centers would decrease the solemnity of future military deployments.

For any question arising with the field of the antimonies, the honest answer is "nowhere to run to, baby, nowhere to hide." We'll have to do the best we can with what we have, assuming we can agree toward what end this activity is directed but keeping in mind that any answer we achieve will be provisional and open to revision.

We find little honesty within legal discourse, however, about what we do and don't know. When we look closely, we see instead that the postmodernist philosophers (notably here, Foucault) were right in identifying the "economy of knowledge and power" as the stuff of which the world is made. When it suits the status quo, knowledge is impossible, such as when we need a decision about the cruelty of the death penalty for minors and the mentally retarded. And when it suits the status quo, certainty is scientifically achievable, even when the scheme of proof is manifestly made up in a manner that consistently benefits the wealthy friends of those who are assigned the task of making up the criteria for truth. As noted in the epigraph to this chapter, power results from collusion among knowledge, ignorance, and opacity.[15]

For the remainder of this chapter, instead of talking about "evaluative" questions, such as what constitutes "cruelty" or "religious" belief, I want to focus on "facts." Specifically, I will explore another of those Kantian puzzles in some depth: the judicial evaluation of causation.

This issue is like a metaphysical bad penny: for all the innumerable efforts to revise, reconceptualize, and streamline rules for determining causation, it keeps re-presenting itself in ever more complex forms. This seems particularly so in "mass tort" and/or "toxic tort" cases. The toxicity left by human enterprise is only recently being appreciated, and research cannot keep up with the synergistic effects of the toxic soup in which we live.[16] From thalidomide to asbestos to Vioxx to the as-yet-unanalyzed concoctions that belched out of the World Trade Center on September 11, 2001,[17] how can the law meet the needs of persons injured by exposures that are difficult to isolate?

I believe that at least in federal courts, judges are deploying a baroquely configured fake objectivity in a way that actually discourages corporate actors from promoting public safety. That is the political result. My theoretical point is that the federal courts in mass tort cases have confused the distinction between epistemology and ontology when addressing questions of causation in mass exposure situations.

These are fancy words, but I don't think one can appreciate the problem of toxic causation as a subset of the hegemony of "facts" without understanding them. "Epistemology" means the study of knowledge, of the criteria by which we measure the usefulness of any assertion of fact. "Ontology," on the other hand, is the study of being, of what is actually "out there." Ontology is the question of whether there is furniture in the universe, and what it might look like.[18] Without maintaining the distinction between epistemology and ontology, one is apt to confuse a method for calibrating the practical reliability of a claim of fact with the eternal word of God.

Specifically, the federal courts[19] have allowed a Rule of Evidence (a rule about what will count toward "knowing," an epistemological rule) to decide profound questions of metaphysics and social policy. The critical event was the U.S. Supreme Court's 1993 ruling in *Daubert v. Merrell Dow Pharmaceuticals, Inc.* The Court interpreted the requirements of Federal Rule of Evidence 702, which allows for testimony of "scientific, technical, or other specialized knowledge" that will assist the trier of fact. In order to be admissible, the *Daubert* Court stated, scientific evidence had to be grounded "in the methods and procedures of science," a "condition [that] goes primarily to *relevance.*"[20] Whether or not it was the Court's intention, lower federal courts in toxic tort cases have used their *Daubert* "gatekeeping" power to exclude plaintiffs' scientific evidence as irrelevant, which has led either to summary judgment for defendants or to the overturning of jury verdicts for plaintiffs where such evidence had been admitted.[21]

What does a claim of causal connection really amount to? Is causation really a matter of fact? If empiricism is the guide, then all causal claims are indeterminate, according to a three-part analysis devised 250 years ago by British philosopher David Hume.[22] First is the relationship in space and time between alleged cause and alleged effect. We could refer to this aspect of causation as "closeness." Second is what Hume called "constant conjunction," what we can refer to as "frequency"—how often we observe the alleged effect after the alleged cause.

But the third aspect of an allegation of a causal relationship is not observable. That is the "necessary connection" between alleged cause and alleged effect. It is only this third aspect that turns mere *correlation* into *causation.* Because of the impossibility of observing the necessary connection, what we call "causation" is really just a habit of inference, a habit humans will exercise depending on the persuasiveness of the evidence of closeness and/or frequency. It is a habit we exercise thousands of times each day, in easy as well as hard cases. It is still just a habit, a customary way of explaining our experience. To put it in the grand language earlier used, Hume's point was that judgments of causation are always matters of epistemology (method), rather than ontology (being).

Causal claims that seem strongest are those that have high degrees of both closeness and frequency. The habit of causal inference becomes less comfortable as situations yield fewer indicia of closeness or frequency, or both. We can visualize this decreasing comfort level by addressing three easy thought problems: depending upon gravity, hitting billiard balls, and falling off a bridge.

I feel confident about gravity, the force (perhaps soon observable as "gravitrons") by which masses are pulled to other masses at a calculable rate. Though scientists are now reporting that gravity may be differential,[23] gravity is as reliable as things get. For example, when I let go of my pencil and it hits the floor, I have a good argument that the letting go caused the hitting. My fingers were exactly next to the pencil, and the letting go was temporally smashed up right against the falling and hitting, and, at least so far, every time I let go of my pencil while holding it above the floor, it falls. There seems to be a perfect Humean correlation.

I have only somewhat less confidence when it comes to billiard balls. Adding isolatable lateral forces to the force of gravity is an easy physics problem. Sometimes I'm a good pool player. Other times every angle seems to conspire against me. When I miss I tend not to attribute it to a crooked cue or a warped table, but to my lack of concentration or lack of skill. And I am not led to doubt that, if the stroke is properly executed, the effect will be the sinking of the billiard balls. There will be perfect contiguity in space and time, and there will be absolute constancy in alleged cause and alleged effect.

Beyond that, things are more complicated, particularly as we become cognizant of necessary negative inferences in an analysis. Consider a case from Louisiana. A man, alone and probably drunk, fell off a bridge while walking home at night and was killed.[24] There were no witnesses. The bridge rails were four inches shorter than as prescribed in regulatory documents. There are dual Humean difficulties in this example. We have a fairly confident notion of the spatial closeness between alleged cause and alleged effect (the bridge and the body) but cannot be confident about the temporal closeness. The man may have bounced off the perfectly sufficient rail many times before he decided to backtrack, climb up, and jump over. He could have been thrown off by someone else. Many things could have happened.

The more important Humean problem, though, is lack of frequency. It is manifestly untrue that every time an intoxicated person walks over that bridge at night, he falls to his death. Indeed, in the Louisiana case, there were no prior instances of similar casualties at the insufficient bridge. The "constant conjunction" aspect of Hume's test utterly fails (not to mention the fact that the dead man may have fallen even if the rails had been four inches higher). Nonetheless, the Louisiana Supreme Court allowed the trier of fact to make the causal judgment in favor of the plaintiff.

Here's the point: determinations of causation in toxic tort cases are not necessarily more difficult than causation determinations in garden variety torts. We let triers of fact make those determinations all the time. Some causal cases are just more unfamiliar than others. But in toxic tort cases, the federal courts typically take fact-finding authority away from the jury by privileging frequency over all other possible indicia of causation. The real explanation of why toxic torts get treated differently, I suspect, is that the defendant industrialists don't like losing.

It is worth studying the elaborate epistemological choreography at work here. The rigid burden on plaintiffs in toxic torts cases has two parts: "general causation," that the toxin in question could cause a harm like that suffered by plaintiff, and "specific causation," that the toxin in question did cause this plaintiff's harm.[25] The first question is easy with respect to toxins that produce "signature diseases." That is, although not everyone exposed to the toxin will develop the disease, every time the disease appears, the patient has been exposed to that toxin. The disease is not known to be associated with anything else. The paradigm signature disease are adenocarcinoma, the vaginal cancer observed only in daughters of pregnant women who took DES to prevent miscarriage, and mesothelomia, the respiratory cancer observed only in persons who have been exposed to asbestos.[26] In these circumstances, the "frequency" aspect of the Humean model is satisfied, for there is no incidence of disease in the "background population" to which the frequency of disease among plaintiffs can be compared. In such cases, plaintiffs almost always satisfy the requirements for general causation. But those are not the typical cases. In the vast majority of toxic injuries, the disease suffered by the exposed plaintiff is a disease that occurs "naturally" in the population, even among those who have not been exposed to the toxin at issue. For example, birth defects can occur even among newborns of mothers who did not take the antinausea medication Bendectin during the twenty-seven years that it was on the market. The questions are whether Bendectin sufficiently increases the probability that an infant will be born with a birth defect (general causation), and whether Bendectin was the cause of the defect suffered by the child of this particular Bendectin-ingesting mother (specific causation).

And here is where we've let industry, the defense bar, and their judicial friends blind us with science. To prove "general causation," the plaintiff is expected to put on epidemiological evidence. Epidemiology is the science of establishing an association between a toxic agent and a disease by comparing the incidence of the disease in the "exposed population" against the incidence of the same disease in the "background population." In general, a toxic tort plaintiff needs to introduce at least one study of how many people got a disease after a particular exposure to a toxin compared to how many people would have had that disease anyway. Moreover, and most artificially, the epidemiology presented has to reach a very specific result: the study must show a "relative risk" of at least "2," often called the "doubling of the risk" standard.

The relative risk is an estimate, expressed as a ratio, of the incidence of disease in the exposed group compared to the incidence in the nonexposed group. Put simply, if ten newborns in the Bendectin-exposed group had a specific sort of birth defect, and ten newborns in the unexposed group had that same defect, the relative risk would be reported as "1." That would suggest no difference in the rate of birth defects between the groups, and would therefore suggest no correlation between Bendectin exposure and that sort of birth defect. If, however, thirty infants in the exposed group suffered the defect, and only ten in the unexposed group suffered it, the relative risk would be reported as "3," suggesting that an exposed infant was three times more likely than an unexposed infant to suffer that defect.[27]

That sounds fine, but one needs to appreciate how seldom epidemiologists reach a relative risk of "2" or greater. That is so even among the populations of Hiroshima and Nagasaki exposed to huge amounts of ionizing radiation by U.S. atomic bombs in 1945. Almost sixty years later, among the dozens of diseases commonly suffered by those residents and their descendants, there has been a demonstrated relative risk of greater than "2" only for breast cancer and stomach cancer.[28]

Any relative risk greater than "1" actually indicates that exposure to a toxin increases the risk of getting a disease, and we let juries consider evidence of "mere" increase of risk in all manner of cases.[29] An epidemiological study with a relative risk result between "1" and "2" may not itself show a strong association between a toxin and a disease, but it certainly does not disprove causation. Though courts simplistically liken the doubling of the risk requirement to the "preponderance of the evidence" burden in civil cases,[30] it is actually closer to proof "beyond a reasonable doubt."[31] As some scientific critics of courts' misapplication of epidemiology have put it, scientists would consider epidemiological studies regardless of the "relative risk" calculation. "They might ignore the results because of poor study design, or because confounders might explain the findings when the rate ratio is less than two, but they would not find the study to be 'irrelevant.' "[32]

So, for example, a study introduced in the silicone breast implant litigation showed a relative risk for autoimmune disease among women with implants of "1.24." Even Dr. Marcia Angell—who has been vociferously critical of the implant litigation—had to admit the relevance of the study. It could mean, she said, that for two out of twelve sick women with implants, "the implants were the sole cause of their disease and in the other 10 they played no role. Or it could mean that implants played a major role in 3 or 4 women and a very small one in the others. Or it could mean that implants contributed a varying amount to the disease in all 12."[33] With all due respect, how can courts denigrate such evidence as irrelevant? Angell's modest interpretations are suggestive at the least of the need for further study, rather than reasons for breast implant plaintiffs to be forever shut out or for the FDA to reconsider allowing silicone implants to be used.

Nonetheless, epidemiology with a specific result has become the sine qua non in mass exposure cases. If epidemiological evidence showing a relative risk greater than "2" is unavailable or otherwise inadmissible, the plaintiff's case is over.[34] Other evidence that might show a general association between a toxin and a disease, such as animal studies or toxicological testimony, is ordinarily not admissible at that point. And the plaintiff will not get to "specific causation" at all. No jury will ever get to hear about the relationship in space and time between the plaintiff and the toxin; will not hear about the dose of the toxin this plaintiff received; will not hear about consistencies between the latency period of the disease and plaintiff's disease; will not hear whether plaintiff can eliminate other sources of the disease; and will never hear anything from the plaintiff's own physicians, no matter how qualified they are.

Judges distort the nature of causality, stack the deck for risk-imposing defendants, and overreach their powers when they allow epidemiology to become the evidentiary sine qua non in mass exposure cases. Epidemiology could speak only to Hume's second criterion for an allegation of causation: the frequency of appearance of both an alleged cause and an alleged effect. Epidemiology begs the question on Hume's first criterion, the "contiguity in space and time" between a specific alleged cause (the conduct of a defendant) and a specific alleged effect (the harms suffered by a plaintiff) because every epidemiological study constructs from the beginning what spatial and temporal boundaries will be considered. To throw out everything on the grounds of alleged epidemiological insufficiency is rather like saying the jury can't know the drunken man was crossing the bridge, because fewer than half the people who crossed it before hadn't fallen off.

Epidemiology has a special place in the pursuit of scientific progress. It allows for tracking and predicting patterns of diseases, and is perhaps the single most important indicator for how medical research should be directed. However, epidemiology is a conservative science that errs dramatically in the direction of false negatives.[35] Epidemiology is also an extraordinarily expensive, time-consuming, and complex enterprise, including many controversial variables. Those variables include defining the disease or diseases of interest; determining the demographic contours of the relative populations; ascertaining the exposure levels of the exposed population; controlling for "confounders" (other sources of the disease); and devising measurements of the scientific robustness (including "statistical significance") of the study.[36] Many plaintiffs will face a statute of limitations years before a meaningful epidemiological study of an alleged toxin could even be designed. Yet they are unable to get courts to see the difference between "no correlation" and "not yet any epidemiological evidence" of correlation between alleged cause and alleged effect. Even if there is time, no plaintiff to date has been in a position—financial or otherwise—to conduct his own studies. Studies do not happen in a vacuum, and in litigation or potential litigation contexts are often conducted by the defending interested parties.

Epidemiology is simply not a neutral tool of legal analysis. It is therefore critical for courts not to conflate methodologies with conclusions—not to conflate epistemology with ontology—a conflation particularly audacious because judges are making claims about the natural world that scientists would not make.

Some scientists and lawyers are attempting to engage courts in more honest conversation about the nature of causal judgments. Much philosophical and legal commentary revolves around the problems of what information, in what different contexts, should be deemed "necessary" or "sufficient" or "necessary and sufficient" in order to justify a judgment of causation.[37] Perhaps most revealing about the real stakes and processes at issue are discussions of a hugely influential article, in which Sir Austin Bradford Hill identified nine "points of view" that can be brought to bear on a causal hypothesis in the toxic exposure context.[38]

It is worth taking a brief look at these because they tend to expand in the toxic exposure context upon what Hume identified as the observable aspects of any causal assertion, as well as upon the pragmatic nature of human knowledge and the feminist method I espouse.

First in Bradford Hill's list is temporality. The event or exposure hypothesized to be causal must precede the effect in time. Second is experimentation; the hypothesis must be testable by scientifically designed methods. Third is consistency. That means that the results of experiments must be replicable if at all possible. Note that epidemiological results can never be exactly replicated because epidemiological cohorts are never strictly "controlled"; no two test populations in successive studies can ever be exactly the same.

Analogy informs Bradford Hill's fourth point of view. The scientist should consider the biological activity of disease agents similar to what is known about the toxin at issue. Here again, the point is not dispositive because biological pathways are only partially understood—if understood at all—for many toxic agents.[39] Fifth in the list is consideration of the "biological gradient." The concern here is the dose-response ratio: what degrees of exposure would we expect to see with what effects? This is a complex curve, difficult to establish, and never established for many powerful toxins, for example, the antimiscarriage drug DES. Sixth to be considered is the strength of association in available studies. Among criteria are "statistical significance" and evaluation of various "confounders," those other influences acting on populations and individuals that could be alternative explanations for disease. Seventh is biological plausibility, that is, the explicability of the causal hypothesis in terms of known mechanisms of disease. Eighth is coherence, an assessment of how the hypothesis fits with, or the degree to which the hypothesis does not displace, all that is known about this toxin and this disease. Ninth is specificity, meaning the degree to which this hypothetical cause and effect can be isolated. Of course, this last point of view underscores the largest difficulty: in other than "signature disease" situations, no one cause is ever isolatable.[40]

Bradford Hill's points of view overlap, are suggestive with respect to one another, and are necessarily cumulative. Evaluation of a causal hypothesis depends on consideration of all the points of view. I cannot overemphasize the conclusion of Sir Bradford Hill's analysis: "None of my nine points of view can bring indisputable evidence for or against the cause-and-effect hypothesis and none can be required as a sine qua non."[41] I would suggest that Bradford Hill's conclusion in the context of toxic causation resonates with the great recent contributions of philosophy from Wittgenstein through the American pragmatists to the postmodernists: *nothing* can be postulated or required as the sine qua non of *any* critical issue of knowledge or social policy.

That admonition notwithstanding, the defense bar has largely succeeded so far in transforming the Bradford Hill "points of view" into just further regressive and authoritarian hoops that plaintiffs have to jump through.[42] An illustration of the circularity in the legal standard is a case involving Parlodel, a drug taken by women postpartum to suppress lactation. The court granted summary judgment against the plaintiff, who had never had hypertension but who suffered several strokes after taking Parlodel. The parties had agreed that no meaningful epidemiology existed regarding the drug. Plaintiff's expert proposed to rely on items of evidence that would inform several of the Bradford Hill points of view, and explained the meaning of the Bradford Hill methodology as well as its scientific recognition. The court, however, accepted the drug company's argument that the Bradford Hill factors were useful only after a toxin/disease connection had been "established" by epidemiological evidence.[43] Either disingenuously or ignorantly, the court went on to state that "by requiring an epidemiological study as a starting point for application of the Bradford Hill criteria, the court is not requiring [plaintiff] to provide an epidemiological study in order to establish causation."[44] Of course, the reality is that epidemiology is required not because of the scientific usefulness of epidemiology but because it occupies the place of "necessary connection"—the aspect of causation Hume showed was never demonstrable—in the judicial imagination. Perhaps "imagination" is not the right word. A mind-set so narrow as to require that sort of privileged mysticism is stuck in a Newtonian or even pre-Newtonian world. It cannot deal humanely or rigorously with problems beyond the billiard balls.

This chapter is not about the many alternatives proposed to the archaic treatment of toxic torts currently imposed by U.S. courts. There is a vast literature on that, suggesting everything from more legislative compensation schemes[45] to science courts to more modest procedural and evidentiary reforms. Because the tort system is an incredibly inefficient health care regime, universal health care would solve some of the present hysteria. And the present system must become much more preventative. As it is, the requirements of courtroom proof actually discourage manufacturers from conducting sufficient premarket testing that might indicate a danger from their products.[46] That is unacceptable; surely, a consistent and compulsory measure of good science prior to consumer exposure, such as is emerging in the law of the European Union, would be preferable to endless fights about what is good science once we're at the mercy of the rickety U.S. torts system.

I am not saying that the law can't have standards and guideposts. I cannot say often enough that I am not encouraging judges simply to make stuff up. It is fanciful to suggest that they do, or that existing institutions give them much room to do so, or that anybody teaching law thinks it would be fine if they did. And I am not saying that there aren't "facts of the matter," which are sometimes simple to ascertain and that undeniably decide cases. Rather, I've described how intractable metaphysical questions tend to pop up again and again in law, and that even on questions of "scientific fact," certain interests are reliably served at the expense of others. I understand judges' frustration with the astronomical inefficiencies in the common law resolution of toxic torts. But that does not justify the embrace of scientistic dogmatism. It is not that plaintiffs should win all of these cases; it is that they ought not be stuck in the basement with the alleged furniture of the universe jammed under the doorknob.

The reader may wonder what this has to do with feminist jurisprudence, and the answer is "everything." The institutions, the rules, and the "facts" are all engineered by people who, consciously or not, are serving the patriarchal corporate masters. There. I said it. Let the reader note that almost every example of toxic tort injustice to which I've referred has special relevance for women: thalidomide—the anti-morning-sickness drug that causes birth defects; Bendectin—the anti-morning-sickness drug that causes birth defects; DES—the antimiscarriage drug that causes cancer in both daughters and sons (and possibly the grandchildren) of the mothers who took it; Parlodel—a lactation-relief drug that causes strokes; silicone breast implants—the product that causes autoimmune deficiencies; Fen-Phen, a diet drug taken mostly by women that causes strokes; antidepressants, the drugs that have multiple and lethal side effects and that are overwhelmingly prescribed to women, and, given the examples just listed, who can blame women for needing them? I haven't even referred to other sex-specific toxic torts and the injuries arising from them, from birth control pills to various IUD's to killer tampons.

Is there a conspiracy in the tort system against women? Various studies confirm that women are hugely disproportionately hurt by the toxic torts regime and the law of torts generally,[47] and several scholars have shown how that happens.[48] But "conspiracy" connotes consciousness. It would be fairer to say that scientific establishments and the torts system have ignored women because women are not persons within their learned habits of social investigation.[49] Women have been relatively expendable subjects of "after-market research," the sell-and-see-later approach encouraged by U.S. tort law.

The real sex discriminatory regime is this: women take the toxins into their bodies because society tells them to; men are externally exposed to toxins in their jobs. Of course, that is not uniformly true: all sufferers from arthritis are internally exposed to the risks from Vioxx and similar drugs; women in blue-collar jobs are externally exposed to industrial toxins; I do not denigrate the class-oppressive connotations of the jobs on which men are most often exposed. But the "voluntary" taking into the body of various toxins by women in order to fulfill social expectations of womanhood is a fundamental feminist issue. Among the contexts of special concern are the burdens of reproduction and child rearing on women; the medicalization of reproduction; the commodification of women's bodies and concomitant pressures on women to conform to those images; and the chemical manipulation of women's minds so that we don't go crazy (and that if we do, we won't be too threatening). Industry's participation and profit in all of that are feminist issues. Therefore, the disproportionate impact of courts' treatment of causation in toxic torts is a feminist issue.

Some princes in the court of privilege have argued that causation is just "an inarticulate groping for economically sound solutions."[50] I am dismayed by the extent to which judges, lawyers, and law students believe that. It isn't true; causation is not just that. Not without explicit description of the nonmonetary economies at issue.

I am all for recognizing the indeterminacy of causation, and the indeterminacies inherent in many other legal questions. I am against easy answers such as "economically sound solutions." What will it take for all lawyers and judges, in Professor Mari Matsuda's immortal words, to ask the next questions? What will it take for every student, teacher, lawyer, and judge to submit every assertion of causal or other fact to scrutiny under the lenses of historical inequality?

In any case, the way to deal with intractable questions is not for courts to pretend to scientific expertise or any other authority over questions that have stumped the human mind for millennia. The way to deal with intractable questions is to recognize them as such, to affirm that the law can't avoid them, and then to attempt and refine methodologies that by definition lead only to provisional answers, with primary and honest focus on the purposes of the laws giving rise to the ambiguities.

In this book, I want to expand the notion of toxicity. To my mind, sexism, racism, homophobia, and all the other instruments of manipulation of human fears, are toxins just as powerful as plutonium. They are the ultimate weapons of mass destruction, and the law cannot be legitimate without addressing them head on.

4

The Limits of Liberalism

How she longed to get out of that dark hall, and wander about among those beds of bright flowers and those cool fountains, but she could not even get her head through the doorway; "and even if my head would go through," thought poor Alice, "it would be of very little use without my shoulders."

—Lewis Carroll, *Alice in Wonderland*

So far, this book has criticized some of the conventional explanations for legal power that initially attract lawyers, judges, and students. In chapter 1, I related how institutional justifications—such as the magisterial invocation of "the rule of law"—are meaningless without commitments to the principles implied thereby. In chapter 2, I described how approaches regressing always to radical doubt need to get over themselves in order to be helpful in legal disputes. Allowing that doubt will always be with us regarding particular questions, I focused in chapter 3 on how what we call "facts" are themselves elaborate social constructions that serve existing economic interests. In this chapter, I expose the empty refuge of philosophical liberalism—the structure by which law lets us live in our heads.

Given the difficulties described so far, one wonders why the U.S. legal system has worked at all. I believe U.S. law can attribute apparent successes to the pervasive and usually invisible theoretical underpinnings of "liberalism." It is the unofficial politics, ethics, and psychology of the United States. "Liberalism" is simply a philosophical theory, born of the eighteenth-century Enlightenment, reappearing in multiple incarnations since. It is important not to conflate *philosophical* liberalism with *political* liberalism. Indeed, those who in daily politics we call "liberals" and "conservatives" are all philosophical liberals who agree on almost all fundamental ideas, and whose disputes occur within a narrow field. Three attributes of liberal government have given it staying power: its very specific ideology passes as neutrality; it makes its narrow conflicts look broader than they are; and very little actually changes amidst all the sound and fury.

Liberal Human Nature and Liberal Society

So what is liberalism? Most political theory has an underlying theory of human nature, and that is crucially so for liberalism. All features of liberalism follow, however, from one powerful idea: individualism. First, liberalism holds that the individual exists prior to society. The structures of society are made of the bricks of individuals, and are simply the sum of those parts. Second, all individuals—at all times and at all places—share certain characteristics. The individual is a rational creature. Moreover, individuals are naturally self-interested. They will use their rationality to achieve their individual needs and desires. Humans have the capacity for altruism, but any such inclination is in tension with the more fundamental pursuit of self-interest. Third, the power of reason is possessed in approximately equal amounts by all humans. But having this level playing field rarely means that the score will be tied. Instead, individuals must invest their own industry in order for their desires to be achieved. The natural result of equal capacities unequally utilized will be social inequalities.

Liberal political theory brings this picture of humanity to another assumption about the world: resources are and will remain scarce. Thus, individuals are naturally in competition for available resources, and the individual's program for fulfillment of desires is subject to constant interference from other individuals and their competing programs. The political question is therefore how to organize society best to protect opportunities for self-fulfillment and to resolve inevitable conflicts.

In the classical liberal conception, people create governments because we can't get along in the "state of nature." The purposes of government are to provide defense from external threats, and domestically only to provide conditions conducive to peaceful coexistence and self-fulfillment of all of the individuals thus described. This "night watchman" theory of the state defines political power by its limits. It is a given that the individual is primary and his self-determination must not be encroached upon unless absolutely necessary. Moreover, because the program for self-fulfillment is determinable only by each individual himself, there is no basis on which the state could prefer some efforts at self-fulfillment over others. The state must act, or appear to act, neutrally. In light of all this, liberalism is constantly engaged in differentiating legitimate exercises of state power from illegitimate exercises of state power.

Most of Western philosophy is organized around dualisms, and the one most central to the liberal theory of limited government is the distinction between public and private realms of life. The state may regulate the former when necessary, but may not "interfere" in the latter. Liberals dispute among themselves which activities are public and which are private, but they don't dispute the centrality of the public/private distinction. This is what I meant about the short distance between political liberals and political conservatives: they agree on the liberal theory of human nature, and they agree about the theory of limited government that follows from it. They disagree only about the specific circumstances when the state may justifiably encumber individual preferences.

All of this is so engrained that, when recently rereading John Locke's Second Treatise of Government,[1] I felt as I felt the last time I saw a production of *Hamlet.* It was so familiar that it was as if Shakespeare had just strung a lot of clichés together.[2] Similarly, the story of liberalism is practically second nature for lawyers. It is the plot in the dispute between Federalists and Anti-Federalists during the drafting of the United States Constitution: which structure of government would tend less toward encroachment upon individual actions?[3] It is the story of "the Lochner era" in the first third of the twentieth century: could worker protections ever trump individual freedom of contract?[4] More recently, this mythic struggle was embodied by the threat or the promise, depending on your point of view, of the Warren Court. That Court "loosed" the equality principle, declaring in 1954 that black children and white children had to go to public school together, in spite of individual choices to the contrary as codified by representative bodies.[5] The question of the subsequent two decades was to just what degree governmental power could limit individualism, importantly including enjoyment of the fruits of individual industry. The Warren Court came scarily or thrillingly close, depending on your point of view, to articulating a constitutional requirement for the redistribution of wealth.[6]

In more general terms, twentieth-century liberal thought began to move slightly away from the "night watchman" theory of the state in recognition of the fact that the playing field is not really level. The first area for adjustment of opportunities was the market economy, which is not surprising, given the joint historical and theoretical heritage of liberal theory and capitalism. When liberalism emerged, it expressed the self-image and political needs of the simultaneously emerging bourgeoisie. The political theories of John Locke and John Stuart Mill worked in lockstep with the economic theory of Adam Smith. The presumption of scarcity and the focus on fulfillment of self-interest justified and protected the institution of private property. Twentieth-century mitigation of classical liberal assumptions has been in response to the excesses of capitalism: as the rich got so much richer and the poor got so much poorer, liberalism could not maintain its purely abstract egalitarianism.

The Dimensions of Liberalism

In demonstrating the narrow range and utter predictability of public debate on allegedly profound disputes, Professor Catharine MacKinnon has helpfully identified "the five cardinal dimensions of liberalism" as individualism, naturalism, voluntarism, idealism, and moralism. Professor MacKinnon illustrates how these dimensions work in the context of the usual justifications for "men's magazines." In this litany, a model who spreads her legs for a camera is acting voluntarily; she is a self-determined individual and we should honor her choices. Moreover, her photogenic body is a simple fact of nature, "prior to its social construction through being viewed," that is merely captured on film like any other landscape. When anyone criticizes men's magazines, they become "thought police," hysterically attempting to regulate mere ideas when everybody knows ideas have a harmless life of their own. Finally, critics of men's magazines are dangerous to the American way of life; they are attempting to shove their morality down everybody else's throat, when liberalism has taught us that morality can be nothing more than individual opinion.[7]

If you are a law student, take down any casebook and select any case. Odds are that you can find at least one of these "cardinal dimensions" in argumentation, if not dispositive of the matter at hand. I took a quick look through the casebook I'm now using in my Torts class. Individualism: Three hundred drug companies made DES, an antimiscarriage drug that caused cancer in children of pregnant women who took it. It all happened long enough ago that it cannot be proven that a given woman took doses manufactured by any particular company. Each company wanted to defend on the ground that whoever did it to this mother's daughter, it wasn't them, and even if that company acted negligently, it is just un-American to hold anyone responsible (keeping in mind that corporations possess most of the rights of individuals) for some specific harm unless it can be shown that that company individually did it.[8] Naturalism: a man's wife and friend had a sexual affair; the man wanted the court to agree that the conduct was just transparently outrageous, thus satisfying that element of a claim for intentional infliction of emotional distress.[9] Voluntarism: a thirteen-year-old girl committed a suicide that her high school officials might have prevented; the high school defended on the ground that suicide is "a deliberate, intentional and intervening act" for which no one else should be held responsible.[10] Idealism: a civically active man received anonymous and threatening telephone calls over the course of twenty months. The court said there was no harm done where there was no threat of physical injury in the imminent future.[11] Moralism: a casino patron keeled over with a heart attack. The casino had an intubation kit but no one was trained to use it. Too bad for the plaintiff. The law imposes no obligation to act in the aid of others. Where would such a morally intrusive doctrine end?[12]

Silicone breast implants are another dramatic example. On the question of individualism, popular discourse wants to hold women to the claim that our bodies are our own. When some of us augment our breasts, we are customizing our bodies like other people customize cars; we are expressing ourselves. On the naturalism front, at one point large breasts were said to be "essential to women's mental health." Flat-chestedness causes a "total lack of well being," amounting to a disease called "micromastia."[13] Because the deformity was unnatural, so surely was the corrective desire natural. Which leads us to voluntarism. It is true that silicone implants were rushed to market without adequate testing. It certainly appears that breast implants are a recent chapter in "a virtually uninterrupted history of painful alteration of the female body" for beauty's sake.[14] But cosmetic surgery is an elective change to a healthy body. It is not even a choice of competing therapeutic treatments. No one is forcing her to do it.[15] And because beauty is in the eye of the beholder, this is all about idealism. One woman's self-objectifying excess is another woman's décolletage. In the peroration of the liberal argument, those feminists who criticize the breast implant industry are un-American moralistic hysterics. The counterargument captures the limits of liberalism: why is it that so many women decide to rebuild themselves? Aren't the forces at work a bit murkier than liberalism wishes to acknowledge?

The liberal tradition has both ennobling and depressing aspects. We partake of the best part of liberalism when we express admiration for a person's accomplishments, particularly when she captains her own ship through stormy waters. On the other hand, liberalism masks the nature of accomplishment and belief. Everything worth doing takes a village. No beliefs are formed in a vacuum. The radical individualism at the heart of liberalism obscures the group-based nature of human enterprise, and encourages a race to the bottom in public discourse.

The radical relativism in liberal thought also tethers us to slow-moving majoritarian politics, which itself transpires with agonizing disingenuousness. Perhaps most destructively, liberalism makes it systematically difficult to perceive or take responsibility for systematic violence and power imbalances. These beliefs affirmatively discourage recognition of the group-based nature of social problems. Liberalism leads us to think that every spilling of literal or figurative blood is an "isolated incident."[16] If some (surely tiny!) subset of women "chose" to have silicone breast implants because they had been socially beaten down just for being women, and were desperate for any pathetic measure of self esteem, and were also (completely unrelatedly, of course) unlucky enough to develop debilitating autoimmune diseases, that's just the way the liberal cookie crumbles.

Consequences for the Guarantee of Equality

I've chosen to illustrate the consequences of liberal thought with equality law, not just because it has been the focus of my law practice but because "equality" is the biggest thorn in liberalism's proverbial side. In traditional liberal discourse, the predominant tension is between "liberty" and "equality." Take the situation of a country club, say, Augusta National. It may exclude women from its golf course, be perfectly open about that, and even enjoy widespread respect, so long as it is a private organization. In the United States, when the value of "equality" bumps up against the value of "liberty," liberty interests usually win.[17]

The 14th Amendment to the U.S. Constitution guarantees to every person the "equal protection of the laws" but doesn't define what "equal" means. The language doesn't tell us how to decide real cases. In the United States, the measurement of equality has been based upon Aristotle's notion of justice: like cases must be treated alike. But how do we know when cases are alike? What must be equal with respect to what? Maybe every person should have exactly the same amount of money in all conceivable circumstances. Maybe all persons whose last names begin with "S" should be compelled to wear pink socks. I won't get many votes for those interpretations. A socially useful definition of equality requires multidimensional considerations that will necessarily vary from case to case.

We can usefully consider the kinds of commitments that are called for in equality law with reference to a spectrum, the left end representing the least "governmental intrusion" into individualistic ordering, and the right end representing the most.[18]

FORMAL EQUALITY——SUBSTANTIVE EQUALITY——ABSOLUTE EQUALITY

This equality spectrum is a sort of "Goldilocks" problem: formal equality is not enough, absolute equality is too much, but substantive equality is *just* right.

Formal equality is just that, a matter of pure form. The word "equal" in the Constitution connotes only a logical relation. If $2 = 2$, then both "2's" must be treated exactly the same. However, $2 \neq 2.000013$. Therefore, the numbers 2 and 2.000013 can justly be treated differently. How would this play out in law? If any difference can be discerned between any two individuals, they may justly be treated differently. A former student named Sherry had a bushy head of red hair. I don't. Suppose the Governor gave Sherry a Snickers bar and didn't give me one. That would be "just" in a formal equality regime because she has red hair. Sherry and I are at least as different from each other as 2 and 2.000013 are from each other.

This argument probably doesn't convince anyone. You cannot imagine yourself standing up in court and arguing that red-headed people are legally entitled to more peanut products covered with creamy nougat, caramel, and chocolate. In U.S. constitutional law, we require that any difference asserted to justify different treatment be at least "rational." It would be fine if Sherry got the Snickers bar because I have diabetes and she doesn't, but not because I don't have red hair and she does.

Like formal equality, "absolute equality" (sometimes called "assimilationism") is fairly useless as a tool of social policy. In its extreme form, absolute equality holds that no group-based differences should ever count in figuring out the appropriate distribution of governmental burdens and benefits.[19] The perceived differences among people have no inherent meaning. The significance of any difference is simply what we attach to it because of habit, laziness, or anxiety to impose order—however artificial—upon a senseless existence. Thus, the Aristotelian formula is inherently circular. Cases are as "like" or as "unalike" as we choose to make them.[20]

In an assimilationist mode, one could argue against laws that impose much lower speed limits for vehicles in school zones. One could say that these laws are destructive indulgences. Everyone needs to learn how to dodge traffic, don't they?[21] Hmm. That doesn't work any better than giving preferential treatment based on hair color. Laws are generated by purposes, and we have to have clear ways of talking about them. When the government gives a functional reason for different treatment (younger children are less capable of dealing with traffic), when that reason is genuine (not a subterfuge for accomplishing some nefarious purpose) and does not involve any historically suspect classifications, we're pretty much fine with that legislation. We don't need to go much further in the justification game. This is why we have legislatures, to make choices to protect public well-being.

Law looks not just for a difference but for a difference that makes sense. Having now rejected the concepts of both "formal equality" and "absolute equality," we are ineluctably left with the question: how much sense does a difference have to make? How good does the reason for different treatment have to be? According to our spectrum, we would seem to be in the land of "substantive equality," but what substance are we talking about?

There are no obvious logical answers here, just functional and historical ones. The historical reasons are far more contentious than functional ones regarding, say, speed limits in school zones. That is, some differences used to justify different treatment are bogus for historical reasons: over time, some groups have gotten a raw deal. Thus, when those bogus differences are asserted, there has to be an underlying good reason (as opposed to a merely "rational" one) to justify a difference in treatment between individuals.

To posit an unlikely scenario, suppose Sherry and I are otherwise equally qualified for a job on the police force. It turns out that Sherry is a U.S. citizen, and I am a resident alien. Historically, it is undeniably true that legal immigrants have been denied a range of advantages. Because of that, the police have to give a good reason to hire Sherry and not me. According to the U.S. Supreme Court, they do have a good reason: it makes enough sense for police personnel policies to assume that citizens will have a greater investment in the fair and efficient enforcement of law than noncitizens.[22] Give us your tired, your poor, et al., so long as they don't want to be cops. Here is why the discourse of equality law conventionally conflicts with the individualist rhetoric of liberalism. My country of origin notwithstanding, I may actually be the superior U.S. patriot. Sherry may be a pinko infiltrator but gets away with thwarting my program of self-fulfillment and individual achievement by an accident of birth.

Some of the historically suspect reasons are more suspect than others. In U.S. equality doctrine, the closest we have come to "absolutely equality" is with regard to race discrimination. Although it is not true that race never counts, it is true that race rarely counts in legal argument as a justification for distinguishing among persons or situations. If a racial difference is asserted to justify different treatment of individuals (or groups of individuals), there has to be not only a rational reason for it, and not only a good reason for it, but a damn good reason for it. Let's say that Sherry is an African American woman, and that I'm a white woman. Suppose we also live in a place where Sherry has access to publicly funded sickle-cell anemia screening and I don't. If I complain about that, I will lose. Sickle-cell anemia is a medical condition endured almost exclusively by persons of African heritage. Screening everybody else would be medically meaningless and a waste of public funds. If the health department denies me this service because of my race, it has a damn good reason.

But now we're out in lawyer woo-woo land. There are a few race discrimination cases involving sickle-cell anemia.[23] Though sickle cell anemia will gain civil rights traction as genetic testing becomes common, the existing cases are hardly historically representative of racism in action. The reason that race discrimination demands a really damn good justification is because in United States history, the reasons for treating races differently were not only bogus, but evil.

Slavery and the complex social institutions that followed from it were not mistakes of differentiation, or overreactions to real biological differences, but atrocities. It is for those reasons that race discrimination is paradigmatic of the meaning of inequality in this country. Remedying histories of demonstrated persecution of groups of people is the entire point of the guarantee of equality. Skin pigmentation is a proxy for historical persecution. When law disappears the history and focuses on all the possible permutations of "difference," the guarantee of equality is worse than futile; it is a monumental diversion of our resources.

So we have to focus on what we might mean by "substantive equality," what versions of the guarantee of equality might be available in that logical middle ground. It might be useful to visualize another spectrum:[24]

MERITOCRATIC EQUALITY OF OPPORTUNITY	———	EDUCATIONAL EQUALITY OF OPPORTUNITY	———	CANADA AND BEYOND

The first two of these are probably familiar to you, because they encompass much of the territory contested in the context of affirmative action. The "meritocratic" part is the notion that persons being compared are otherwise "equally qualified" (or "equally in need," or what have you). If so, it is acceptable (within very narrow limits) to "take into account" their race (or sex, or what have you) to give a tiny boost to the otherwise equally qualified persons who have suffered historical discrimination. This is the "similar situation" requirement in U.S. Equal Protection doctrine. You can't get equality rights unless you show that you are like the people with respect to whom you're being treated worse.

"Educational" equality of opportunity focuses slightly less on the requirement of "similar situation." The idea is that the law can intervene (again, within narrow limits) to alter environments, recognizing that environments can preclude individuals (note the consistent focus on individualism—we are still firmly rooted in liberal turf here) from reaching a stage of development that could give them a plausible shot at being equally qualified with, or similarly situated to, individuals from more privileged backgrounds or living in circumstances that give them disproportionate power. As of now, this is where public discourse in the United States stalls.

Other hot issues in U.S. law fall under this rubric. One example is the attempt by some cities to provide public education for groups at risk. Detroit had ample data that its African American adolescent males were a population in considerable danger, but that city was not allowed to provide all-male schools for them.[25] Young women face their own multiple risks. As an obvious example, pregnancy is closely correlated with high school dropout rates. The city of New York has opened the Young Women's Leadership School in East Harlem.[26] It has not yet produced a legal challenge.

The most contentious example right now is legislative reapportionment, the power of state legislatures to configure voting districts every ten years (or more often, in the case of Texas[27]) in order to reflect demographic changes revealed by the Census. Though reapportionment is not about education as such, I include it as an instance of "educational equality of opportunity" because it involves explicit recognition of group-based historical discrimination, and empowers government—at least in theory—to give a leg up not based on a prior showing of "similar situation." That is, the Voting Rights Act of 1965 requires that states assure appropriate representation of racial minorities in the House of Representatives, though of course the states must do so within the terms of the act and constitutional limits. That's where the problems have come. The United States Supreme Court has made rather a mess of it. Disappearing history again, it has allowed states to tinker with voting district boundaries when to do so will dramatically stack the decks for one political party,[28] but the Court has imposed ever-more-stringent requirements on reapportionment decisions that would likely increase representatives of color.[29]

It turns out that neither meritocratic nor educational equality does much for real equality. Because of the radical individualism at liberalism's core, these "improvements" are not very far from formal equality at all. In the next two chapters, I will focus more specifically on equality, and describe a vision of it that actually focuses on how structures of domination by some groups over other groups were historically created and are currently maintained. The feminist approach described there dares to name the oppressions, dares to talk about white supremacy and male supremacy, and heterosexism and global capitalist exploitation—

systems that are astronomically and multitudinously effective in combination—without cowering before the charges of political correctness or moral imperialism.

These days, systems of oppression are not usually consciously maintained. That is where the tenets of liberalism get in the way of progress for equality; because the harms of existing power structures are not done intentionally, as it were, individuals are offended by what looks like them to be efforts to deprive them of what they are and have become all on their own initiative, individualism being the ultimate value. And from the usually subconscious point of view of socially powerful people, that is really the beauty part. The power grid is invisible *and* it really works.

The Canadian Vision

On the doctrinal level, we have instructive articulations of the principle of "substantive equality" from Canadian courts. Canada ratified its own Constitution only in the early 1980s, and since then, the Canadian Courts have often looked to but rejected U.S. interpretations of similar constitutional provisions. Consider seven principles, or my compilation of seven features, of Canadian equality law that challenge the hegemony of liberal thought.

First, Canada has a broader view of which groups, as groups, get socially shafted. Section 15(1) of the Canadian Charter of Rights and Freedoms prohibits discrimination on the bases of "race, national or ethnic origin, colour, religion, sex, age or mental or physical disability." But the list is not exhaustive. A plaintiff states a constitutional claim if her complaint is based on "analogous grounds," that is, if her grouping is characterized by stereotyping, prejudice, and historical disadvantage. It is pursuant to the "analogous grounds" doctrine that sexual minorities enjoy full constitutional protection in Canada.[30]

Second, not just anybody gets to claim that he or she is unequally treated. You can't just be some optician in Oklahoma[31] who wakes up feeling unequal one morning in order to invoke constitutional equality protection. You have to be a member of an enumerated group or show that your group (or individual situation contextually conveyed) meets the "analogous grounds" test.[32] In the last decade or so in the United States, I've been amazed by how often privileged people and entities describe themselves as victims, even as they decry the "victimology" supposedly practiced by people who can actually demonstrate their own historical disempowerment.[33] Undoubtedly, it would help to unclog U.S. courts' dockets if we tightened access for those who are historically privileged from asserting equality claims.

Third, in Canada, affirmative action is specifically allowed in the Charter of Rights and Freedoms.[34] I can't think of anything that more directly expresses a society's recognition that individualism is not the be-all and end-all of the social contract, in any of its dimensions.

Fourth, in Canadian constitutional law, there are no "levels of scrutiny." Once any constitutional claim has been stated, courts engage in an explicit balancing test, to wit, asking whether a constitutional infringement once proven is "justified in a free and democratic society," as required by Section 1 of the Canadian Charter.[35] Some commentators see this as a dispositive difference between American and Canadian constitutional adjudication[36] that may even justify U.S. lawyers' ignorance of Canadian law. But that criticism doesn't really clock the reality of American practice. What we have in the United States is just perpetual *implicit* balancing in all manner of constitutional cases, inefficiently delayed and undemocratically obfuscated by the Byzantine regime of preliminary tests.

Fifth, and usually most astonishing to U.S. lawyers, Canadian equality law has no requirement of a showing of "similar situation." The Canadians get that equality is a comparative concept but have accepted that locating the relevant comparative group is not a matter of logic but of examination of the context in which a claim arises.[37] This difference from American law made it relatively easy for the Canadian Supreme Court to overcome one of the most embarrassing constitutional "principles" of U.S. law, that pregnancy discrimination is not sex discrimination.[38]

Sixth, constitutional adjudication in Canada is expressly purposive, what U.S. lawyers sneeringly call "result-oriented," so that decisions have explicit political content and are explicitly provisional. As former Canadian Chief Justice Brian Dickson stated, "[I]t is only where the law is interpreted by an independent judiciary with vision, a sense of purpose, and a profound sensitivity to society's values, that the rule of law, and therefore the citizen's rights and freedoms, are safe."[39] I don't know about other U.S. legal scholars, but I'm ready to add vision, purpose, and sensitivity to the rather reticent U.S. understandings of the rule of law described in chapter 1. And we should also include Canada's relative fearlessness of majority rule in constitutional matters: that country's commitment to making equality real includes a willingness to order provincial legislatures to bring their games up to speed.[40]

Seventh, finally and most important from my point of view, in Canada there is no requirement to find intent to discriminate in order for a constitutional equality claim to be proved.[41] Think of how different U.S. constitutional lawyerly lives would be if we didn't have to show intent in constitutional equality cases.

I don't want to exaggerate Canada's success. The Charter is not perfect, its interpretations are not perfect, and many Canadian scholars are working to ensure that people like me don't overidealize the Canadian example. But working with Canadian equality law is refreshing because Canada is simply not deterred by the alleged obstacles to doing better that U.S. lawyers take as gospel. For example, in deciding that a claim under the U.S. Equal Protection clause required a plaintiff to show the government's intent to discriminate, our Supreme Court dragged out a slippery slope argument that generally produced knowing nods from the U.S. constitutional professoriate:

> A rule that a statute designed to serve neutral ends is nevertheless invalid, absent compelling justification, if in practice it benefits or burdens one race more than another would be far-reaching and would raise serious questions about, and perhaps invalidate, a whole range of tax, welfare, public service, regulatory, and licensing statutes that may be more burdensome to the poor and to the average black than to the more affluent white.[42]

The (perhaps idealized) Canadian response to this prospect is "great." Let's get after those discriminatory tax, welfare, public service, regulatory, and licensing statutes as soon as possible! Canada has done so and there are no visible cracks in the foundation of that republic.

Beyond Liberalism

There is a lot about liberalism to love. Its historical emergence was intertwined with the demise of feudalism and immortal manifestations of the human spirit in art, science, and politics. There is no reason that some of liberalism's ideas and commitments should not be retained. However, there are lots of other ways to think about our species' possibilities. It may take some therapy for our national solipsism, but we need only look around to see the possibilities. It will also take some willingness to name problems out loud. Improving upon liberalism means to expose the structures of privilege, that is, to recognize that all of law is already an affirmative action plan for somebody (usually, for whoever got to write the law).[43] To make this case, however, requires at least some consideration of alternatives to the tenets of liberalism.

Individualism. The self is a necessary but unprovable construct in law as in life. The uniqueness of individuals, though a genetic reality, doesn't have a lot of social meaning. The forces of conformity have astonishing and insidious power. Whether by nature or nurture (itself an intentionally obfuscating distinction), our individual identities are permanently fluid and are largely functions of our coordinates in time and space, functions particularly of our group memberships within culture.

Naturalism. Nothing in the world carries around or communicates its own singular meaning. Nothing has to be as it seems to be. Those who argue that some negative features of social life are inevitable almost always have a stake in maintaining those features. There is a reason why fundamentalism in all forms hates evolution theory. Fundamentalisms hold that there can be no change in anything. The central contribution of Darwin was that nothing, not even human nature, is static. The central idea of evolution is that species change, as necessary. It would now seem necessary for the human species to change in innumerable ways and to embrace the processes of change, both to avoid military annihilation and to flourish.

Voluntarism. "Choice" is one of the most highly contested concepts in the legal world,[44] and so I discuss the concept more fully in chapter 7. In the meantime, though there may be some genuine determinists still around—those who believe that free will doesn't exist—the whole notion is probably much more complicated. We do make choices and do have responsibility for them, but one of those responsibilities is that we must radically interrogate what we believe our choices to be. In much of life, what we "consent" to is what we are conditioned to accept. We are normalized—by popular culture, social norms, politicians, and histories of violence—"willingly" to undertake or accept lots of things that aren't good for us, our neighbors, or the planet. In many circumstances, we are so constrained by social forces that we choose choicelessness. Whenever the concept of choice or consent is invoked as legal justification, let's take a closer look at what is really going on.[45]

Idealism. Whoever convinced us that words and ideas don't have an impact on reality had an incredible impact on reality. It is amazing that we still entertain this axiom, when every advertiser and other practitioner of *realpolitik* knows the opposite: if you say something often enough, people are increasingly likely to believe it is true. An alternative to liberalism accepts that words and ideas matter a great deal, and are in fact constitutive of reality.[46]

Moralism. I don't think that the distinction between moral judgments and other judgments has much use any more. In referring in this book to the emerging field of "virtue ethics," I am asking the reader to reconsider the human "virtues" described by Aristotle. The original list that he so admirably explained—honesty, courage, wisdom, and generosity—needn't be understood as an essentialist final word on ethics. We don't even have to call the listed items "virtues." But Aristotle's is a pretty good list, a set of topics that inform pragmatic thought as well as describe whatever our species has gotten right. Whatever you want to call it, there is no way around moral dispute. The cardinal dimensions of liberalism are thoroughly moral, in the sense of representing choices about the way the world should work and the way people should behave or aspire to behave. People seem to require norms and mythologies to help us find our way about. But morals, norms, and myths are only and ever products of communication rather than of individual invention.

It was only in the 2004 election season that I grasped the profundity of President Franklin Roosevelt's admonition that "the only thing we have to fear is fear itself." Heated moral sloganeering has displaced discourse. That fundamental stupidity is a function of our fears: fears of contingency,[47] of unimportance,[48] and of our inevitable dependency on others.[49] Only participation in "moral" discourse allows us to go beyond fear. The ethic of communication must be to resist dogmatism, particularly in subconscious or invisible forms. Good-faith communication requires, ironically, a return to individualism of a sort, a perpetually questioning individualism that liberalism actually inhibits.[50] And that aspiration is inexorably a function of community identification. The late great Andrea Dworkin put it this way:

> The fundamental knowledge that women are a class having a common condition—that the fate of one woman is tied substantively to the fate of all women—toughens feminist theory and practice. That fundamental knowledge is an almost unbearable test of seriousness.[51]

If it is worth our participation at all, the rule of law cannot be just a sedative, or a shroud for greed. Nor am I willing to settle for the depressive "vision" of liberalism, that law serves only to regulate the competition among self-interested individual entities. I am not a fundamentalist. I believe that the principle of evolution applies to institutions and individuals as well as to biological events. A more evolved, more mature legal system will be feminist in the sense that it will comprehend the complexities of equality. Just as individual maturity requires reexamination by every person of many perceived slights—comprehending among other things that you don't shoot people or have a fit or file a lawsuit just because you woke up feeling unequal today—legal maturity requires the incorporation of feminist insights.

We will all be feminists when we embrace the world-making responsibilities of language users, and thereby learn how to participate in communities. Not just in any one community, but with all communities as communities, whether or not we belong to them, in compassion and solidarity.

PART II

Places beyond Stuckness

Feminist Notions, Controversies, and Promises

5

Feminist Legal Theory

People sure get nervous when a woman's free.

—Trisha Yearwood

Everything I know about being a lawyer has been through the emergence of what came to be known as "feminist jurisprudence." What I call "feminism" is not a way of thinking confined to persons born female. Rather, this feminism is the concrete analysis of systematic oppressions, which analysis has led to a critique of objectivity in epistemological, psychological, and social—as well as legal—terms. There is no "female point of view" nor any "male point of view" corresponding to an individual's membership in a biologically defined group.[1] Rather, there is a socially constructed process that conscripts people into a gendered way of seeing the world. This process includes not only rites of genderization for individuals but also habits of thinking that are contingent but powerful. Among those habits is the division of the world into knowing subjects and known objects, that is, the habit of dividing perceptions between those that are subjective and those that are objective.

In the understandable rush to render feminist work acceptable in traditional terms, it is sometimes suggested that feminist lawyers ought to advertise our insights as the best among competing revivals of the Legal Realism of the 1930s. All outsiders are surely indebted to the Realists for their convincing demonstration that the law could not be described, as the formalists and positivists had hoped, as a scientific enterprise, devoid of moral or political content. The Realists' description of the influence of morality, economics, and politics upon law is the first step in developing an antidote for legal solipsism. In the end, however, Realism was not courageous enough for feminism. The Realists did not revolutionize the law but only expanded the concept of legal process.[2] The Realists did not press their critique deeply enough; they did not bring home its implications. In the face of their failure, the system has clung even more desperately to objectivity and neutrality.

As described in the previous chapter, liberalism is the unifying theme of most contemporary jurisprudential debate. The Ronald Dworkin slightly-left liberals, the Antonin Scalia pretty-far-right liberals, the Law and Economics scholars—all of these people share classic liberal assumptions. Liberalism has the lure of the abstract and the universal. It purports to rise above the grime of detailed daily life. It holds the promise of objectivity.

The legal feminism emerging in the 1960s began in that liberal mode. It involved challenging the exclusion of women from equal opportunities of all sorts. The thrust of the approach was to argue for neutrality in legal standards, that is, for a legal rule regarding women that "did not take sex into account." That led a group of feminist scholars in the 1970s and '80s—it surely led me[3]—to waste a lot of time bickering about rules and standards in the abstract. I thought that if feminist lawyers could just set out our principles precisely enough, if we offered a new, improved equality standard just one more time, then there would be justice in the world.

The equality standard did change,[4] but the world didn't, except for the privileged few. It was a time of stuckness for me, until I read the book Catharine MacKinnon wrote in 1979, called *Sexual Harassment of Working Women*. In it, she demonstrated that the engine of the liberal machine is the "differences approach."[5] If women ask to be treated the same as men on the grounds that we are the same as men, then we concede that we have no claim to equality in contexts where we are not the same as men, whether as matters of biology or as matters of social fact. Slowly the people doing this work came to realize the need to resist abstraction, to realize that perception is not just given but is directed by socially constructed power relations. Thus we also learned the need to resist domestication of our own thought.

In the liberal realm, the engine of the struggle for equality has been Aristotelian. Equality means to treat like persons alike, and unlike persons unlike.[6] In this system, everything depends upon accuracy in assessing the similarities and differences among situations. The deficiency in the system is always brought home to me by the fact of how recently the U.S. Supreme Court let women in the equal protection door. That was in 1971, in a case invalidating an Idaho statute that preferred males over females for appointment as administrators of intestate estates.[7] In

Reed v. Reed, the Court held that the state of Idaho could not presumptively deny to women the right to administer estates. With respect to such activities, the Court saw that women and men are "similarly situated." That is, no discernible difference between the sexes justified treating them differently.

In the evolution of the differences approach, all was going swimmingly until the Court had to face situations where the sexes are not, or do not seem to be, similarly situated—situations involving pregnancy, situations involving the supposed overpowering sexual allure that women present to men, and situations involving the historical absence of women.[8] When the differences approach was applied in those cases, the plaintiffs lost. Feminist legal scholars then devoted enormous energies to patching the cracks in the differences approach. The debate was arduous. Which differences between the sexes are or should be relevant for legal purposes? How does one tell what the differences are? Does it matter whether the differences are inherent or the result of upbringing? Is it enough to distinguish between accurate and inaccurate stereotyped differences? Or are there situations where differences are sufficiently "real" and permanent to demand social accommodation?

It was not possible, ultimately, to describe a theory of women's rights that fit the discrete, nonstereotypical, "real" differences between the sexes. Attempting to do so exacerbated the underlying problem—the objectification of women—and enlisted us in reification of the vocabulary, epistemology, and the political theory of the law as it is. The judicial diagnosis of the problem in *Reed v. Reed* was an example. It assumed that some mistake of differentiation had occurred. It amounted to saying, "Gee, come to think of it, there really isn't a very good reason to prevent women from administering estates in Idaho. What was Idaho thinking?" And once the Court discovered that "mistake," it needed to construct an "objective" rule to govern it, a rule that appeared to transcend results in particular cases.[9]

Philosopher Carol Gould has named this aspect of liberal theory, so central to the U.S. constitutional approach, as "abstract universality."[10] In order to apply a rule neutrally in future cases, one must discern *a priori* what the differences and similarities among groups are. But because there are an infinite number of differences and similarities among groups, one must also discern which differences are relevant. To make this determination, one must first abstract the essential and universal similarities among humans; one must have strict assumptions about human nature as such. Without such an abstraction, there is no way to talk about which differences in treatment are arbitrary and which are justified.[11]

Thus, somewhere in the nature of things there must be a list of differences among people that matter and those that do not. Notice, however, that abstract universality by its own terms cannot arrive at such a list. It has no "bridge to the concrete"[12] by which to ascertain the emerging and cultural qualities that constitute difference. It is a conception of the world that takes "the part for the whole, the particular for the universal and essential, or the present for the eternal."[13]

As workers in this project became more familiar with structures of power, we saw how abstract universality made those with power the norm of what is human, and did so *sub rosa,* all in the name of neutrality. Maleness defines human; whiteness defines human; heterosexuality defines human. And the values held by powerful people are made to appear as if they were qualities inherent in a world "out there." By this subterranean system, the "relevant" differences have been those that keep less powerful people in their place.

With the allegedly anonymous picture of humanity thus painted, women, for example, are but male subjectivity glorified, objectified, and elevated to the status of reality. So goes the process of objectification: the winner is he who makes his world seem necessary. Professor MacKinnon expressed this insight in one of her most famous passages:

> [M]ale dominance is perhaps the most pervasive and tenacious system of power in history . . . it is metaphysically nearly perfect. Its point of view is the standard for point-of-viewlessness; its particularity the meaning of universality. Its force is exercised as consent, its authority as participation, its supremacy as the paradigm of order, its control as the definition of legitimacy.[14]

Long ago, I wrote that "[f]eminist analysis begins with the principle that objective reality is a myth."[15] This assertion struck some commentators as proof that feminist legal theorists were dangerous fruitcakes.[16] That reaction strikes me in turn as exemplary of the "totalizing" nature of liberalism and its fearful resistance to anything that is not an example of dichotomized thought. I never said that the notion of "objective reality" was useless, either strategically or practically. My description of objective reality as mythic was not necessarily to denigrate it, for myth can be a positively transformative category of communication.[17] My characterization was simply to underscore the need for modesty in matters of knowledge. Not only can our species often not "know" what the facts of the world are but claims to "objectivity" are often cover for dogmatism. "Knowledge" is always open to revision. Vigilance about that insight can dethrone those aspects of "objective reality" that cover for human misery.

Among the most pernicious of these myths—right up there with the belief in "objectivity"—is that the domination of women reflects a natural biological order.[18] The paradigm of the will of the father informs rationality at every historical stage. For example, Aristotle's description of woman as partial man[19] was prototypical of justifications for domination, from Christianity to Freud, through social Darwinism, and including economic and scientific explanations of the social order. The narcotic influence of the notion of objectivity dulls alertness to that historical theme of partiality.

I consider it significant that the demise of legal formalism—the idea that neutral legal rules could be mechanically applied to objectively known facts to determine a result—was concurrent with the rise of modern physics. For example, *Palsgraf v. Long Island Railway*,[20] the case that firmly displaced legal causation from the arena of objective fact into the arena of "policy" judgment, appeared at the same time that Werner Heisenberg formulated his uncertainty principle.[21] Physics, the same field that for centuries exemplified the dichotomy between individual mind and external world, said with Heisenberg's voice that the two were inevitably interrelated. According to Heisenberg, the more precisely an observer tries to take one measurement of electron status, the more the accuracy in another measurement is skewed. Put more broadly, the observer inevitably transforms the observed system. After Heisenberg, there was no longer any clear division between the knowing subject and the known object. The demise of the subject/object split on the quantum level suggests that lawyers should at least *acknowledge* its contingency on the legal level.[22]

A legal system must attempt to assure fairness. Fairness must have reference to real human predicaments. Abstract universality is a convenient device for some philosophical pursuits, or for any endeavor whose means can stand without ends, but it is particularly unsuited for law. Law is, after all, a social tool. It is only extrinsically important. Its actual value depends upon its success in promoting goals that people decide are worth promoting. By inquiring into the mythic structure of objectivity, we see that abstract universality explicitly contradicts the ideal of a "government of laws, not men." Our task, therefore, is to construct a system that avoids solipsism, that recognizes that the point of view of the law-maker is not the whole of reality.

Feminist thinking has evolved dramatically in the past twenty-five years, from an essentially liberal attack on the absence of women in the public world to a radical vision of the transformation of that world. The demand for "gender neutrality" that served valiantly in the legal struggles of the 1970s has inevitably become a critique of neutrality itself, a critique which proceeds by an admittedly nonneutral method. Explanations of our method usually provoke the charge of nominalism, such is the staying power of the ideal of objectivity. Feminist method would appear to be an easy target for that weapon. The feminism I practice does not claim to be objective because objectivity is the basis for inequality. Feminism is not abstract because abstraction when institutionalized shields the status quo from critique. At the risk of incurring the scorn of the *Wall Street Journal,* I will even admit that this feminism is result-oriented. However, I believe that to be a very modest claim. It means only that the law's actual effect in the world matters more than the law's simply being in the world. It means that if society is not getting positive results from law as it is, society needs to rewrite or reinterpret the law.

The next step for theory is therefore to demonstrate that feminist method leads to "principled adjudication" and more dignity for everybody. Power relationships manifest themselves by negating that which is not powerful. Thus, both male supremacy and white supremacy define self and other important concepts by that which is nonmale and nonwhite. In order to be a valorized self, there must be a negativized "other."[23] As postmodern theories have demonstrated repeatedly, the prevailing notion of rationality divides the world between all that is good and all that is bad—between objective and subjective, light and shadow, natural and unnatural, white and nonwhite, man and woman. For all of these dichotomies (and there are scores more), the goodness of the good side is defined by what it is not. The approach I endorse rejects the objectification—the "othering"—of parties to disputes. This approach has the virtue of expanding the context of disputes, of following the connections among people and events. It does not insist upon uncovering an essence of the problem but looks for a solution that is coherent with the rest of experience. This is not a choice between male domination and female domination. The choice is, rather, between a compulsion to control reality and a far less anxious understanding of how language users actually function in their environments.[24]

Philosophical Relief

When I was in college, and torn by the antimonies of philosophy described in chapter 3, I was rescued by the philosophy of Ludwig Wittgenstein. Wittgenstein is fun to read and spells relief regarding some persistently knotty concepts akin to objectivity and universality. Consider Wittgenstein's explanation of the concept of "games." It is a concept we all use with great success. But let's mystify it in a lawyerly way.

Suppose you are a judge. Suppose there is an ordinance prohibiting the playing of games in the park. Suppose further that the ordinance doesn't define "games," but that a citizen has been given a ticket for doing a crossword puzzle on a park bench. Was the citizen violating the statute? In conventional legal debate, it is assumed that you need to shine some sort of pure light of reason on the concept of "games" in order to distill the essence of the concept. Legal thought assumes further that the legislature, when using the word "games," was acting on some essentialist basis. In that idealized world, that is what legislatures do: they identify the unique facts of some matter, and then create a policy to respond to those facts. The legislature just rearranges the furniture of the universe.

Is this how legislatures and judges really go about their businesses? In our example, is this how you as the judge should conceive of the situation? Wittgenstein would think that approach was a waste of your time.

> [L]ook and see whether there is anything common to all [games]. For if you look at them you will not see something that is common to all, but similarities, relationships, and a whole series of them at that. To repeat: "don't think, but look."[25]

Language doesn't point to some essential reality. Language is, instead, what our species *does*. And the way we do language is an incremental process.

> [W]e extend our concept . . . as in spinning a thread we twist fibre on fibre. And the strength of the thread does not reside in the fact that some one fibre runs through its whole length, but in the overlapping of many fibres.[26]

As the judge in the crossword puzzle case, you may hope that there is a legislative history that tells you what sort of games the legislature was worried about. But there may be no legislative history, or what there is may not help in a particular case. You're going to have to consider more than the words, and even more than what the legislature supposedly intended by them. Consider another Wittgensteinian example:

> Someone says to me: "Shew the children a game." I teach them gaming with dice, and the other says "I didn't mean that sort of game." Must the exclusion of the game with dice have come before his mind when he gave me the order?[27]

In this variation on our hypothetical, you're the person who has to decide whether Wittgenstein should be charged with corruption of minors. It doesn't depend on whether the legislature actually considered playing with dice as an example of corruption. Your decision does not depend upon whether gaming with dice falls neatly within the statutory term, nor upon any objectively determinable similarity or difference between this activity and others that the legislature considered as instances of corruption. Your decision depends upon a larger context that is not neutral or objective at all.

Law, like language that is its medium, is a system of classification. To characterize similarities and differences among situations is a key step in legal judgments. That step, however, is not a mechanistic manipulation of essences. Rather, that step always has an evaluative crux. It requires a sophisticated theory of differentiation, something that feminism is particularly adept at doing. Finding the crux depends upon the relation among things, not upon their opposition. By looking around, language users acquire examples by which they can grasp a concept. Then language users recognize other examples, not because of a shared essence, but because of some purposive analogy. The scope and limits of any analogy must be explored in each case, with social reality as the guide. This is a normative but not illogical process. Any logic is a norm, and cannot be used except with reference to its purposes.

Wittgenstein believed that his work with language was obvious, that he was supplying "observations which no one has doubted, but which have escaped remark only because they are always before our eyes."[28] As a linguistic enterprise, law has the tools of language available to it, including rules, standards, categories, and modes of interpretation. All of these tools are merely means for economy in thought and communication. They make it possible for us to pursue justice without reinventing every wheel at every turn. But means must not be turned into ends.

In feminist thought, deciding what differences are relevant for any purpose does not require objectifying and destroying some "other." This feminist approach does not elevate some point of view to the level of principle and then define others out of existence. This feminism takes the variousness in point of view as constitutive of social life. It sees differences as systematically related to one another, and to other relations, such as exploited and exploiter. It regards differences as emergent, as always changing.[29]

Consider the extended Wittgensteinian example above but substitute the concept of "inequality" for the concept of "games." Is there an essence of inequality that we will spot if we think hard enough? No. Oppression is not a descriptive mistake, and we can't think our way out of centuries of refinements in its mechanisms and fluidity in day-to-day manifestations. When the priority is to understand differences and to value multiplicity, lawyers are obligated to discern between occasions of respect and occasions of oppression. Those are judgments we know how to make, even without a four-part test to tell us for every future circumstance, what constitutes inequality.

By definition, the concept of inequality is inexact.

> Only let us understand what "inexact" means. For it does not mean "unusable."[30]

> One might say that the concept "game" is a concept with blurred edges. —"But is a blurred concept a concept at all"—Is an indistinct photograph a picture of a person at all? Is it even always an advantage to replace an indistinct picture by a sharp one? Isn't the indistinct one often exactly what we need?[31]

A precise picture of a fuzzy scene is a fuzzy picture. Inequality comes in many forms. Its mechanisms are so insidious and so powerful that we could never codify its "essence." The approach that uses no ostensibly neutral formula but that points to the crux of the matter in a social context is exactly what we need.

The admonition that lawyers should engage in explicit evaluative debate sounds scary because we have been taught to distrust metaphysics. But I am not asserting that this enterprise is governed by any foundational norm; I am not asserting that there is a right answer or even necessarily some correct contours of debate. When lawyers are faced with hard cases, it is almost always my experience that everybody knows exactly what the real stakes are, even if we don't always know how to talk about them. The business of living and progressing within our disciplines requires that we give up on "objective" verification at various critical moments, such as when we rely upon gravity,[32] or upon the existence of others,[33] or upon the principle of verification itself. Law needs some epistemological and psychological sophistication. Jurisprudence will forever be stuck in a postrealist battle of subjectivities, with all the discomfort that has represented, until we confront the distinction between knowing subject and known object.

My admission of result-orientation does not import the renunciation of all standards. In a system defined by constitutional norms such as equality, we need standards to help us make connections among norms, and to help us see "family resemblances"[34] among instances of domination. Standards, however, are not means without ends. They never have and never can be more than working hypotheses.[35] Just as it would be shocking to find a case that said, "The petitioner wins though she satisfied no criteria," so it must ultimately be wrong to keep finding cases that essentially say, "Petitioner loses though the criteria are indefensible." In legal situations, a case is either conformed to a standard or the standard is modified with justification. That justification should not be that "we like the petitioner's facts better"; rather, it is that "on facts such as these, the standard doesn't hold up."

A Better Standard

Why not have an equality standard that focuses on the issues of domination, disadvantage, and disempowerment instead of on the issues of difference? I endorse a standard proposed by Professor MacKinnon that she calls the "inequality approach." The test in any challenge should be "whether the policy or practice in question integrally contributes to the maintenance of an underclass or a deprived position because of gender status."[36]

This would not be a hugely radical departure. Back in 1979, when Professor MacKinnon proposed this standard, she identified the extent to which U.S. equality law had essentially already embraced it. To be sure, there was and is a somewhat fractured consciousness about inequality in American law. To me, the encouraging part is that we already have this progressive standard out there on the interpretive turf.[37] It has not completely lost out, and its presence has not caused discernible damage to other ideals that the legal system holds dear. Moreover, other democracies have adopted interpretations of their constitutional guarantees of equality that look a lot like the MacKinnon standard.[38] Those interpretations are confirmation of the practicality of her approach.

Such a standard would not immediately dispose of all recurring problems but would analyze them differently. Consider the problem of stereotyping. The notion of stereotyping connotes various often overlapping problems,[39] including falsification of group characteristics, oversimplification of group characteristics, inattention to individual characteristics, lack of seriousness, and invariance. Even the differences approach could attack stereotyping without difficulty when the challenged practice is based upon an untrue or overbroad generalization. Only the inequality approach, however, can address two other problems of stereotyping: first, the need for a reliable approach to generalizations that are largely true (either because of biology or because of highly successful socialization, what Professor Anthony Appiah calls "normative stereotypes"[40]), and second, the need to distinguish between beneficial and burdensome legislation.

In the gender context, the "normative stereotypes" that the differences approach reinforced were often tied to biological differences between men and women.[41] Thereby, the reasons for having antidiscrimination laws have been seen as reasons to allow discrimination. The inequality approach unravels the tautology. Under the inequality approach, different treatment based upon unique physical characteristics would be "among the first to trigger suspicion and scrutiny."[42] It makes no sense to say that equality is guaranteed only when the sexes are already equal. The issue is not freedom to be treated without regard to sex; the issue is freedom from systematic subordination because of sex.[43] Thus, the inequality approach would reach not only false stereotypes but also stereotypes (such as women's unequal child-rearing responsibilities) that have largely made themselves true through a history of inequality.

The inequality approach provides a more historical and less deterministic analysis of beneficial classifications—what in the United States we agonizingly debate as "affirmative action." When a preference is provided for members of an historically disenfranchised group, the only "stereotype" definitely being "reinforced" is that the group has been historically disenfranchised. The only indelible message is that history counts, and can't be stipulated away by adherence to a nineteenth-century universalist notion of human nature and human capabilities. Seriousness about recognizing and condemning supremacist systems requires seeing how systems work. Disadvantage replicates and legitimizes itself. It is unhelpful to become hysterical about how members of these groups can do it themselves and ought not be stigmatized for not having done it themselves thus far. There is nothing wrong with getting societal help. Indeed, formerly disenfranchised groups could not have become enfranchised without the actions of surrogates.[44] That has not required that the groups thus assisted conform for all time to the surrogates' perceptions of them (or even to their own perceptions of themselves).

Injustice does not flow directly from recognizing differences; injustice results when those differences are transformed into social deprivation. Surely, affirmative action ought not be a slapdash undertaking. Affirmative action requires some discernment about how history has operated. Insofar as an affirmative action program oversimplifies, however, it is an oversimplification in the service of a profound complexity, as is any well-drafted policy. Such a program evinces laudable seriousness toward the problem, especially if the program assists in the recognition and relinquishment of privilege. And such programs are not invariant. By definition, they point to stereotypes for the purpose of undoing them. When allegedly beneficial classifications do not have this form,[45] or when once beneficial schemes cease to have it, the inequality approach would prohibit them.

The inequality approach requires an investigation that must delve as deeply as circumstances demand into whether the challenged policy or practice exploits gender status. To worry in the abstract about which standard should be applied at what time is to replicate the fallacy of the differences approach. Logic is no obstacle to the implementation of the inequality approach. The obstacles are, rather, perception and commitment.

If perception can be facilitated, which I believe it can, and commitment can be serious, which I know it is, it doesn't matter so much exactly what feminist lawyers call this approach. We do, however, need to avoid both underinclusiveness and overinclusiveness and otherwise not fall for the traps of domestication. For example, I noted in the introduction that because the term "feminism" sometimes triggers hostility,[46] perhaps the sort of understanding I support should be called something else—perhaps "gender mainstreaming" or "antisubordination theory" would be better.

I noted that "gender mainstreaming" is the name given by the member states of the European Union to its admirable commitment to sex equality, but I also warned that the gender mainstreaming notion seems to carry on its face a threat of domestication. Although some people regard feminism as too oppositional, gender mainstreaming may be insufficiently oppositional, in that it does not name existing social institutions such as male supremacy for what they are and what they do. The image conjured is of mainstream society bumping merrily along while gender is also happening somewhere along the margins. The solution is just to come on in here, little lady, and tell us what's up. Some of the participants in the European debate understand this danger and rightly see the tension in all of feminism, caught as it historically has been "between being a political movement and [becoming] a part of institutionalized mechanisms" of political theory.[47] Surely it is true that permanent struggle—otherwise known as political consciousness—must remain a part of the feminist project, whatever we call it.[48] I am just disinclined to slap the happy-face title "gender mainstreaming" on it before we have a sense of what it will achieve.

What is generally known as "antisubordination theory," on the other hand, presents less of a threat of domestication. While antisubordination theory has a distinguished feminist heritage,[49] it is now used productively in a variety of antidiscrimination contexts.[50] I am daily heartened by these proliferations and creative articulations, and I definitely consider myself an antisubordination theorist, practitioner, and teacher.

It is still critical, however, both to avoid the conflation of different aspects of social subordination and to deepen understanding of the complexities in how systems of subordination reinforce one another.[51] Earlier in this chapter, I emphasized the dichotomization of the world that underlies existing structures of social power, including the structure called "reason." I don't think progressive people should reify or reconstruct those axes[52] but do think we must appreciate that in the present scheme of things, different axes reinforce somewhat different structures of social control, and have somewhat different emphases. The gendered axis, for example, separates out not only male from female but also society from nature, enterprise from homeyness, and history from love.[53] This has given us a society built around what Aldous Huxley called "organized lovelessness." The enterprise of making history becomes a "compulsive concentration on what can be predicted, controlled, manipulated, possessed and preserved, piled up and counted."[54]

Feminism brings a number of psychological lenses through which we might consider these large questions of history making. Of course, all subordinations produce and are produced by psychological scar tissue. It cannot be only gendered pathologies that cause our species' habits of subordination (and even of being subordinated).[55] There do seem to be common psychological aspects to the strategies of othering and group devaluation that existing structures of domination and subordination exhibit. From a psychoanalytic point of view, it is likely that those institutions share spooky erotic/thanotic roots.[56] In terms of the football metaphors that public figures cannot refrain from using, maybe each of these social failures is another "broken play" en route to a losing season.[57]

It is possible that we're just a loser species, but I'm unprepared to embrace suicide as destiny. Psychology is atop the fields that must resist essentialism. Particularly in psychoanalytic thought, morbid aspects of human nature are portrayed—hence, justified—as unavoidable and unchangeable. But even if not structurally necessary, psychological habits *are* morbid. They can't be merely wished away. So I would ask some indulgence in using the terms of psychoanalysis because they help to illustrate an example of feminist legal theory in action, as it were: women in the military.

The recurring issue of women in the military—which is itself a subset of the fundamental social issue of the uses and abuses of military power—presents a near-perfect illustration of the potential of feminist legal theory. How could anyone possibly explain what war is and why it still exists without some reference to gendered realities? Both "manhood" and "womanhood" are mythic vortexes. Historically and in most cultures, both "manhood" and "womanhood" require conscription into and endurance of rites of genderization. In twentieth-century Western intellectual history, surely Sigmund Freud's accounts of becoming male and female are most familiar. Those accounts are unnecessarily static and depressing, not to mention their role as elaborate justifications for patriarchal violence. But the cruelty in Freud's descriptions of genderization rings true for many people.

For present purposes, to the brutality of the Freudian account I would add Simone de Beauvoir's analysis of the symbiotic nature of sexual pathology. Both sexes, at least in their gendered roles, keep the world crazy. A person in the feminine role—as nurturer, worrier, and lamenter—may have no say in decisions of historical importance, but she does get benefits: she gains the approval of those who are powerful, and, of course, she does not have to take responsibility for making ugly historical decisions.[58] A person in the masculine role—as warrior, as history-maker, and as keeper of woman—avoids moral responsibility for his actions and need not admit the ugliness of aggressive behavior. He has women there to ventilate the difficult emotions. In this story, women do the weeping for the world, while the mad megamachine rolls on.[59]

With that pathology in mind, let's look at the present situation of women in the U.S. military. After the tribulations of Vietnam, in 1973 the United States ended the military draft. The all-voluntary armed forces got some public attention in the 1980s, when President Jimmy Carter decided in response to the Soviet invasion of Afghanistan that young people should at least be registered for military service. If the United States had to reinstate the draft, at least the cards would be correctly filed. Carter and his military advisors had originally sought registration of both men and women, but Congress got cold feet about that, and subjected only men to the registration requirement. In a 6-3 vote, the Supreme Court decided that the male-only registration was constitutional; the Court deferred to "military judgment" on the matter.[60]

Fifteen years later, because of the U.S. wars in Afghanistan and Iraq, the all-volunteer armed forces are again garnering public attention. There are not enough troops. As one recruiter put it with admirable brevity: "The problem is that no one wants to join."[61] Front lines are increasingly staffed by "part-time soldiers" from the Reserves and the National Guard. Guard forces are being stretched thin enough to worry Governors that their states will be short-staffed in the event of natural disasters.[62] The "don't ask, don't tell" regime—the U.S. rule that forces gay and lesbian soldiers to be closeted or else be discharged from the military—is proving costly.[63] Eligibility requirements and recruiting practices are changing: the Pentagon is considering older recruits; Congress has involved the Peace Corps for the first time in military matters; and recruiters are encouraged to bend the rules—ignoring criminal records, fixing medical reports, even achieving the application of a man just released from psychiatric commitment for having been a danger to himself and others.[64] The official story is that the United States will not reinstitute the draft; officers closer to the realities of recruitment believe that some sort of conscription must be considered.[65] In response to these difficulties, the armed forces are becoming increasingly privatized, a strategy that drives up costs and drives down accountability.[66]

In all of this mess, the issue of the roles of women in the military has again surfaced. At present, women can serve in combat support units but cannot serve in combat,[67] a distinction without a difference in the war without a discernible front in Iraq. To date, forty female soldiers have been killed in Iraq, a number equal to the number of U.S. military women killed in Korea, Vietnam, and the first Gulf War combined.[68] In the summer of 2005, some members of Congress wanted to restrict female participation but backed down due to military concern about conflicting messages that might be sent to the troops. As the Army leadership wrote to the House Armed Services Committee, "This is not the time to create such confusion."[69]

From a militaristic point of view, however, it may be more accurate to say that now is not the time to dispel a very profitable confusion. As I wrote some years ago, a militaristic worldview requires women to be *in* the military (for sound logistical reasons) but also requires that women cannot *be* the military because, "when you get down to it, you've got to protect the manliness of war."[70]

Feminists do not agree about whether or to what extent women should participate in the military. Some argue that because military service entails political respect (or rather, lack of military service often entails a political discount), women must become fully integrated into all aspects of war-making. Others believe that the equation of military service with credibility and respect is itself the problem. In this view, acceptance of women by the military is the surest sign of cooptation. Women must resist militarism, and should encourage everyone to resist militarism by every available means.

These are complex economic and political matters, and a worthy exploration of the points of view awaits another book. Most striking to me about the debate among feminists, however, is how little there is of it compared to other matters of public concern. Indeed, particularly when troops are being killed abroad, even the most progressive people become complicit in a conspiracy of silence about what militarism is and does. This would be the truth in the otherwise tiresome allegation that progressive people are "soft on defense."[71]

To me, the promise of feminist legal theory resides not only in breaking the silence, as all antisubordination theories aim to do, but also in focusing the psychological stakes in a relentless examination of military realities. The debate cannot occur without discussions of masculinity and femininity and the relationships of those concepts to violence. For too long, those discussions have become diffused by the conventions of abstraction and fear of being accused of male-bashing.[72] Sex-neutral terms such as "domestic violence" obscure the gendered nature of intimate violence,[73] just as patriotic sound bites obscure discussions about militarism and the gendered nature of international violence. If anything good can be said about the present U.S. wars in Afghanistan and Iraq and how they deplete both U.S. credibility and genuine defense needs, perhaps it is that these wars ensure that the debate *must* occur. The politeness and abstraction of liberalism have to give way to a habit of naming the stakes, including the psychological ones, and trying different social strategies, including the feminist jurisprudence that I advocate.

I didn't invent the insights of feminist jurisprudence. The literature is already rich. To me, the challenge is to sustain in daily practice the insights already achieved. The challenge is to develop consistent methods that help to keep in focus.

6

Feminist Legal Method

A hand or something passes across the sun. Your
eyeballs slacken,
you are free for a moment. Then it comes back:
this
test of the capacity to keep in focus
this
unfair struggle with the forces of perception

—Adrienne Rich

If it is true that law is a discourse about epistemology, ethics, and politics, the next project is to *inform* the epistemology, ethics, and politics of legal decision making. Chapter 4 explained why difficult legal projects can't be informed by the rhetoric of liberalism. Chapter 5 described a feminist way of understanding law that takes history, suffering, and context seriously. At the end of that chapter, I spoke of the difficulty in keeping feminist insights in focus.[1] In this chapter, I would like to talk more precisely and practically about how the feminist theory I describe would actually operate. I would like to suggest eight ideas (or steps) that inform a practical analysis of a legal problem. It will strike some as a wrongheaded "structuralist" effort, but I mean only to indicate recurring places in practice where confusion creeps in, where bad habits take over, and where cases are lost.

1. Don't Get Bogged Down in Conventional Political Divisions

As I explained in chapter 4, most political controversy in the United States occurs within a narrow field. In my lifetime, the biggest changes in the polity were wrought by Ronald Reagan and his pro-big-business agenda. Those changes can be understood within the tradition of philosophical liberalism. With regard to the role of the state (whether the state is conceived as a mere night watchman or as something slightly more), those changes can be seen as tilting the balance among philosophical liberals to the right, far in favor of the concentration of wealth and against measures designed to "level the playing field." The George W. Bush administration continues that legacy, and may end up going well beyond it.[2] The differences among the contestants costumed for daily political battle, however, are magnified beyond their meanings. Nobody with political clout is seriously talking about changing very much. Redistribution of wealth is certainly happening, but toward the already rich. Environmental protection is merely an irritation to private property, rather than a real threat of deprivation of it. And so on. The debates are nickel-and-dime stuff, mostly.

Don't get me wrong. Nickels and dimes matter greatly. The scope of political theories that contest those nickels and dimes is just not very profound, and it is a real waste of talent and energy when we let ourselves get sucked up into that furious little vortex. The left-versus-right spectrum is largely an artifact, and serves primarily as a smokescreen that contributes to the forces arrayed against transformative political coalitions.

Lawyers get comfortable being aligned with particular sides. In civil practice, for example, it is common to identify as a defense lawyer or as a plaintiffs' lawyer. A legal community might be momentarily surprised to hear that so-and-so is on the other side of a particular case, but it wouldn't be the death knell for that person's reputation. Nonetheless, when it comes to progressive coalitions, it is commonplace to hear that a whole movement is wrongheaded, because its proponents are "in bed with" some crowd supposed to be inherently hostile to the proponents' real interests.

During the "porn wars" of the 1980s, for example, the paradigmatic "strange bedfellows" moment occurred pursuant to the allegation that the antipornography feminists were in bed with President Reagan's attorney general Edwin Meese, and similar conservative opponents of sexual freedom.[3] Today, sexual harassment law presents similar opportunities for strange-bedfellow allegations. Unsurprisingly, female speakers are in the foreground in the endless reiteration of familiar arguments against sexual harassment laws. Some of these critics say that proponents of sexual harassment law are prudish anti-sex schoolmarms.[4] Others accuse us of participating in an incoherent and misguided effort which is a "clumsy substitute for manners."[5]

This is familiar territory. Obviously, just like any other category of cases, sexual harassment cases are neither all meritorious nor all frivolous. The envisioned onslaught of sexual harassment cases that threaten the desexualization of life has not come to pass so far. Any appearance of that onslaught will call upon the proponents of sexual harassment law to demonstrate again what it is and is not there for. If it happens, it will be another aspect of interpretive competition. The "strange bedfellows" charge is a way of making innovators believe that they can't survive every next wave of that competition.

As a longtime participant in feminist debates, I'm accustomed to this sort of challenge and have learned to see challenges that would formerly have been most threatening as the most interesting opportunities. In a rush to distance ourselves from the "morality" that informs right-wing politics, for example, feminists lose an opportunity. Andrea Dworkin argued that right-wing women participate in moral crusades because they perceive that it is their best protection from male violence.[6] It is vital for progressive people in all political analyses to attempt to fathom the fears and insecurities that motivate their opponents. If we can understand and speak to those concerns, we may learn something, and find allies.

Strange bedfellows charges fly about too often, even in arguments with ourselves. Over the years a number of my students, both male and female, have said things like, "You know, I'm not a feminist, I'm actually quite conservative, but my friend complained about her boss hitting on her and now they are making her life miserable and it really ticks me off." Often, such statements are accompanied by a sense of insecurity or inauthenticity, as if one were forbidden to hold or to express seemingly contradictory opinions. You are a strange bedfellow when you sleep alone.

These students' opinions are contradictory only in terms of the socially acceptable limits of political debate. Their discomfort signifies some possibly illuminating point that can't shine through the shame of contradiction. They are strangled by conventional systems of thought, systems so complete that a refutation of any part can instantly be transformed into further proof of the system.

We live in an era of strange bedfellows. From the demonizing of governments so recently on the arms-trading friends list to the sudden solidarity of evangelical Christians with Israel, both definitions of the issues and formerly predictable political alignments are giving way to different ways of understanding the present and imaging the future.

2. *Eschew Neutrality*

The illusion of "neutrality" has been a primary topic of this book so far. The impulse behind the principle of neutrality is a noble one. The idea is that justice is achieved only when blind, only when the stations and characteristics of those before the law are ignored. But there is no logical sense in this idea. A truly neutral position draws *no* lines nor authorizes any action according to differences among situations. The law, however, is all about drawing lines, contrasting behaviors and making classifications—to an incredibly detailed degree.

Neutrality makes sense only when we ask, "Neutral in what respect? Neutral as compared to what? Which aspects of this situation should be consequential, and which not?" Having voiced those questions, we are plunged neck deep into the grime of politics. Better to relinquish neutrality as a surrogate for justice because the ideal of neutrality obscures more than enhances the debate. As Professor Lon Fuller said, "There is indeed no frustration greater than to be confronted by a theory which purports merely to describe, when it not only plainly prescribes, but owes its special prescriptive powers precisely to the fact that it disclaims prescriptive intentions."[7]

As described in chapter 5, the pretense to neutrality presents special obstacles to women and other historically disempowered groups. This is due not just to the historic equation of rationality with maleness but also to the colossal privilege that allows those in power genuinely to believe they are acting neutrally. Usually the ideal of neutrality converts someone's comfortable version of experience into an "objective" fact. Moreover, neutrality drains reality of history. From that comfortable point of view, a given injustice can be converted into an isolated incident. The useful notion in what is called neutrality is that, in a given disagreement or class of disagreements, there are some situational aspects that should be similarly discounted or similarly evaluated. The ideal of neutrality, however, doesn't tell us which aspects those are.

Consider the portrayal of the world in a famous sexual harassment case, *Rabidue v. Osceola Refining Company.*[8] Vivenne Rabidue's Title VII claim against her former employer was based in part upon the display of pornographic materials in the workplace. The United States Court of Appeals for the Sixth Circuit pronounced that this is a pornographic world we live in, a fact merely reflected in the defendant's environs.[9] Thus was *Rabidue* the *Bradwell v. Illinois* of the twentieth century.[10] Ms. Rabidue didn't even get a chance to show how her economic well-being was harmed because her injury transpired against the allegedly neutral background of the way the world is.

I see that a few features of collective life could be described as neutral. Gravity, maybe, but not pornography. I understand why it is tempting to characterize a practice that seems out of control as a fact of nature, and to postulate that it affects everyone the same way. But it is affirmatively disabling to legal analysis to describe existing social imbalances as the neutral background of experience.

3. Challenge False Necessities

Most of philosophy and law is organized around a set of bottom lines, presented as unquestionable. These false necessities are present all the time in daily political discourse. Thus, the alleged lack of choices for patients in anything except the existing for-profit health care system stopped health-care reform in the 1990s. Marriage supposedly just *is* the union of one man and one woman. The march of liberty requires killing in Iraq. This sort of conversation stopper reminds me of a 1990s TV commercial: "When you say 'Bud,' you've said it all." If you thought you had something to add about beer selection, think again and shut up.

When such a conversation-stopping argument is lobbed out, however, that should signal an important beginning for conversation, rather than the end. In addition to the false necessity of "objectivity" or "neutrality" discussed previously, I would like to mention two other commonly lobbed bottom lines: the postulation of dispositive false dichotomies, and the slippery slope argument.

False Dichotomies

Chapters 4 and 5 were largely devoted to an explanation and critique of false dichotomization in categories of understanding. Legal thinking, in particular, is organized around bottom-line dichotomies: law versus policy, public versus private realms, expert versus lay opinion, civilian governance versus military necessity—there are lots of them. These dichotomies constitute law's binary logic: when a situation falls on one side of the line, it is actionable, or otherwise of consequence; when a situation falls on the other side of the line, it is unactionable, someone else's business, or inconsequential.

In sexual harassment law, a salient binary is between welcome and unwelcome sexual conduct: a plaintiff has the burden of showing that the conduct was "unwelcome." Among claims that turn on unwelcomeness, there is a subset where the plaintiff had a voluntary sexual relationship with the alleged harasser before the harassing began. By itself the prior sex tells us nothing.[11] How about a case where a plaintiff had an affair with her boss, and didn't complain until after the boss's wife found out about it and convinced the husband to fire her? Compare that to a case where a plaintiff dated a coworker for a month, then broke up with him, then ultimately complained because in trying to get her back he constantly came on to her at work and hassled her at home.

Being trained to look for bright-line rules, lawyers would like for these cases to fall neatly on one or the other side of the unwelcomeness divide. But neither of these cases is neat. In the former, just after what turned out to be the last episode of consensual sex, the supervisor terminated the relationship and plaintiff's employment because his family "disapproved." The supervisor suggested that plaintiff "call his wife at her therapist's office and 'beg' for her job back." Plaintiff did so, to no avail. The court said the fruitless begging was "at most, a degrading and humiliating episode which occurred after the sex and the termination."[12] In the second case, though the court held that the prior sexual relationship did not constitute a "free pass" to harass the plaintiff, it described the plaintiff's burden as showing the difference between harassment and "personal animosity."[13] One could argue that using an employee for sex and playing her off against the family is a tried-and-true strategy of gender exploitation. One could also undertake to show the systematic ways that women provoke animosity—personal and otherwise—when they exercise their own sexual agency.

But in unwelcomeness cases like those described above, we wouldn't be doing anything different or more difficult from what lawyers do in any interpretive challenge, whether it be the meaning of "reasonableness" in a negligence case, "good faith" in an insurance case, or "interstate commerce" in a federalism case. If the rules and standards explained themselves, lawyers would be unnecessary. It is unhelpful to pretend that reality is sliced up like a ham.

Slippery Slope

Though the slippery slope argument gets trotted out in many contexts, it is ubiquitous in First Amendment discourse. You know how it goes: if we allow juries to award civil damages for injuries proven to be inflicted by racial hate speech, tomorrow they'll be censoring Oprah and packing her off to the pokey. It is crucial, however, to consider the concentration of media ownership and the way the First Amendment game is actually played. It doesn't often look like real censorship.[14]

Oprah, bless her heart, has gotten a lot of mileage out of the attempt at censorship threatened by the cattlemen of Amarillo. Oprah Winfrey was sued, *inter alia,* under the Texas "False Disparagement of Perishable Food Products Act" for negative statements about hamburger and Bovine Spongiform Encephalopathy (otherwise known as mad cow disease) made on her television program. During the six weeks of trial, Oprah broadcast her show from Amarillo, and America was supportively tuned in to Oprah's Texas adventure. The judge dismissed the primary claims on First Amendment grounds.[15]

A more recent demonstration of the value of "censorship" is the suit brought by the Fox News Network against Al Franken and the publisher of his book *Lies and the Lying Liars Who Tell Them: A Fair and Balanced Look at the Right.*[16] Among other things, Fox claimed that its trademark on the phrase "fair and balanced" was infringed because consumers might be confused about the affiliations among Franken, Fox Network, Bill O'Reilly, and Ann Coulter.[17] After a ridiculous hearing, the Southern District of New York denied the preliminary injunction and Fox dropped the case. In the meantime, due in large part to the lawsuit, Franken's book became a best seller.[18]

Slippery slope arguments should flag your skepticism for three reasons. First, doctrinal line-holding notwithstanding, we have long been wallowing near the bottom of some slippery slopes. As one example, in 2003 CBS got intimidated out of airing a miniseries called *The Reagans.*[19] That was a shame in that non-premium-channel-subscriber TV viewers missed another boffo performance by Judy Davis, but it did not exactly signal new weapons' development in the culture wars.

Second, the slippery slope is often disingenuously invoked. In structure, the slippery slope argument concedes the innocuousness of regulating the instant case but posits impossibly harder cases down the road.[20] For example, the popular press tried to illustrate the danger of sexual harassment law by reporting that in their training, some trade workers were taught the "five-second rule," according to which male workers ought not look at a female coworker for more than five seconds because it might constitute sexual harassment.[21] The idea here is that sexual harassment may be bad, but the law is too hard to apply, and we just can't tell the difference between meritorious and nonmeritorious claims. I'd be interested to read a case holding that the sixth second of staring made the difference, but I can't find one.

Third, the engine of the slippery slope argument is a fear that decision makers in later cases either will not understand or will ignore the distinctions that drafters of regulations have tried to explain.[22] Sexual harassment law is also a rich source of these fantasies. Take the hapless victim character played by Michael Douglas in the movie *Disclosure*.[23] The character played by Demi Moore was not nice, coming on to Michael and making his life miserable when he refused her advances. This fantasy leads to an equally fantastic collapse of the republic. Every male executive across the land will begin to imagine that every woman in his office is coming on to him. All these guys will sue, judges will end up having to segregate workplaces by sex, and both heterosexuality and the economy will come to a dead stop. Whoever follows the mainstream press's bombardment of sexual harassment law knows that I am not hyperbolizing their fantasies very much.

Of course, there is some slippage in every articulation of thought, and in every legal dispute there lurks the possibility that a decision maker will purposely skew the necessarily flexible language of rules and doctrines to wreak havoc on cherished institutions. This is familiar argumentative terrain, but there is no necessity for such a grim view of lawyers' powers of articulation and judges' capacities for discernment. There are real slippery slopes; there are massive gray areas; but not every case is a hard case.

4. *Deconstruct the Status Quo from the Level of Knowledge*

The term I use in classes that most frustrates students is "epistemology." But it isn't really that hard. As described in chapter 3, epistemology is that branch of philosophy that investigates the origin, structure, methods, and validity of knowledge. Legal results are generated, though sometimes very loosely, by determinations of facts. The analysis of "what the facts are" is too often taken for granted. How do we know the facts? What does it mean "to know"? In a complex factual determination such as causation in toxic torts, we can see how mechanisms of proof and habits of inference can be hijacked to serve the interests of the powerful.

The interrogation of claims to knowledge is also at the heart of feminist legal method. Because existing social arrangements are expressed, recapitulated, and reinforced by claims to knowledge, the feminist method is concrete. It emerged from women's accounts of their experiences of oppression. Though no one seriously asserts that law is separate from experience,[24] the feminist claim to knowledge of "real" women and "actual" oppression has been treated as controversial. Granted, no one gets to decide what reality ultimately *is;* no one can finally describe the furniture of the universe. Lawyers and law really are on the surfboard of infinite regress, however, if we say that mountainous evidence of oppressions isn't worthy of evaluation and possible redress. The key is to question what counts as knowledge. What appears true, is even accepted as true according to the rules of evidence, sometimes requires deeper interrogation. And that cannot be done through invocation of pseudoobjectivity but only through historical contextualization.

When in legal discourse we deconstruct from the level of knowledge, we find that the facts are often open to multiple interpretations. And when varying factual accounts are alleged, no one has to be lying. Divergent factual accounts may make perfect sense within their own sets of cultural determinants. Professor MacKinnon illustrated this in the context of rape prosecutions where the defendant claims that the sex was consensual. In these cases, MacKinnon asks, "[I]s a woman raped but not by a rapist?"[25] To the woman, the action was a violation and an injury. To the man, it was sex. His belief may even be reasonable in this society where sex is largely what women are for, and therefore can seldom be an injury, and where men are encouraged not to have to know what women want. Many women, too, have a powerful internal censor when it comes to registering or expressing our own desires.[26]

The law needs a more dynamic conception of reality and a more sophisticated epistemology than that allowed by the assumption that there is one objective truth of the matter. To allow that there are multiple realities is not to deny the possibility of agreement or progress or even what contextually serves as truth. Rather, this approach whenever possible "remains content with multiplicity as an end in itself"[27] and otherwise engages in making "increasingly complex adjustments to novel stimulation."[28] Individual dignity is a goal worth pursuing. Serious pursuit of it requires coherent experiences of group membership, and that requires rearrangement of the institutional mechanisms of knowledge. Questions of knowledge cannot always be answered by burdens of proof or rules of evidence. Some questions of knowledge also require the investigation of relative epistemological privilege. This leads to the next step in my list. When two or more good-faith accounts inform a dispute, whose reality shall prevail?

5. Look to the Bottom

Professor Mari Matsuda suggested the phrase "looking to the bottom" as part of an improved jurisprudential method.[29] The "bottom" does not refer to the merit or capacity of any actor but to the situation of an actor among the usually obvious structures of social hierarchy. Looking to the bottom requires a painstaking historical, contextual analysis of whose subjectivity has been relatively unfettered and whose has been systematically constrained. Looking to the bottom includes at least three historical, political, and moral judgments. First, it recognizes that some groups and group members have had epistemological privilege, including the power to define, appropriate, and control the realities of others. Second, looking to the bottom incorporates the moral principle that at some point, it is just that members of that group relinquish their epistemological privilege in favor of the point of view of the theretofore epistemologically unprivileged. Third is the proposition that it is appropriate for the law to undertake this epistemological redistribution.

Looking to the bottom is anathema to mainstream liberal jurisprudence because it brings a big dose of purposive interpretation of rules and allegations, so leads yet again to accusations of subjective decision making. I have tried throughout this book to show the dead-endedness of the subject/object divide, and the need to get beyond it in order for law to serve as a useful social instrument. Whatever features you would include in the rule of law, I would include the promotion of equality as the basic aim, as the feature without which law is largely pointless. And a signal feature of inequality is in the maldistribution of the power to label a perception as truth. Thus, a legal system committed to equality must have the ability to evaluate relative truth-labeling powers. This is an example of what progressives mean by referring to *systematic* inequalities. Being able to undertake this sort of analysis is what makes legal guarantees more than trivial.

I'm confident that we can identify the nonprivileged point of view in a given case. When the law must choose among realities, the principle of equality requires that we look to see whose dignity is most at stake, whose point of view has historically been silenced and is in danger of being silenced again,[30] and that, in the ordinary case, we choose that point of view as our interpretation. That is why, for example, the unwelcomeness of the conduct in all sexual harassment cases, and the severity and pervasiveness of the conduct in hostile environment cases is measured from the point of view of the harassed, not the harasser.

The method of looking to the bottom does not refer simply to conflicts in evidence. It can help as well to identify kinds of subordination, to appreciate the harms arising from varieties of subordination, and to direct the interpretation of rules to address those subordinations and those harms. Perhaps most famously in litigation and academic literature are the problems that have arisen when women of color have sought to bring claims *as* women of color. For a long time after the civil rights achievements of the 1960s, most courts were hostile to those claims. One court accused women of color of attempting to create a sort of "super remedy,"[31] seeking greater standing than that enjoyed by other litigants. Another envisioned an onslaught of "combination claims," which it characterized as a "many-headed Hydra."[32] Those courts embraced mechanical resolutions of plaintiffs' claims, placing some items of evidence into the racial pile, some into the sexual pile, and pretending that the piles had nothing to do with each other. In those cases, not only were women of color often left with no remedy but their experiences of discrimination were distorted, artificially parsed, and rendered invisible.

The courts are slowly coming around on this. In the sexual harassment context, a turning point was *Hicks v. Gates Rubber Company*,[33] a case brought by a black female plaintiff. In 1987, the United States Court of Appeals for the Tenth Circuit decided that the trial court could aggregate evidence of racial hostility with evidence of sexual behavior in determining the pervasiveness of the alleged harassment. The *Hicks* court did not comprehensively address the historical interdependence of sex-based racism and race-based sexism by any means,[34] but did turn on a tiny light bulb for other courts. Eventually, the courts began to understand that what happens to women of color is not mere "combination" discrimination but synergistic discrimination. For example, in *Lam v. University of Hawaii,* the Ninth Circuit Court of Appeals ruled in favor of a Vietnamese woman in a law school hiring case, reversing the district court's grant of summary judgment to the university in part because it had improperly separated the plaintiff's sex discrimination claim from her race discrimination claim. "[W]here two bases for discrimination exist, they cannot be neatly reduced to distinct components. . . . Rather than aiding the decisional process, the attempt to bisect a person's identity at the intersection of race and gender often distorts or ignores the particular nature of their experiences." In support of this reasoning, the Ninth Circuit cited articles by Professor Kimberlé Crenshaw and Professor Judith Winston.[35] I hope to see more of that.

As always, I don't want to paint a happy face on this relatively positive turn. Courts are just beginning to grasp intersectionality and the ways that the method of looking to the bottom can work. In *Hicks,* the intersectionality provisionally being grasped, the plaintiff was not able to prove her case after remand for reasons that were all too familiar. Her credibility was impugned, the alleged harassment got characterized as just bad manners, and the potentially actionable conduct got transformed into isolated incidents.[36] Perhaps the best that can be said about *Hicks* is that consciousness was raised and then fell over again. But it and cases like it are confirming that the steps I outline are viable moves in legal judgment.

6. Find the Best Answer for Now

Finding the best answer for now means to generate as many options as possible about how to deal with a situation. Then, based on information learned from the prior steps, choose the best option. The crucial idea of this step is that any option chosen can be provisional. Solutions once embraced can cease to be useful or can be coopted by others for bad ends. Therefore, this step requires constant vigilance about when the best answer for now becomes a bad answer for the future.

Sometimes, empirical and political conditions mandate "the best answer for now." Abortion is the best example. Anti-choice forces have popularized the phrase "abortion on demand," as if women, left to our own murderous devices, would become pregnant just for the fun of increasing the abortion rate. Contrary to this implication, no one desires to have an abortion as an end in itself. Rather, abortion is a necessary interim option pending the changes that would dramatically decrease the need for abortions: women's control of sexual access to their bodies, equal participation in child care, economic parity between the sexes, and meaningful access to health care. Abortion is a necessary option for now, and feminists should portray it as such. Honesty is the best strategic policy.

Often, the "best answer for now" strategy entails the careful use of stereotypes. Legal liberalism tends to say that stereotypes are always bad, without acknowledging its own extensive use of them.[37] As discussed in chapter 5, however, stereotypes can sometimes be useful. Some stereotypes are true, if only temporarily; some stereotypes describe group characteristics that tend to be true, if only statistically. The obstacle to the proper use of stereotypes is the circularity that emerges when the law tries to curtail activities that produced the stereotypes in the first place. When, for example, proponents of abortion struggle to keep abortion available to teenagers, we reinforce the stereotype that teenaged women are not sexually self-possessed. Because of existing social arrangements, however, it is often true that young women are not in control but, rather, are buffeted by a swarm of contradictions emanating from moral commands, sex education curricula, images of popular culture, and the demands of their male peers. It does not hurt those young women worse to describe the social facts. Abortion is an interim remedy for pregnant teenagers, while we all work on the social arrangements that put them in the position of having unwanted pregnancies in the first place.

The "best answer for now" strategy requires the same historical thoroughness and self-trust that I mentioned in the discussion of looking to the bottom. It is critical in all cases to discern the origins of stereotypes, and to use extra care when dealing with new, very sweeping, or truly self-replicating ones. As lawyers become comfortable with feminist legal theory, they will come to trust themselves with those discussions.

7. *Practice Solidarity*

Solidarity means other-directedness on different levels. At a minimum, solidarity means our thinking through, as professionals and as activists, how legal decisions affect other people. It is too easy in the practice of law, even while engaged in the representation of clients' worthy causes, to make bad law that will do harm down the road.

The storm around same-sex marriage illustrates the problem. I am among many feminist lawyers who believe that the devotion of so much time and so many resources to the goal of marriage was a mistake for many reasons. If a few lawyers and clients had not committed us to the goal of marriage a decade or so ago,[38] who knows what divisions might have been avoided or minimized? Who knows what other legal protections might have been achieved? It stuck in my craw that, on the same day that the U.S. Senate passed the Defense of Marriage Act, the Employment Non-Discrimination Act, which would have prevented employment discrimination on the basis of sexual orientation, failed to pass by one vote.[39] Now the marriage advocates are admitting that straight citizens needed to get to know us better before we laid the marriage trip on them. What better way to get to know us than around the watercooler in workplaces where we needn't fear disclosure of our sexual orientations?

Actually, I'm done being cranky about the marriage deal. I know that same-sex couples will be guaranteed the right to marry, if not in my lifetime, then soon. I'm glad I won't have to litigate the cases or write much more about it. I just wish that the original lawyers and plaintiffs had thought the thing through more carefully, regarding what resources would be consumed and whose interests might actually be harmed, before the rest of us were dragged into their agenda. Lots of people who have no interest in the marriage goal *did* back it. I've given lots of speeches and interviews, trying to explain the constitutional context, because solidarity is more important to me than my disagreement with the agenda.

Thinking these through in the way I advocate is a big challenge because it requires understanding the connections between your own life and the lives of other people. It requires seeing how you have benefited from privilege, including by never having to notice it before. It requires understanding that group identities and characteristics and histories can be nodes in systems of oppression—whether or not consciously perpetrated—rather than falling into the habit of seeing injustices as "isolated incidents."[40] It requires uncompromising study of how our lives and well-being are tied together, and requires resisting any reform that implicitly reincorporates systems of hierarchy.

On another level, solidarity means trying unfamiliar strategies informed by unfamiliar voices. Anybody can think up a million reasons, for example, that the foundations of the republic would crumble if a pornography civil rights ordinance[41] were put into effect. But really, how do we know that? How do we know that everyone's quality of life, and the free marketplace of ideas itself, wouldn't be enriched? It is possible that pornography regulation would cut into the vicious cycle of gender hierarchy. The social construction of gender could change, and that would be to everyone's benefit.

Finally, and most difficult for us verbal types, I believe that at some points, solidarity requires privileged voices to back off, give up the floor to different perspectives, and see if somebody else can do a better job.

8. Keep the Law in Proper Perspective

Being a lawyer sometimes leaves one feeling that the only choices are nihilism or conformity to the dreary, overcautious status quo. In my experience, that stuckness is critical to the maintenance of law's self-importance, and is fueled by a weird legal pathology.[42] As a partial remedy for this syndrome, keep in mind that legal decisions are mere snapshots of ongoing social processes.

Lawyers have learned to view a legal dispute as the beginning and end of a controversy. But that is usually not true. It is a mistake, for example, to imagine abortion as an abstract constitutional conflict. Rather, the constitutional controversy is incidental to the social arrangements that produce unwanted pregnancies. Relatedly, feminist lawyers have learned the hard way that merely winning abortion cases is not nearly enough. Even before the recent storm about Supreme Court appointments, the right to abortion was a mere abstraction for most women.[43] If the federal right goes away, the matter will move back to the states and the streets. I suspect that feminists like me haven't yet had the opportunity to appreciate exactly what sort of snapshot *Roe v. Wade* was. This is one of those situations where I suspect I'll tire political muscles that I didn't know I had. Even the work done in losing litigation is important. Those snapshots we took, and the preparation that went into them, are invaluable educational and organizational items. It all contributes to changes in consciousness rather than mere changes in rules.

In developing the eight methodological steps contained in this chapter, I want to give further texture to the MacKinnon equality standard endorsed in chapter 5, but I also want to go beyond the boundaries of what lawyers usually understand as equality law. I want to suggest that the steps I describe could benefit legal analysis in all manner of legal disputes, not just those illustrative "women's issues" that I've primarily relied upon in this chapter.

Let us revisit, for example, the problem of causation in toxic torts that was the primary focus of chapter 3. Many of the controversies are *de facto* women's issues because an extraordinary number of the contentious litigations have involved products that are used exclusively or disproportionately by women. But let's talk about a toxic tort issue that is nominally sex-neutral, say, the increase in violence to self and others allegedly caused by commonly prescribed antidepressants. In brief form, the analysis might go like this.

Avoiding conventional divisions. The contest in the antidepressant cases is not between a few whiny plaintiffs (with their greedy lawyers) and the heroic scientists (employed by pharmaceutical companies) whose sometimes risky innovations undoubtedly improve lives. The plaintiffs are not "in bed with" enemies of science, such as school boards who insist that "intelligent design" be taught alongside the theory of evolution.

Eschewing neutrality. Remember Heisenberg: the observer changes the observed system. Science is not a pristinely neutral endeavor. The present sine qua non in toxic tort cases, epidemiology, is also a purposive rather than a neutral enterprise. It is concerned as much with how to model populations and diseases as it is with finding final answers about the relationships between populations and diseases. It is a science in search of other scientific paths, rather than a description of the furniture of the universe. In any case, the fact that a "background" population commits violent acts doesn't make it OK that the plaintiff population commits those acts. It isn't OK for the background population either. The law is another purposive enterprise that should design its relationship to science in accord with its own conscious aims. When social practices and institutions, including pharmaceutical companies, participate in causing violence, the law gets to regulate those practices and institutions.

Challenging false necessities. Courts don't have to choose between deciding on one hand that an antidepressant was *the* cause of a plaintiff's harms (what Aristotle might call the "final cause") and on the other hand that an antidepressant was unrelated to those injuries. Courts decide only *legal* cause, a term that can have whatever meanings the law needs to ascribe to it. In determining the criteria for legal cause, courts also get to decide what constitutes expert opinion, and which experts' testimonies are more germane than the testimonies of other experts. The slippery slope argument is usually a red herring in these cases. If a jury decides that a specific injury was caused by a specific antidepressant, it means neither that a given manufacturer will be liable for all injuries allegedly associated with its antidepressant nor that all manufacturers will always be held liable for any injuries that can be merely statistically associated with their products.

Deconstructing from the level of knowledge. This is the real focus of chapter 3: what counts as knowledge and who gets to decide the criteria for deciding what counts as knowledge? Pharmaceutical cases are special cases, among other reasons because drugs are marketed only after supposed scrutiny by the federal government. In reality, the manufacturers conduct their own studies, and usually disclose to the government (and to shareholders and consumers) only positive results. Antidepressants are a textbook problem in that regard.[44] Importantly, the studies that exist about profitable, still-patented pharmaceuticals are *clinical* studies, that is, observations based upon populations prospectively identified and compared. Epidemiological studies don't exist for most pharmaceutical drugs still on the market; by definition, epidemiology concerns postexposure effects of a toxin in more general populations, and the studies take time. The more time, the more reliable the study. Nonetheless, plaintiffs in antidepressant cases usually cannot even get to a jury because they cannot present epidemiological evidence that by definition could not exist or could not be reliable.[45] Here is the simple methodological question: who should decide the significance of the nonexistent or incomplete epidemiological evidence, the non-scientifically-trained judge or the non-scientifically-trained jury?

Looking to the bottom. The reason for the development of product liability law in the first place was to shorten the immense distance between twentieth-century consumers and the manufacturers of the products that can inflict mass injuries.[46] Talk about epistemological privilege! Consumers can't test products before they go on the market (accompanied by astonishing advertising budgets), and manufacturers pretty much disclose what they want to disclose. Particularly when manufacturers did know or should have known about dangers and didn't disclose them to consumers in a meaningful way, whose version of the facts should be given most attention?

Finding the best answer for now. There is lots of dispute about whether judgments for damages deter the design, manufacture, and marketing of dangerous products in a general and consistent way. But is that the standard? There are a number of ridiculously dangerous products that are now off the market because of the efforts of injured plaintiffs and their lawyers, products that wouldn't have been removed by legislative or administrative or market-regulatory means. Particularly in the United States (where there is no universal medical coverage nor any consistent mission for regulatory agencies), we won't soon agree upon a final and comprehensive answer about the role of lawsuits in the service of the goal of consumer safety.

Why not make some provisional changes in standards and doctrines? Judges (sometimes with the help of legislators) vary tort doctrines all the time. It is commonplace to tinker with burdens of proof, especially by the creation of burden-shifting doctrines on questions of causation.[47] Remedies are another rich source of provisional solutions. All plaintiffs' recoveries are "odds-based" in several senses, and the recent development of odds-based *partial* recoveries[48] could be expanded. And what would be so bad about provisional adoption of the proposals, for example, that create presumptions of liability (or presumptions of proof on the causal element) when manufacturers are shown simply to have failed adequately to test their products, intentionally or not?[49] Exceptions could still be made for experimental lifesaving products, and lawmakers could change those provisional rules when they appear not to work anymore.

Practicing solidarity. This admonition is somewhat complex in the toxic tort context. The defense bar, defense experts, and the insurance companies that finance them are virtual monuments to the success of coordination of efforts. Plaintiffs and their lawyers are becoming more organized, as well. Solidarity, however, connotes more than coordination with those on your own side. Solidarity probably requires that plaintiffs' lawyers refrain from bringing "frivolous" suits, and that defense lawyers refrain from defending dangerous products. But these are mere platitudes without, first, a norm of disclosure about tests and risks, and second, an understanding of the "life cycle" of tort litigation. Every lawsuit is a snapshot in a long story, including years of testing (or not testing) products, marketing products, discovering injuries from products, and testing the judicial waters in the first cases involving such products before an equilibrium emerges among judgments, settlements, and product withdrawal.[50] The best that could be hoped for at this stage, perhaps, is agreement that such stories are the most inefficient possible way of regulating dangerous products. Solidarity on that conclusion could lead to a different regime of premarket testing, regulatory streamlining, and normalization of litigation longevity.

Keeping the law in proper perspective. In the United States, we have a particularly odd view of the relationship between law and health care. Health care industries are largely deregulated on the front end, and law steps in only after injuries have occurred through the filing of malpractice and products liability suits. This setup doesn't deserve the name "social policy." We give the common law (and lawyers and judges and insurance companies) too much power. By regulation through lawsuit, we get problems like the practice of defensive medicine (driving up health care costs) and huge inequities in the distribution of damages for similar injuries from malpractice and toxic treatments. Among all social problems, perhaps the problems of health care cry loudest for reevaluation of the role of law. In my view, the righteous feminist position is to argue strenuously for getting over the existing litigation system and trying different approaches. At the same time, keeping the law in perspective argues for supporting the plaintiffs who take the risks of bringing suit. That is, one proper perspective is to celebrate what litigants achieve in calibrating social norms.

I invite the reader to look to her own areas of legal interest as tests of the eight methodical steps I've described. As the exegesis on the application of those steps to toxic torts indicates, perhaps my steps are just ways of organizing familiar arguments. But I believe the reader will find that those steps point to places where such arguments *consistently* present themselves as serious obstacles. My point is to show that these consistent possible pitfalls needn't always nab us. Lawyers can decide to go beyond them, and can do so with vigilance directed toward elimination of bad habits and delusional choices.

7

False Consciousness

Everyone in this room is wearing a uniform.

—Frank Zappa

In previous chapters, I've repeatedly come back to the concept of choice. It is a fundamental tenet of legal liberalism—that the individual is the only meaningful unit of social measurement and that the individual captains her own ship, makes her own bed, and is the self-determining protagonist in a number of nonmetaphorical endeavors as well. Choice is also an intractable problem in philosophy. There is no way that our human minds could ever know for sure whether what we experience as choice actually determines any events in our own lives or elsewhere. We could be mere cogs in an eternal universal unalterable plan. Or maybe what we understand as our choices have some partial effectuality—maybe nature and nurture and physics and the gods and human dignity are all ingredients in a cosmic stew. We just can't know for sure.

I've also referred the reader to how the concept of choice has particular poignancy for women and other "others." This chapter is a meditation upon the matter of individual choice, and specifically upon how feminist lawyers have dealt and not dealt with the concept. Though my discussion goes well beyond the specific term, I've called this chapter "false consciousness" because the term signifies—not always precisely—a continuing source of feminist infighting and paralysis. "False consciousness" is both a philosophical term of art and a political epithet, at least these days. Along with the charge that a feminist is engaging in "essentialism," the allegation that a feminist has accused another of "false consciousness" has long been both a conversation stopper and a thought stopper. That happened when any of us began to think beyond liberalism. If individual perception and evaluation *aren't* the measure of all things, if political success *isn't* just the provision of equal individual "opportunity," what standards should feminism provide to replace those? People who grew up in the Cold War era, perhaps particularly, were hypersensitized to threats of "thought-policing" by others claiming to have found a better political path.

The idea of false consciousness bounces around in lots of contexts, and at the least seems to mean that someone is missing something important or that someone is accusing someone else of missing something important. Before getting to the heritage and meanings of the idea, let's consider three situations where the matter of false consciousness might arise or has arisen.

First, in London on the morning of November 4, 2004, the *Daily Mirror* ran a front-page picture of the just reelected President George W. Bush with the headline "How Can 59,054,087 People Be So DUMB?"[1] Second, President Bush has appointed Gerald Reynolds as the new head of the United States Commission on Civil Rights. Though an African American, Mr. Reynolds says that he has never clocked race discrimination, at least as practiced against himself: "I just assume somewhere in my life some knucklehead has looked at me and my brown self and said that they have given me less or denied me an opportunity. But the bottom line is, and my wife will attest to this, I am so insensitive that I probably didn't notice."[2]

The third example is a comment from Professor Joan Williams, who in a symposium about the work of caring for others (that most fundamental and usually uncompensated work done most often by women), stated that "the only rhetoric dominance feminism offers for understanding 'choice' . . . is 'false consciousness.' " Williams says that an accusation of false consciousness "is infuriatingly condescending," and asks, "[C]an you imagine a trade book that actually inspired women to think of themselves as responding to social mandates rather than making authentic choices by telling them they suffered from 'false consciousness'?"[3]

I understand that these examples are different in many ways but offer them to introduce a spectrum of talking about the misconceptions of others. "False consciousness" could refer to a wide range of responses to the assertion of an opinion, from "I disagree with you, and believe that with more information or experience you might change your mind," to "you are a total puppet and I am both smarter than and morally superior to you."

The first example is straightforward. Of course, the British press has always enjoyed hyperbole, and it is no secret that Europe is fed up with the United States. I don't think, however, that anyone in Europe actually believes that a majority of U.S. voters have low intelligence. Rather, the November 4 edition of the *Mirror* wonders why the voters failed to use that intelligence, and acted instead against what the editors regard as the self-evident interests of the citizens of the United States and everyone else in the world.

The second example is more complex. In quoting Mr. Reynolds, the *New York Times* didn't bother saying that "this guy doesn't get it." It instead implied that perhaps the top civil rights official should be sensitive to racism, at least sensitive enough to notice it. In addition, the report about Mr. Reynolds invites us to consider the motives of the Bush administration. This President's father, President George H. W. Bush, was thought by some to have acted cynically or delusionally in appointing Clarence Thomas—an African-American man vehemently opposed to affirmative action—to the Supreme Court, the institution that would decide the fate of such policies. Similarly, some might think that Bush Junior specifically wanted to fill a racial-policy-making position with an African-American man who believes that racism is all in our heads.

But who is cynical? Who is delusional? Are Justice Thomas's and Mr. Reynolds's beliefs genuine? Are those beliefs wrong?[4] Did the Bush administrations think their appointees' beliefs were genuine, and knowing that such beliefs were "wrong," act to exploit those beliefs to keep people of color in their place? Or did the Bush administrations believe their appointees' beliefs, that racists are basically knuckleheads? Are they then *all* wrong? Or, as the Bush administrations would argue, are "the liberals" completely deluded about the benefits of affirmative action and racial awareness? Moreover, do the liberals know they are wrong, and do they argue for affirmative action out of abject cynicism? Are they playing the rest of us for knuckleheads? You see where this is going. Such questions are not just about policy; they are also about probity and paranoia.

The third example is complex in a different way, and exemplifies what has made "false consciousness" such an issue among feminists. Professor Joan Williams's statement accuses an unnamed someone (or someones) of accusing an unnamed someone else (or someones else) of suffering from "false consciousness." Given that Joan Williams is a respected feminist legal scholar, I'm disturbed by her treatment of the problem of delusion. To begin with, this particular quote ignores a fabulous phase of feminist history. She says it is unimaginable that it could be so, yet an actual best-selling feminist trade book about "false consciousness" was Kate Millett's *Sexual Politics,*[5] published in 1970, one of the great political treatises of the twentieth century. Among Millett's central insights was how sex skews the perceptions and interests of both men and women. Millett was among the first to apply the notion of "ideology" to sex. And her book, exposing as it did how deluded we could be, did nothing if not *inspire.* A generation of people who would devote their lives to liberatory causes were changed by Millett's analysis. In 1970, my mother gave that book not only to me (and a perfect high school graduation present it was) but to several of the people with whom she was working, trying to navigate through layers of denial, violence, and weirdness in postdesegregation North Carolina.

What is more important, Professor Williams's comments assume that there is a single understanding of choice offered by "dominance feminism" (if you don't agree with us you are deluded) and that there is an opposite thing called "authentic choices." I cannot find such clarity in a distinction between indoctrination and personal opinion. As explained in chapter 4, the liberal notion of authentic individual choice itself stands in need of radical interrogation.[6] Of course, there is nothing more irritating than having an oafish person get in your face and say, "You know what's wrong with you?" But most exchanges are not like that. And there is more at stake than bruised feelings.

Professor Williams does not provide any citation for the association between false consciousness and dominance feminism, but it is fairly clear from the context that she is accusing Professor MacKinnon of accusing other feminists of false consciousness. It is commonplace to do so.[7] A careful study of MacKinnon's work, however, reveals that not only has she never accused anyone of false consciousness but that she rejects the concept. Here is part of what MacKinnon actually said on the subject:

> Treating some women's views as merely wrong, because they are unconscious conditioned reflections of oppression and thus complicitous in it, posits objective ground. . . . The "false consciousness" approach begs the question by taking women's self-reflections as evidence of their stake in their oppression, when the women whose self-reflections are at

> issue are questioning whether their condition is oppressed at all. The subjectivist approach proceeds as if women were free, or at least had considerable latitude to make or choose the meanings of their situation. . . . The way in which the subject/object split undermines the feminist project here is that the "false consciousness" approach cannot explain experience as it is experienced by those who experience it, and its alternative can only reiterate the terms of that experience. . . . Neither the transcendence of liberalism nor the determination of materialism works for women. . . . Women's situation offers no outside to stand on or gaze at, no inside to escape to, too much urgency to wait, no place else to go, and nothing to use but the twisted tools that have been shoved down our throats. . . . If feminism is revolutionary, this is why.[8]

MacKinnon has been so important to social movements over the last quarter century that we owe it both to her and to the possibility of progress to give more careful consideration than is usually given to the concept of false consciousness.

The actual term "false consciousness" was coined by Karl Marx's intellectual partner, Friedrich Engels.[9] Most political theorists define false consciousness as a belief that is "false," that is both produced by and reinforcing of an oppressive social system, and that conceals and acts against the believer's real interests.

The definition is a mouthful on many grounds, but note that many neo-Marxist and non-Marxist theories posit a notion of "ideology" or "hegemony" that includes a concept of misperception or misjudgment akin to false consciousness. Walter Lippmann, the "Dean of American Journalism," wrote early in the twentieth century about the "manufacture of consent," which he considered a positive part of democratic governance, a notion enthusiastically taken up by the advertising, public relations, and lobbying industries.[10] A recent best-selling book—*What's the Matter with Kansas?*—is an investigation of how the good people of that state have been persuaded consistently to vote against their own economic well-being.[11]

The term "ideology" is used variously in present debates but does not usually refer to a happy part of self-governance. Ideology means a collection of beliefs and values held by an individual or by a group on grounds other than what, upon more careful deliberation, people would usually regard as good evidence. Ideology complements physical force as the primary instrument for the maintenance of social order. The dominant ideas in an epoch reflect the experience and serve the interests of the dominant class. Those can be economic interests, gender interests, race interests, militaristic interests, nationalistic interests, or what have you, and can be in competition. When it is working well,[12] ideology allows the powerful to believe that they deserve to be in power, and induces those not in power to entertain mistaken beliefs about how society works and what is good for them. Ideology induces those not in power to engage in self-policing. Ideology makes the existing order seem natural, inevitable, and/or just, at least to the degrees necessary to quell serious challenges to it.[13]

In the literature about ideology, most familiar to contemporary scholars is the notion of "hegemony," developed by the authors associated with the Institute for Social Research in Frankfurt beginning in the 1930s. Their analysis sought to "unmask" the discrepancies between the proclaimed goals of the powerful and the means by which they actually operate. Ideology is a communicative structure systematically distorted by power relations.[14] Antonio Gramsci famously defined "cultural hegemony" as "the 'spontaneous' consent given by the great masses of the population to the general direction imposed on social life by the dominant fundamental group."[15] This is a complex process, what Gramsci described as divided consciousness on the part of the individual.[16]

Hegemony rules primarily through legitimation rather than force. It thrives on an aura of moral authority established through institutions and symbols instantiating "mainstream" values, norms, perceptions, sentiments, and prejudices. These mainstream items define the existing distribution of all versions of power, and also define the permissible range of disagreement about those distributions. The hegemonic work is arduous, but the payoff is huge. The regime "produces its own image of authority, a form of legitimation that rests on nothing outside itself and is reproposed ceaselessly by developing its own languages of self-validation."[17] That's another mouthful, but think of a simple example: brand-name loyalty. I remember acquiring brand-name loyalty at a very young age, when the issue *was* my father's Oldsmobile. I've read that the average ten-year-old in the United States can identify between two hundred and three hundred brand names. Corporations go to an enormous amount of trouble to make this so, but we help out a lot by wearing corporate logos all over our bodies and paying for the privilege of doing so. Reread the language quoted earlier in this paragraph with any Nike ad in mind.

It is difficult to condense a century and a half of critical theory to describe the mechanisms of hegemony. Still, I have to emphasize three of those mechanisms. First, hegemony limits acceptable discourse. In order to be admitted to debate in the noncrackpot gallery, the contestants tacitly and perhaps unconsciously agree to limits that give away the store regarding some of the most important social issues. Thus, in questions of war and peace, the respectable contestants must assume that the state is benevolent, reacting only to the crimes of others, and that when it acts unwisely, it is only—in the words of Professor Noam Chomsky—"because of personal failures, naiveté, the complexity of history or an inability to comprehend the evil nature of our enemies."[18]

These limits of acceptable discourse mean that pointing out the gratuitousness of a particular war is regarded as merely impolite, perhaps disrespectful to the troops. Suggesting that persons in a particular administration have made it all up, have conspired to create military conflict for political gain is not only uncivilized, it is getting close to treason. Suggesting that *that is what governments do* is lunacy. The limits of discourse mean that one cannot insist too vehemently on an increase in the minimum wage, and cannot talk too openly about the increasing concentration of wealth and the impoverishment that must be imposed to achieve it, lest one be accused of engaging in class warfare. These limits of discourse make feminism always too shrill, too oppositional, because respectable people do not point out the privileges that other people actually have and how those privileges are obtained and maintained.

A second central mechanism of hegemony involves the role of experts. Obviously, with respect to the first mechanism described above, it matters *who* is articulating the limits of acceptable discourse. When experts, pundits, officials, commentators, academics—the credentialed and the confident—are not troubled by matters outside the limits of discourse, why should anyone else be? Thus, in my discussion of toxic torts in chapter 3, it is crucial to the protection of industry that the regime of truth-making devolves from a rule of evidence that describes what counts as *expert* testimony. Practicing lawyers are themselves expert in the manipulation and presentation of expertise. It is not only that you want your guy to have lots of letters after his name, to wear a handsome but unpretentious suit, and to look and sound like Walter Cronkite. There is wizardry involved in elevating his testimony to the level of gospel, and in portraying contradictions as heresy.

Additionally, within a hegemonic system, experts are necessary to create and/or maintain a perpetual crisis-consciousness; a sense of threat to people that will cause them to accept control by others. Experts or those designated as experts have the exposure needed to achieve that. In their 2000 best-selling book *Empire,* Michael Hardt and Antonio Negri rearticulated this insight—perhaps first articulated by Machiavelli—in ways prescient of what would follow the events of September 11, 2001. Ever-enlarging exercises of power require the capacity to define "every time in an exceptional way," the circumstances that demand another exercise of power.[19] There must be a proliferation of indefinite crises.[20] Think of the color-coded "threat levels" the U.S. government created after September 11; recall how often the defense experts changed the threat level, and on what grounds. Having just finished the Hardt and Negri book, I couldn't help but notice that for many weeks after September 11, CNN advertised its 24/7 programming in advance as "crisis coverage." The Department of Homeland Security could be called the Department of Permanent Emergency. My observations are not to minimize the losses of September 11 or to communicate disrespect for the responders. My intentions are exactly to the contrary. In my view, nothing could be less respectful of the bereaved and the valiant than for government to appropriate and manipulate their experiences. Nothing could honor patriots more than to expose political manipulations of them. As Professor Noam Chomsky put it back in 1984, vigilant citizens need to become literate regarding the deployment of expertise. The talking heads' real job "is to prevent the realization that what is happening today is not some departure from our historical ideals and practice, but the systematic expression of the way our institutions function. . . ."[21]

Third, hegemony tends to diminish the opportunities for and possible success of confrontational challenges to the powers that be. Keeping dissent hidden is an ancient tactic that renders the dissent trivial, abnormal, and disconnected from its roots. Due to the distribution of women in society, this has particularly been the case with feminism. Because each new feminist work or insight appears as if from nowhere, as Adrienne Rich put it, "each contemporary feminist theorist [is] attacked or dismissed ad feminam, as if her politics were simply an outburst of personal bitterness or rage."[22]

Think back to the story of the rule of law told by Justice Stephen Breyer in the various speeches that I recounted in chapter 1. Among the morals of that story seemed to be that over the last century and a half, the aftermath of Supreme Court decisions has involved less and less violent resistance or need for military enforcement. Is this an unqualified good, or a sign of the people's political disempowerment? This has long been a worry for me as a law teacher. What I teach my students—particularly in that I teach subjects where litigation is the ordinary means of enforcement of legal norms—is how to act within a closely constrained system of dispute resolution. Particularly insofar as the message is that law is the dispositive arena for every social problem, I am just another messenger for hegemony. File your lawsuits and obey the rules. Otherwise, resistance is futile.

Having discussed the means by which hegemony works, I do not attribute intentionality or even a consistent mentality to institutions, groups, or powerful individuals in society. It is still possible to be critical of whoever benefits from existing arrangements but is unwilling to investigate the ways and means of privilege. I see why the passive participation of the privileged in false consciousness is important to maintain oppression. Everyone wants to think well of themselves, and that is hard if you begin to think that your privileges are undeserved or that you've bought them off someone's back. Indeed, some believe that ignorance is fundamental to the way the world "works." The privileged need ignorance, at least among themselves and preferably among the nonprivileged, in order to sustain the self-confidence they need to keep the wheels turning.[23] In any case, there is always a motive for not knowing, and/or for covering up. Why acknowledge the agonies of prostitution, for example, when you can carry around in your mind the consensually cheerful image of Julia Roberts in *Pretty Woman,*[24] and make movie studios insanely rich at the same time? Get over it and buy some stock in the entertainment industry. Not knowing is where the magic happens.

On the other side, of course, are the negative implications for the dominated of recognizing false consciousness. It connotes complicity in one's own domination, and although the words "complicity" and "collaboration" don't carry the same weight of damnation they did a few decades ago, they aren't very nice. Accusations that people have not acted in good faith or that they lack the capacity to do so—accusations that are inherent in discussions of hegemony—have provoked notable antipathy on the part of U.S. historians over the past quarter century. Those scholars rightfully emphasize the vitality of subordinate cultures, and all the ways that persons and groups without power nonetheless assert themselves.[25] Indeed, enormous strength in social movements comes from celebrating the agency of its members, who have—seemingly against all odds—both recognized the mechanisms of oppression to which they have themselves been subject and spoken with startling clarity about them. Here is how Professor MacKinnon expressed the problem:

> Feminism affirms women's point of view, in large part, by revealing, criticizing, and explaining its impossibility. This is not a dialectical paradox. It is a methodological expression of women's situation in which the struggle for consciousness is a struggle for world: for a sexuality, a history, a culture, a community, a form of power, an experience of the sacred. If women had consciousness or world, sex inequality would be harmless, or all women would be feminist. Yet women have something of both, or there would be no such thing as feminism.[26]

The understanding of consciousness as struggle is the central point, but it is the arduousness of struggle, I suppose, that puts the matter of "false consciousness" near the top of the list of theoretical notions that provoke hostility. Before getting to the psychological aspects of this, I should note that there are at least three analytical aspects of false consciousness that present difficulties. These flow from my earlier definition of false consciousness as a false belief that is produced by and reinforces existing power arrangements in society, and that is held in spite of being contrary to the holder's own interests.

First is the implicit rationalism in an accusation of false consciousness, the implied assertion that there is a "true" consciousness accessible to the critic against which the consciousness of the criticized can be contrasted. This is what Professor MacKinnon was referring to in rejecting the concept of "false consciousness" because it "posits objective ground." The now widespread belief in the social character of knowledge renders suspect any suggestion of objective knowledge about other people's interest or even one's own interests.[27] At the very least, the idea of false consciousness would seem to require the falsifiability of a given belief. That is seldom possible to do. For example, in a 2003 article instructively entitled "The Triumph of Hope Over Self-Interest," the *New York Times* reported that 39 percent of U.S. adults believe that they are or will be in among the 1 percent of richest Americans.[28] It goes without saying that 39 percent of the population are not currently in the top 1 percent in terms of income, but I could not show that any of that 39 percent will never be in the top 1 percent. Far be it from me to quash the American dream.[29]

Second among the analytical difficulties is deciding who are the architects and beneficiaries of "existing power relationships." Even on those days when government and business and media seem most clearly to be forming a synergistic axis of evil, the story of power is not a simple story. Tom DeLay and Wal-Mart and Rupert Murdoch are indeed masters of the universe but are not the only ones with substantial cultural influence. Other arbiters of power and culture are parents, educators, classmates, Starbucks employees, musicians, authors, moviemakers, sports figures, Internet bloggers, and whoever is famous for this and the next fourteen minutes. And of course, there are multiple varieties of influence to be had, each of which waxes and wanes and self-destructs and is reconstituted. Moreover—and this question really does seem to obsess people—cultural influence need not be conscious. I'm certain that some actors set forth deviously and with complex manipulations in mind. However, as noted above, privilege is of far greater value when it is not conscious.

Third among the obvious analytical problems is identifying a person's genuine interests in order to evaluate whether that person is choosing beliefs consistent or inconsistent with those interests. This problem plagues philosophy and social theory. Thus, all versions of utilitarianism—the theories that ground social value on achieving "the greatest good for the greatest number"—founder on the question of what counts as a good, or as satisfaction of a preference, or what weight should be given to each alleged benefit, and so forth. Even if we could presume to interfere in another's interests, what interests would we need to be talking about? Short- or long-term interests? Individual or group-based interests? What interests can we isolate and which should we include? Economic, psychological, communicative, technological, sexual, intellectual, political? Could it never be said that I have a genuine interest in undermining my own interests, or at least in thwarting my own appetites?

Intimidated by the intense "subjectivity" of the realm of desires, philosophers and social scientists have sometimes looked to a calculus of needs rather than wants, in search of firmer footing. But the same kinds of problems present themselves. What needs are included? Can we distinguish on the basis of seriousness, such as basic needs, without which I would perish, versus superfluous needs, without which I would merely be unhappy or dissatisfied? And what about the Freudian distinction between latent and manifest needs? Who will decide when a professed need is a surrogate for a "real" need that I cannot admit, even to myself? And what about my needs for placebos? What about false needs that have become a part of my identity, those "gotta have it" fixes or fixations that make me "me" in my own opinion?

Herbert Marcuse said that false needs are those that people pursue even though they detract from happiness: the needs that perpetuate toil, aggressiveness, misery, and injustice.[30] There is much about that formulation that is attractive. It often seems that existing social arrangements are misery-inducing for oppressors as well as the oppressed, and that these arrangements entail enormous energies to maintain.[31] It would be fabulous to be able to persuade the powerful to chill out and to give up the attributes of power for the sake of their own happiness. I just don't expect them to call me up and ask if I know what's wrong with them.

Given the difficulties in the needs/wants calculus, the most common resolution is just to leave the identification and pursuit of interests, wants, and needs up to each individual. I think of this as the fundamental American freedom to screw up. You just go right ahead and make yourself miserable or whatever, so long as you don't step over very specific boundaries delineating other people's spheres of misery. Chances are that neither you nor anyone else will ever be able reliably to evaluate the choices you are making in your life.

In any case, I am not bothered so much by the analytical issues. These are discussions we have all the time and we carry on whatever the setback *du jour.* Even if we can't establish the "truth" about beliefs (not to mention desires, affections, loyalties, passions, tastes, and even identities), we subject them to critique. We might even change our own minds and participate in other people's changing theirs. Moreover, not only do our desires change over time but we regularly acknowledge that we can be mistaken about them. Almost daily, I hear myself say, "This isn't what I really wanted." I am usually talking about lunch, rather than my career or sexual orientation. Yet, even if I were talking about a serious subject, people would understand what I meant.

Within feminist discourse, the larger problem has been more psychological than analytical. Those who are alleged to have made charges of false consciousness (whether they have or not), are themselves accused of being arrogant, authoritarian, silencing, and elitist. Like pretty much everything else under the sun, this set of complaints is nothing new. Around the time of the Russian Revolution, for example, this problem was called "vanguardism." That is, if the history of workers' consciousness is inexorably moving toward the revolution,[32] why do we need leaders? What role can leaders legitimately play? Vladimir Lenin particularly spent much of his theoretical energy trying to justify the Bolshevik leadership by an educative model, whereby expertise could be provided to the proletariat as they attempted to break free of their enslavement.

The history of Marxism and its variations in the twentieth century provide rich ground for any study of ideology, but the problems of ideology can be generalized. The issue of hierarchy presents itself in all manner of political movements, particularly in urging others that they should and can realign their loyalties. It wasn't just the Bolsheviks urging the workers to struggle against the bourgeoisie but civil rights leaders working to empower people of color to struggle against racial oppression, nationalists encouraging colonized people to struggle against the colonialists, and feminists urging women to struggle against patriarchy. In all of these contexts one could ask, where do these people get off? Do they think they are better than us? Are they claiming to *speak for us?*

Every relationship of subordination and domination is different, and one of the indicia of difference is how ideology plays out in that relationship. The political history of women is generally informed by the distribution of women in society. Women are not their own demographic. In general, they do not live in communities or cultures that are describable differently from the communities and cultures in which men also live. That is true as well of some other historically disenfranchised groups, such as those subjected to subordination because of disabilities or because of gender orientation. The added ingredients in women's political history are sex and the pedestal. The Anglo-European tradition, especially in recent centuries and especially among more affluent classes, has expressed the "separate spheres" ideology. In this version of supposedly natural arrangements, women and men inhabited different worlds, the woman's world having no history-making authority. The inhabitants of that world garnered esteem by their conformity to the closest degree possible to the "cult of true womanhood." In this regime, women's absence from authority was taken as nature itself. Putting women on a false pedestal made it less necessary to deliver express messages of inferiority, at least to aspiring and already conforming females.

Throw into this mix the elaborate structures of sexual objectification and sexual pleasure. Throw in the whole feminist-postmodernist commentary on protecting desire, the erotic, and "the imaginary." Throw in the pleasures and approbation attendant to having and rearing children. Many women resisted, many went crazy, but most went along with the program and I do not criticize them for that. Yet a great deal of feminist analysis has been devoted to showing how this whole regime was a setup for the women involved. The more an individual woman succeeded at femininity, the less she succeeded as a self-determining human being.

It is an old debate. Beginning with de Beauvoir's admonition that "one is not born, but made, a woman," many feminists have argued that femininity is training for subordination, that the very identity as "woman" is disempowering.[33] Particularly, the critique has centered around "male identification," the set of forces that encourage women to surrender themselves to the identities of their fathers, husbands, or sons. Is it false consciousness? Some feminists have thought so, in that the male's power and prestige—or even relative sense of well-being—by definition do not transfer to the female.[34] Other feminists have sharply rejected such an analysis as offensively patronizing, as mirroring Leninist vanguardism, and as denying the complexity of all consciousness, whether raised or unraised.[35]

The debate has been at times debilitating for feminist efforts. I see that there is a lot at stake, including the joys of family life, the release of inhibitions on erotic experience, and the "metaphoric" of gender.[36] I would note, though, that in a sense all group identifications are "false" identifications. I've mentioned several times that "professionalism" seems to be a cover, so that lawyers don't have to think very deeply about what is going on in the multitudinously different worlds in which law has effects. Professionalism has also been a trap for teachers (particularly those in elementary and secondary education), who get meager compensation and have little power in ordering educational systems. I worry particularly about my friends who are nurses; the call of professionalism is incredibly strong when one holds the well-being of others so directly in one's hands, but professionalism doesn't increase your salary, or get you malpractice protection, or buy you a house in a rich suburb with good schools.

Group identifications play overlapping and critical roles in human lives and human history. Whatever one's identifications, it is always possible to conceive of the downsides, including the possibility that one is participating in one's own self-destruction. But, this too, posits a false dichotomy. Group identifications are crucial. Some people have many of them. They shift daily, weekly, contextually, generationally. It is a pervasive mistake to force the choice between individualism and group identification, just as it is a mistake to force a choice among group identifications.

If it were up to me, I would arrange that all dialogue were characterized by tact and respect. The part that *is* up to me is wanting to learn when I am wrong, or when I can do better. I pay some people a lot of money to help me out with this project. A wise physician, therapist, lawyer, handyperson, friend, or even theoretician—all those helpers are worth their weight in gold. When I have thought of people (especially those I like and otherwise trust) as being wrong or deluded, my conclusions tend to follow from having observed similar mistakes or delusions among my own internalized oppressions. I have no doubt that it is my responsibility to continue to take that self-inventory, nor any doubt that I will uncover more sources of self oppression. Just as surely, however, I believe that others suffer from similar self-delusional aspects of the human condition.

More particularly, just because allegations of false consciousness abound and have been a source of controversy doesn't mean that hegemony is not a killer. The responsibility of being a political actor, a lawyer, an author, a teacher, a parent—a human—is to find evidence and good arguments and alternatives in every situation where it appears that a person or group could profitably reinterpret her or their own experience. And it is never that "you are completely wrong and worthless." These interactions are always partial; it is *this* aspect of experience that could be reinterpreted, or *that* aspect of group identification that could be recast.

I suppose that we could agree just to get rid of any concept of "false consciousness." I'd rather that we understand what the concept has meant or could mean. For all the postmodern critique and other sources of destabilization of political action, we have got to have some concepts (and names for) the traps and, yes, falsehoods, that invite people without power to participate in their powerlessness. All three interconnected terms—false consciousness, ideology, and hegemony—have taken a beating and have diffuse meanings. I would welcome the introduction of new terms or the clarification of existing terms—we've had some luck with social mystification, internalized oppression, manipulated consensus, and information management—that would allow us to talk about these things without having to reinvent the wheel every single time we sit down to talk.

The good news about hegemony is "counterhegemony." Even when I agree with what postmodernists have to say, I would almost never express things the ways they tend to do. Nonetheless, along with postmodernist philosophers such as Paul de Man and Jacques Derrida, I have to agree that even the most successful hegemonic regime grows the seeds of its own destruction, that every hegemonic text can subvert its own meaning. The messages of white supremacy, of male supremacy, and of American military/capitalist supremacy are incontrovertibly false and incontrovertibly vulnerable, if only because they take so much energy to maintain. Even though I don't always see those messages subverting themselves, I do see how they have to give way. The consciousness of people is the water; the structures are the stone.

Existing power structures end up letting books like this be published. And this is not a revolutionary book. It is just a familiarly subversive book, insofar as it sticks to the claim that everything we think we know is contingent. That is not, however, just an intellectual position. It is a necessity. The constant bombardment of messages that put us each in our respective isolated places must be resisted because they are not going to stop. As Chomsky said, "For those who stubbornly seek freedom, there can be no more urgent task than to come to understand the mechanisms and practices of indoctrination."[37] In any case, counterhegemony—or whatever less fancy word you want to insert here—is a pretty good way of being in the world. Per Alice Walker, resistance *is* the secret of joy.[38] It sure beats feeling crazy.

I was blessed while in private practice to work for a small firm in Los Angeles that did movie-star divorce work, which was fun, and which also helped to finance Title VII plaintiffs' work. One of my beloved bosses there, Blanche C. Bersch, had previously served as a regent for the California State University system. Blanche reported that in her first regents' meeting, after some person had said something aggressively unhelpful, she burst out with "That's bullshit." Blanche says that in the intermission of the meeting, then-Governor Jerry Brown took her aside and told her, "Blanche, regents do not say 'bullshit.' Regents say 'I am not persuaded.' "

There are words we use and words we don't use, depending upon the situation. There are better and worse ways of persuading people. It is always best to say only what we know, and to refrain from claims of certainty even then. When matters of importance are being discussed, we need to open our minds to new information and perspectives, and to entertain the possibility of changing our positions. There are even times to be silent.

8

The Future of Legal Feminism

> The result of men constantly, fervently and publicly thanking God that they are *not* women has been to make it hard for women to thank God that they are.
>
> —Richard Rorty

> We're not crazy. We're just discouraged.
>
> —Stan Laurel

In the feminist law teaching business, there is an exercise all teachers and students eventually go through. It is called "How should the case have come out?" This exercise is not the usual law school class discussion about how doctrine and facts interact. This feminist exercise is about how legal disputes *should* come out in terms of the bigger pictures of social relations and systems of disadvantage. The exercise has become more complex as feminist legal theory has become more complex, drawing into question legal strategies that once seemed sound, and allowing for results to be reinterpreted in myriad ways.

Thus, for example, what of a case that forced a state-supported military college to open its doors to women, only in 1996, after a century and a half of producing male "citizen-soldiers" in a culture that can be described only as women-loathing?[1] What of the fact that Justice Ruth Ginsburg, formerly a crusading feminist litigator, consistently referred to that institution in deferential, even glowing, terms?[2] Is opening the college to women what a commitment to sex equality required? If it were technically possible as a constitutional remedy, shouldn't the Virginia Military Institute have been closed or deprived of any public support? Wouldn't it have been far better to seal over that particular abyss once and for all? As noted in chapter 5, militarism is a context where feminism focuses discussion in a particularly acute way.

As another episode in this exercise, consider the Supreme Court decision holding that peremptory challenges to potential jurors cannot be based on sex. The matter happened to involve the exclusion of male jurors in a case seeking to establish paternity and an obligation for child support.[3] Like the decision forbidding race-based peremptory challenges on which it followed, this 1994 decision caused a great deal of consternation among those trial practitioners who thought the entire point of peremptory challenges was to get rid of jurors for any reason whatsoever, the more prejudicial the better, in some sense. Even if we can administer the notion of "any reason at all except these reasons," on what grounds must juries be race- and gender-integrated, if law is race- and gender-blind? Most important from my point of view, what of Justice O'Connor's "intuition that in certain cases a person's gender and resulting life experiences will be relevant to his or her view of the case?"[4] In half-joking conversation, women have often noted that because men haven't done such a swell job running the world, maybe women should get a turn. Just to see how it would go, and without necessarily making any essentialist commitments, does anybody have a problem with having all-female juries for a while? How about half-and-half juries, or a half-and-half Congress, or a rotating White House?

I don't know whether these proposals could be structured in serious or plausible ways. Perhaps formal equality and administrative difficulties shut them down before anyone could advance the conversation any further. There's another kind of critique, however, that I'd like to reach here. That kind of critique might be called the matter of "gender trouble."[5] It describes the set of problems we buy when we rely on any fixed gender notions at all.

The insights collectively called "gender trouble" can loosely be identified as "poststructuralist." That tag encompasses a lot. The "post" part refers to a stage beyond something called "structuralism," a set of twentieth-century efforts to go beyond mere skepticism. In the struggle described in chapter 2, by the early twentieth century there were no longer metaphysically authoritative sources—neither religious nor scientific nor philosophical sources—of comfort for human anxiety. "Structuralism" was a movement arguing that though we may not be able to discover or depend upon any universal laws of epistemology, ethics, or politics, perhaps we can locate in language some consistencies that reveal the "deep structures" of our species' ways of getting through. Led by the Swiss linguist Ferdinand de Saussure, the structuralists identified a relationship between signifier and signified—between words and what they discuss—independent of both individual language users and any possible underlying "furniture of the universe." But structuralism led to a set of binary propositions about signifier and signified that were rather inflexible, that were, in the contemporary phrase, "overdetermined."

Poststructuralism refers to the group of intellectual efforts—including postmodernism, postcolonial theory, antiessentialism, deconstruction, and queer theory—that celebrate the lack of reliable boundaries in life. Poststructuralism is about exposing and subverting supposed deep structures. Of most salience to this discussion is "postfeminism," the aspect of poststructuralist thought that inquires whether "the construction of the category of women as a coherent and stable subject [is] an unwitting regulation and reification of gender relations."[6]

That is, postfeminism (or poststructuralist feminism) wants to inculcate a permanent questioning of gender categories, and wants to suggest that prior feminist approaches—I resist the term "feminist orthodoxies" —make matters worse by focusing on existing structures of gender, as if those categories weren't "always already" completely contingent. Let's add this to the "How should the case have come out" exercise with reference to an area of feminist effort that has been often been a target of poststructuralist thought: sexual harassment law.

Among U.S. sexual harassment cases, a notable site of contention has been *Oncale v. Sundowner Offshore Services, Inc.*,[7] in which a unanimous Supreme Court held that male-on-male sexual harassment was actionable under U.S. civil rights statutes, regardless of the absence of allegations or proof of the sexual orientation of the victim or the perpetrators. I happen to think *Oncale* is the best case ever decided by the U.S. Supreme Court in the cause of gender liberation, but it has produced considerable criticism from ostensibly progressive legal theorists. Notably among them is Professor Janet Halley, who argues that *Oncale* could signal a new regime of "homosexual panic," and be the occasion for an onslaught of persecutions of gay men. *Oncale* is an invitation to employers and employees to target sexual minorities, in a process of imagining (maliciously or otherwise) that suspected queer coworkers are coming on to them.[8]

I've not been able to find any evidence that this has happened, but I would both expect and accept some such cases. Hysterical reversals of law's meaning have followed every progressive development. I haven't kept track of the proportion—but it was large last I looked—of cases of sex discrimination brought by male people and cases of race discrimination brought by white people.[9] The fact that ostensibly progressive scholars have become exercised about "homosexuality panic" in the sexual harassment context has led others to think that they may suffer from "sex equality panic."[10] To make a long story short, in the *Oncale* context, the "How should the case have come out" exercise leads directly into the feminist/poststructuralist debate about law's relation to sexuality. Some poststructuralists think some feminists are censorious, prudish regulators of sexuality;[11] some feminists think some poststructuralists are defenders of male supremacy and eroticizers of sexual hierarchy and pain.[12]

I am not able to resolve that debate, but I don't have to in this context. My point is that *Oncale* was important because it got the judiciary off the dime on complicated questions of gender. That is, sexual harassment law made it possible, first, to see that something that had theretofore been portrayed as a fact of nature might actually be an artifact of culture. Second, sexual harassment law made it possible to see that the practice of imposing economic inequality through sexualization of the workplace was sex discrimination, even though it could happen to both sexes. Third, in *Oncale* specifically, courts could understand the injury and see the connection with "gender performance." Particularly after *Oncale,* different aspects of judicial understandings of gender are on a happy collision course. The U.S. federal courts are close to a deeper understanding of gender nonconformity as a prohibited ground for discrimination.

This prospect is demonstrated by comparing cases from the Ninth Circuit, the first being a garden-variety "grooming case" in which the plaintiff lost. In *Jespersen v. Harrah's Operating Company, Inc.*, the court denied the plaintiff's claim that she had been sex discriminatorily fired by Harrah's casino for not wearing makeup. Ms. Jespersen had been a successful Harrah's bartender for nearly twenty years. She hated wearing makeup and thought it interfered with her job.[13]

Before 2000, Harrah's had encouraged but not forced its female employees to wear makeup. A policy begun thereafter is loaded with grist for our mill. It was called "a brand standard of excellence." It required beverage servers to be "well groomed, appealing to the eye, be firm and body toned, and *be comfortable* with maintaining this look while wearing the specified uniform."[14] Female beverage servers had to have their hair "teased, curled, or styled" and to wear "foundation/concealer and/or face powder, blush, mascara, and lip color." Here's an astonishing part. Harrah's called its standards the "Personal Best" program. The employer took pictures of employees when all dolled up, and maintained those pictures as the standard to which each employee should thereafter conform. Ms. Jespersen refused to comply with the new standards, and was fired. The Ninth Circuit panel ruled against her claim that male and female employees had been treated differently.

However, it was also the Ninth Circuit that recently decided gay-friendly sexual harassment claims, regarding the rights of gay men to be free from sex discrimination based upon their nonconformity to gender norms.[15] In the more recent *Rene v. MGM Grand Hotel,* the plaintiff was an openly gay butler on a VIP floor at the hotel. He was taunted, his coworkers would "touch [his] body like they would to a woman," they grabbed his crotch and goosed him. Similarly, in *Nichols v. Azteca Restaurant Enterprises, Inc.,* the openly gay plaintiff was verbally harassed—called by multiple pronouns, called a "faggot" and a "female whore." He was mocked for carrying his serving tray "like a woman." The Ninth Circuit expressly held that this was sex stereotyping precluded by the U.S. Supreme Court in *Price Waterhouse v. Hopkins* way back in 1989.[16]

The difference among the Ninth Circuit cases is not any difference between sexual harassment and other sex discrimination doctrines. As is often misunderstood, sexual harassment is a subset of sex discrimination law. *Price Waterhouse* was *not* a sexual harassment claim but an ordinary sex discrimination in employment case, where the female plaintiff was not made a partner in the accounting firm because she was insufficiently feminine. Check out the pattern: it is illegal to force a female plaintiff to do a gender performance (thou must be more feminine) and illegal to persecute male plaintiffs for their gender performance (thou must be less feminine). Based on that pattern, surely the panel decision in *Jespersen* is incorrect. The only difference in the pattern is that the plaintiffs in the sexual harassment cases were male, and that probably had some psychological power.[17] Of course, should any judges clue into that particular difference, they will have to conclude that the pattern of their own cases is sex discriminatory.

Judge Sidney Thomas, dissenting in the *Jespersen* case, got it. What Title VII prohibits, said Judge Thomas, are appearance requirements "that rest upon a message of gender subordination."[18] I believe that the collision of the grooming and the harassment cases will result in the elimination of the obviously gender-based "grooming code" exceptions to employment law, which could throw gender expectations into a tailspin, and thus tend toward greater legal protection for sexual nonconformists. We weren't getting anywhere very fast going after the grooming cases *qua* grooming cases.[19] *Oncale* was the key that turned this particular lock. The *Oncale* Court came close to understanding that the issue was not that Joseph Oncale was harassed because he was a man but harassed because *of the kind of man he was perceived to be*.[20]

In this focus on how gender manifests in the world, and on the importance of shifting perceptions of it, lawyers (who are feminist whether they know it or not) are implementing that aspect of poststructuralist queer theory that emphasizes gender as "performativity," a notion given the greatest currency by Professor Judith Butler. According to her, having a gender is "constituted through discursively constrained performative acts that produce the body through and within the categories of sex."[21]

Among examples of feminist/queer theory victories are relatively new legislative prohibitions on discrimination based upon "gender identity." I participated in one such legislative project. Among my activities as a lawyer has been working with Equality New Mexico, a gay/lesbian/bisexual/transgender (GLBT) organization in Santa Fe. In 2003, we succeeded—on the twelfth try—in getting the New Mexico legislature to amend the state Human Rights Act to include "sexual orientation" as a prohibited basis of discrimination. It was only the first try, but we also got the legislature to include "gender identity" as a prohibited ground. The definition of "gender identity" that we helped to draft states:

> "gender identity" means a person's self-perception, or perception of that person by another, of the person's identity as a male or female based upon the person's appearance, behavior or physical characteristics that are in accord with or opposed to the person's physical anatomy, chromosomal sex or sex at birth.[22]

So far so good. The votes were very close. Some of the legislators were puzzled about why it is was necessary to list any prohibited grounds of discrimination *at all*;[23] others were confused about how "sexual orientation" and "gender identity" might cover different groups. The bill we pushed seemed chaotic and dangerous to them, invoking the specter of drag queens in nun outfits showing up for work at banks.[24] Actually, I have no idea whether the New Mexico law would protect that. It does not contain an "appropriate appearance" exception, as some other statutes and ordinances have, allowing employers to insist on, say, business attire in business settings. Moreover, the very few cases interpreting similar "gender identity" protections have been very narrow, and may be said to have missed the point. Thus, the New York Appellate Division dismissed a transgender case because the complaint alleged "not that the transgender individuals were selectively excluded from the bathrooms . . . but that they were excluded on the same basis as all biological males and/or females are excluded from certain bathrooms—their biological sexual assignment."[25]

These problems about various understandings of "gender identity" recurring now have a familiar ring. Is it a matter of sex discrimination? ("Defendant argues that [its] restroom policy segregates restroom use by genitalia, not by sex."[26]) A question of choice? A fact of nature? A matter of self-expression? A disability?[27] When I hear these discussions, I am transported to 1974, when Professor Wendy Williams and the rest of us in the legal feminism business were temporarily struck dumb after *Geduldig v. Aiello,* the case essentially holding that a failure to underwrite disability insurance for pregnancy was not sex discrimination so long as both pregnant men and pregnant women were denied coverage.[28] Back then, we had to wonder. Of course pregnancy was not itself a disability but could temporarily disable a pregnant woman. Of course pregnancy was voluntary, but not really like cosmetic surgery. Of course pregnancy was "natural," but does that inexorably mean "beyond legal protection"? What existing legal category could pregnancy be bludgeoned into?

The answer turned out to be, pregnancy is pregnancy. What the struggle over the categorization of pregnancy taught us was that it is possible legally to address a complex social reality without analogizing it to anything. I expect that at least in the legal realm, we will come to some sort of similar resolution to the question of gender identity. Gender identity is what it is, or rather, is what individuals feel and manifest on a complex and shifting basis. Again to quote Professor Butler:

> There is no ontology of gender on which we might construct a politics, for gender ontologies always operate within established political contexts as normative injunctions, determining *what qualifies as intelligible*

> *sex,* invoking and consolidating the reproductive constraints of sexuality, setting the prescriptive requirements whereby sexed or gendered bodies come into cultural intelligibility.[29]

I emphasize the above phrase, "what qualifies as intelligible sex," because it is exemplary of the problem of legal rules. Most poststructuralist philosophy is unhelpful to law. There may be no ontology—no furniture of the universe—that tells us once and for all what qualifies as sex, or gender, or race, or anything else. But the law has to use such categorical terms, if only provisionally. And the complications are strategic as well as structural. I agree with Butler's characterization of "gender trouble," but I cannot picture myself talking to legislators about the need to "safeguard the uncontrollability of the signified"[30] and to open paths for the subversion of gender norms by parody. I can't imagine telling them why the nun costume on the biologically-born-male bank teller might be a social good.

Working in law is an opportunity for exploring the intersections among structuralist and poststructuralist approaches. The law is, by definition, a structuralist enterprise (or a pre-poststructuralist enterprise).[31] It posits what qualifies as intelligible sex, or intelligible racial considerations, or intelligible gender behaviors. And then, having posited these descriptions, it starts asking itself interminably what it meant to do with them. Legislatures enact what they want, but at least by the time we add petitioners and courts to the picture, the interpretation of every law is a foregone inconclusion. Good lawyers I know were already epistemologically poststructuralist. They already understood that they were re/presenting a text (what some call "cases" or "clients") in a vortex of interpretational fluidity.[32]

Of course, lawyers must be extraordinarily careful not to fortify the structures of oppression that we formally resist, but simply identifying those structures in the prescribed terms of legal discourse does not constitute such reinscription. That is, legal categories identify historical realities, and some (perhaps all) categories of non-discrimination identify calcified social performances. The fact that a category is listed among prohibited classifications means that someone has seen how the category is itself a "masquerade." But that is not the same as claiming to know, or as seeking to impose on anyone else one's own perception of "what precisely is masked by masquerade."[33] The fact that any legal category is approximate and fluid is why I insisted among the aspects of feminist legal method in chapter 6 that any legal answer be regarded as *provisional.*

I do not regard conversations between feminists and poststructuralists as a zero-sum game, or, as Professor Ruthann Robson might say, anything involving pie.[34] However, in every such conversation we do seem to re-cover a lot of well-covered ground. It is sometimes good to do so, but I'm wondering whether there might be some aspects of discussion that we could conditionally agree upon. The following list of eighteen themes could be a springboard for collective forward motion.

1. Metaphysically, nothing is certain, not even gravity, nor even the notion of certainty.
2. Distinctions, boundaries, and borders are linguistically, culturally, and psychologically "constructed." Those constructions are contingent.
3. There is no "outside," nothing beyond the world of human discourse to stand on when participating in social life, including participation in law and philosophy.
4. Poststructuralist thought, including postfeminism and queer theories in their postmodern forms, is philosophically unassailable. (As are all versions of skepticism.)
5. Conversation is nonetheless possible. It necessarily proceeds by processes of categorization.
6. Categorization is itself a contested concept, even in—or perhaps particularly in—the natural sciences.
7. The most important legal conversations involve discussions about when particular categories are necessary or possible or mistaken or in need of abandonment. In this regard, I recall a largely forgotten aspect of Professor Angela Harris's 1990 article that became famous for its attack on feminist "essentialism."[35] The article began with two epigraphs, one quoting the U.S. Constitution's invocation of "[w]e, the people,"[36] and the other quoting a wonderful story by Jorge Luis Borges about a person who remembered everything in complete detail (such as how each leaf on each tree looked on a certain date at a certain time), and could only recount experience by taking as much time as it took to live it.[37] In short, Professor Harris was not condemning all categorization. Rather, she was contrasting "essentialism," on one hand, understood as a kind of overgeneralization, with what

philosophers call "radical nominalism," on the other hand, understood as a kind of undergeneralization that leads to communicative failure. Harris was talking about the need for conversation always to proceed in the territory between saying everything and saying nothing. Professor Harris gets too little credit for identifying the nominalist, merely liberal, and politically hopeless place to which some poststructuralist thought leads.

8. Categories are contestable. The categories of race, ethnicity, and culture are contestable. The categories of gender, family, marriage, man, woman, male, female, masculine, feminine, homosexual, heterosexual, gay, lesbian, bisexual, transgender, and queer always have been, are now, and always will be *contestable.* As described in chapter 2, contemporary ethics—hence much of legal discourse—can be understood as engaging in these contests in good faith, not just with due regard for the arguments proposed by others but understanding the insights of others in order to improve one's own.
9. We have to include in the list of contested concepts those of left, right, progressive, and *status quo.* Almost all feminists, antisubordination theorists, and poststructuralists want to regard themselves as progressive. The challenge, of course, is to explain or justify a claim to political progressivism in light of skeptical critiques, including our own.
10. "Gender" is "performative." Gender, in all its manifestations, is also a function of existing social power. In all the ways that reality bites, but to a degree of gruesomeness that is impolite to acknowledge, gender hurts.
11. Suffering exists.
12. Suffering is itself a contested concept,[38] but should include "mere" psychological injuries on a wide scale. I mean emphatically to include among separate generously compensable injuries those caused by living under systems of inequality. Equality claimants must be re-cognized as "special attorneys general," doing society's work in their courage to come to court, whether or not they have proven other specific damages to themselves.
13. It is a legal, political, and ethical good thing to do whatever one can to reduce suffering, one's own and that of all others. Why is that so? I cannot resolve the issue of "altruism" in this book, or any book. It has been a matter of debate for centuries. I believe,

however, that there is substantial agreement among feminists, including postfeminists,[39] that the point of our work is to figure out the conditions for all individuals to have livable, and even dignified, lives.

14. "Statism" is not the point. In conventional political debate, "left" versus "right" has largely been a matter of peoples' relationship to state power. Conventionally, for progressives, the state was always the bad guy. But there are no longer clear distinctions that can be drawn solely on that basis. The basic tenet of feminism has been that "the personal is political," and the opposite is also true. Power exists in many shifting forms. It is not statism to ask government to intervene on behalf of people who do not possess power on their own in the world as now constituted. Thus, although we should continue debate about the nature and limits of invocations of state power, it is naïve to accuse feminists of "statism," whether we are called "feminazis" by Rush Limbaugh, or proponents of "Governance Feminism" by people we know and love.[40]
15. Access to government, however, is not automatically cool. Professor Ruthann Robson has been right in her original and prolific work, consistently illustrating the "domesticating" effects of voluntarily engaging with and seeking legitimation from the law.[41] Perhaps particularly in the litigation context, where the few may affect the many, deliberations of clients and their lawyers should always account for the limits of law and potential harms of legal decisions. For example, the inestimable commitment of resources to the same-sex marriage issue was caused by a few plaintiffs and lawyers, who in my view exhibited an appalling lack of solidarity.
16. Solidarity is possible.
17. Solidarity is also the only viable option for progressive people. The liberal ideal of absolute individualism makes no sense in a world of inevitably interdependent language users.
18. Solidarity requires constant reevaluation of issues and constant rejuvenation of commitments and coalitions.

With these eighteen themes in mind, I'd like to highlight a contemporary solidarity imperative: the right to abortion. In the future, other issues may carry greater urgency, but as I write, abortion is on the block. It is for sale to political contributors, and is subject to other kinds of blocks: chopping, mental, and stumbling. In my view, in the United States, abortion is the queerest issue there is, for at least four interrelated sets of reasons.

First, abortion regulation is the most salient example of "disciplining" the body. Consider how much legislative and judicial energy has been consumed with consideration of whatever restrictions on access to abortion can be thought up and fine-tuned to be constitutional. That history is an astonishingly detailed discourse about which mechanisms of social control ensure the (re)productivity of women's bodies. Restrictions on abortion are also chartable as a list of permissible and impermissible reasons for deciding to terminate a pregnancy. One is ineluctably reminded of the ongoing kerfuffle about what "causes" homosexuality (and what causes heterosexuality and so forth). It is convenient to the powers-that-be to portray homosexuality as an unconstrained "choice" that could simply be reversed by an act of individual will, or as a biological defect, that can be remedied by the advances of science. Abortion is another prominent occasion on which to safeguard the uncontrollability of the signified: reasons to have abortion vary hugely, and simply must not be constrained by some legislature's schedule of acceptable considerations.

Second, that bodily control is scarily demographic—if not eugenic—in character. The federal right to abortion was substantially decimated by 1980 because of the cases in which the U.S. Supreme Court held that governments didn't have to provide funding to indigent women, even for medically necessary abortions. In one of those cases, the Court said that the State might wish to encourage childbirth due to "demographic concerns" that are "basic to the future of the State."[42] What concerns are those? Enlarging the tax base? Increasing congressional representation? Providing cannon fodder? Similar arguments against same-sex marriage[43] and parenting by GLBT people helped me see that the concern is also propagandistic. "Barefoot and pregnant" is not a great social policy in every respect, but it accurately describes women's dependency under present social arrangements, and is a stereotype that requires endless modeling. Likewise, though there are no data to indicate that children actually do better when raised by heterosexual couples, the state seems confident that heterosexual couples will more successfully conscript children into the gendered system.[44]

Third, a subtext of the abortion debate is the enforcement of sexual conformity. The need for abortion is associated with (women's) sexual promiscuity. They have to pay for that, because they have breached the social contract. Never mind that the actual terms of the contract—that a woman has to be simultaneously sexually accessible and virginal—are impossible to meet. The damages consist in making that impossibility visible. This is also a familiar argument in the queer universe: go ahead and do it, just don't flaunt it. In legal terms, after having subjected you to constitutionally enshrined hatred for seventeen years, go ahead and have your queer sex.[45] Just don't expect your intimate relationships to be publicly valued or subsidized as other relationships are.

Fourth, the drumbeat about the evils of abortion serves to remind women that any life, even a potential life, is more valued than theirs. As one of my students put it in an immortal paper title, "Gentlemen Prefer Fetuses."[46] I am not speaking here about doctrine; I'm aware that—at least as of now—abortion restrictions must have "exceptions" to protect the life of the mother.[47] I'm talking instead about the more existential messages. Be ashamed. Remember that most public discourse does not even weigh the costs to you of nine months of pregnancy and the stresses of adoption or years of child rearing. If abortion restrictions and moral condemnation send you to a back-alley butcher, so be it. This, too, is queerly familiar. I don't have to remind queers about the economy of shame, nor about society's failure to value all that is lost in the closet, nor about the dangers that we face from "gay bashers."

At the moment, abortion is the veritable line in the sand when it comes to disciplining and deploying the body. The barricades will be reestablished, and all the feminists, liberals, and all flavors of poststructuralists need to show up. Matters of reproductive autonomy are not about constitutional doctrine or medical minutiae. They are about making connections with other issues that confront different people differently; they are about the nature and limits of the disciplinary society.

I noted above that as of 1980 the abortion right was virtually extinguished for indigent women. As of 1989, four Justices indicated in *Webster v. Reproductive Health Services* that they were ready to eliminate the right altogether. Justice Harry Blackmun, the author of *Roe v. Wade,* was alarmed: "For today, the women of this Nation still retain the liberty to control their destinies. But the signs are evident and very ominous, and a chill wind blows."[48] Blackmun's language provoked one of two reactions in the lawyers I know: they either rolled their eyes or got the shivers. The eye-rollers were those for whom the right to abortion was about doctrine and doctors (as it was for Blackmun at one time), and thought Blackmun was being over dramatic in using the words he did. The rest of us agreed with Blackmun that the stakes could be described as women's "destinies."

At about the time of the *Webster* case, Justice Blackmun gave a lecture at the University of New Mexico Law School, where I was then teaching. Someone asked him to identify the biggest difference in Supreme Court practice that he had observed over the years. He unhesitatingly replied that the difference was women advocates, both the increased numbers of them and the sort of advocacy they brought before him. He was impressed by their insights and by the dedication that they brought to their causes. He said that their preparedness and their passion had raised the quality of lawyering before the Court to such a level that he was "almost scared of them."

I've always thought that was a telling phrase. Blackmun was a man who was scared of various things at various times, but who always eventually rose to the occasion and attempted to do the right thing. Pursuant to the terms of his will, Justice Blackmun's papers became public only in March of 2004. In the first book derived from these papers, Linda Greenhouse states that "[o]n Harry Blackmun's improbable journey, becoming a feminist icon was perhaps the most improbable destination of all."[49] Greenhouse describes a judge who was initially wary and "a little grumpy" about early women's rights litigation.[50] Nonetheless, his papers show a man paying close attention, grappling with his own biases, and overcoming his own lawyerly reticence and conservative ideology. By the end, as his opinions show, he understood that abortion was an equality issue, and part of a larger vision of human dignity.[51] Blackmun incorporated the arguments of others in ways that improved his own arguments and understandings. He was, therefore, in the terms I have proposed in this book, an ethical judge.

In a liberal mode, one is tempted to conclude that they can't all be Justice Blackmun, but I'm not willing to let judges off the hook. I understand the pressures on them to conform or to pretend to conform to a vision of a Rationalist universe, a world where results are commanded by or must match up with some higher authority that can be identified and unambiguously interpreted. But that is a fantasy of pristine decision making, a wistful desire for life to have more certainty than it does. As Professor Richard Rorty said, "[T]he need for something ahistorical which will ratify one's claims, is itself a symptom of power-worship—of the conviction that unless something large and powerful is on one's side, one shouldn't bother trying."[52] The fantasy of value-free adjudication is not one that should be encouraged.

Neither professional education and prestige, nor even confirmation by the United States Senate, bestows the power of flight. Lawyers can't soar above social life. Our footprints are ultimately discernible on all that we do and don't do. I'm not asking a judge to decide in my favor because I'm big-word-using academic or because my clients' causes are just according to some transcendent standard. Rather, I've read the Constitution, and I see the word "equal" in there. I've mulled over the cases, and see that these legal commands involve essentially contested concepts. Grimy and changing concepts. My loyalty to the rule of law depends on its being able to reach through the grime of history and politics in order to achieve incremental measures of dignity for real people in real life situations. If that is something other than the usual bloodless model of legal principle, so be it. If that is result-orientation, I'm proud of it.

It isn't true that judges can't all be Justice Blackmun. Rather, the future of legal feminism depends upon doing more of that which turned him around. And doing it better. Taking all the complexities into account. This is no time to take a break from feminism. Feminism is a tradition that broke through seemingly polar ice on matters of what it means to get a little R-E-S-P-E-C-T. I don't want to forestall criticisms of feminism. I want to enlarge feminism's range, and I don't even care very much what we call it. Among progressive lawyers and thoughtful lawyers such as Justice Blackmun, who didn't even identify as progressive, the insights of feminist legal theory are already at work. As much as it hurts some to admit it, at least we all *need* to be feminists now. Let's explicitly consider and apply the insights of feminist legal theory, and then get on with all the business at hand.

Notes

NOTES TO THE INTRODUCTION

1. See Ann Scales, "Towards a Feminist Jurisprudence," 56 *Indiana Law Journal* 375 (1981); "The Emergence of Feminist Jurisprudence," 95 *Yale Law Journal* 1373 (1986); "Militarism, Male Dominance, and the Law: Feminist Jurisprudence as Oxymoron?" 12 *Harvard Women's Law Journal* 25 (1989). Some dislike the term "jurisprudence" because it sounds haughty or pseudoscientific. I, too, am critical of scientistic pretense in law (a position developed in chapter 3). I am fond of the term "jurisprudence," however, for two reasons. First, in my mind, it refers to the legal theory generated by lawyers, as opposed to theories about law emerging from other disciplines. Second, the term makes it possible to refer to those engaged in the enterprise as "jurisprudes," and that's fun. In any case, I use the terms "feminist jurisprudence" and "feminist legal theory" interchangeably in this book.

2. See *Black's Law Dictionary* (8th ed. 2004) (under category of "jurisprudence," crediting me with first published use of the term "feminist jurisprudence"); Patricia A. Cain, "Feminist Jurisprudence: Grounding the Theories," 4 *Berkeley Women's Law Journal* 191, 193 (1989–90) (reporting that I coined the term as a student in 1977, while planning a panel for the celebration of the twenty-fifth class of women to graduate from Harvard Law School); Sheila James Kuehl, "For the Women's Reach Should Exceed Their Grasp, or How's a Law Journal to be Born?" 20 *Harvard Women's Law Journal* 5, 7 (1997) (same).

3. Martha Chamallas, *Introduction to Feminist Legal Theory* (New York: Aspen Publishers, 2d ed., 2003).

4. I will refer in this book to most of these variations and achievements, and will offer definitions as needed, but I refer the reader to Professor Chamallas for the basic bibliography.

5. Matthew Brelis, "Law Professor's Murder Still Unsolved a Year Later, Few Leads in 'Classic Whodunit,'" *Boston Globe,* April 5, 1992, at 29; Matthew Brelis, "An Accomplished Life, A Brutal Death," *Boston Globe,* April 14, 1991.

6. Mary Joe Frug, "A Postmodern Feminist Legal Manifesto (An Unfinished

Draft)," 105 *Harvard Law Review* 1045 (1992); Fox Butterfield, "Parody Puts Harvard Law Faculty in Sexism Battle," *New York Times,* April 27, 1992, at A10.

7. For an almost visceral experience of the disappearing of Mary Joe Frug, read Peter Collier, "Blood on the Charles," *Vanity Fair,* October 1992, at 144. Professor Patricia Williams says that what she found remarkable about the parody incident was that discussion of it

> on campus and in newspapers, swirled mostly around whether the editors (who went on to employment as clerks of Supreme Court Justices and associates in powerful rainmaking firms), had the legal right to say it. Indeed they did. That said, the curious culture of sadism that produced it was scarcely addressed.

Patricia J. Williams, "The Disquieted American," *Nation,* May 26, 2003, at 9.

8. See Ann Scales, "Disappearing Medusa: The Fate of Feminist Legal Theory?" 20 *Harvard Women's Law Journal* 34 (1997).

9. Professor Halley has published various articles making the argument. Best known is the one she published under the name Ian Halley, "Queer Theory by Men," 11 *Duke Journal of Gender, Law, and Policy* 7 (2004).

10. My brief talk to the Tenth Circuit is reprinted as "Law and Feminism: Together in Struggle," 51 *University of Kansas Law Review* 291 (2003).

11. Recurring in the debate are Harry T. Edwards, "The Growing Disjunction Between Legal Education and the Legal Profession," 91 *Michigan Law Review* 34 (1992), and the other articles in that symposium issue of the *Michigan Law Review.* See also Alex Kozinski, "Who Gives a Hoot about Legal Scholarship?" 37 *Houston Law Review* 295 (2000); Sanford Levinson, "The Audience for Constitutional Meta-Theory (or, Why, and to Whom, Do I Write the Things I Do?)," 63 *Colorado Law Review* 389 (1992); David M. Ebel, "Why and to Whom Do Constitutional Meta-Theorists Write?—A Response to Professor Levinson," 63 *Colorado Law Review* 409 (1992).

12. For an excellent overview of the sources, see William W. Fisher III, Morton J. Horwitz, and Thomas A. Reed, eds., *American Legal Realism* (New York: Oxford University Press, 1993).

13. "The statement has been made so frequently that it has become a truism to refer to it as a truism." Lauren Kalman, *Legal Realism at Yale, 1927–1960* (Chapel Hill: University of North Carolina Press, 1986), at 229.

14. David Luban, "What's Pragmatic about Legal Pragmatism?" 18 *Cardozo Law Review* 43, 72 (1996).

15. Oliver Wendell Holmes, Jr., "The Path of the Law," 10 *Harvard Law Review* 457, 477–78 (1897).

16. Richard A. Posner, "What Has Pragmatism to Offer Law?" in Michael Brint and William Weaver, eds., *Pragmatism in Law and Society* (Boulder: Westview Press, 1991), at 44.

17. Thomas C. Grey, "Freestanding Legal Pragmatism," 18 *Cardozo Law Review* 21, 26 (1996).

18. Will Rogers, quoted in Joseph H. Carter, *I Never Met a Man I Didn't Like: The Life and Writings of Will Rogers* (New York: Avon Books, 1991), at 186.

19. The jurisprudential views that include lenses of class, race, ethnicity and/or gender are the ones that are usually deemed illegitimate or unhelpful. For example, Judge Alex Kozinski of the United States Court of Appeals for the Ninth Circuit has acknowledged that at least two jurisprudential movements, Legal Realism and Law and Economics, have had profound influences on the administration of the law. He went on to predict, however, that "Critical legal studies and its offshoots—critical race theory, critical feminism, and the like" would not "be accepted." Alex Kozinski, "Who Gives a Hoot about Legal Scholarship?" 37 *Houston Law Review* 295, 317 (2000). I share the perplexity expressed by Professor David Dow about how we go about measuring such acceptance. In any case, as Professor Dow reminds us, at least critical legal studies has had a profound impact in that it has "taught us something about law, and that is the measure of relevance." David R. Dow, "The Relevance of Legal Scholarship: Reflections on Judge Kozinski's Musings," 37 *Houston Law Review* 329, 337 n. 35 (2000).

20. "Two intellectual movements—critical race theory and gay and lesbian legal studies—are currently so closely allied with post-essentialist feminist writings that it is difficult to tell whether all three will eventually merge into a more unified approach (such as anti-subordination theory) or will continue to develop among more distinctive lines." Chamallas, note 3, at 135.

21. A number of papers and reports about gender mainstreaming are available at the Council of Europe Web site, http://www.coe.int.

22. Respectively, they are "The Emergence of Feminist Jurisprudence," 95 *Yale Law Journal* 1373 (1986), and "Feminist Legal Method: Not So Scary," 2 *U.C.L.A. Women's Law Journal* 1 (1992).

23. Richard Rorty, "Pragmatism and Law: A Response to David Luban," in *Philosophy and Social Hope* (New York: Penguin Books, 1999), at 112.

24. Claire L'Heureax-Dubé, "The Importance of Dialogue: Globalization and the International Impact of the Rehnquist Court," 34 *Tulsa Law Journal* 15 (1998). At the time she published this piece, Madame L'Heureax-Dubé was a Justice of the Supreme Court of Canada. She is now retired.

NOTES TO CHAPTER 1

1. John Adams coined the phrase "a government of laws, and not of men." John Adams, "Novanglus Papers, No. 7" (1774), in 4 *Works of John Adams* (Charles Francis Adams, ed. 1851), at 106. For a range of contemporary commentaries, see: George P. Fletcher, *Basic Concepts of Legal Thought* (1996), at

12 ("[W]e are never quite sure what we mean by 'the rule of law.' "); Ian Shapiro, ed., *The Rule of Law: Nomos XXXVI* (1994); Allan C. Hutchinson and Patrick Monahan, eds., *The Rule of Law: Ideal or Ideology* (Toronto: Carswell, 1987); David Kairys, "Searching for the Rule of Law," 36 *Suffolk University Law Review* 307 (2003); Michael Rosenfeld, "The Rule of Law and the Legitimacy of Constitutional Democracy," 74 *Southern California Law Review* 1307 (2001); Jessie Allen, "Blind Faith and Reasonable Doubts: Investigating Belief in the Rule of Law," 24 *Seattle University Law Review* 691 (2001); James W. Torke, "What Is This Thing Called the Rule of Law?" 34 *Indiana Law Journal* 1445 (2001); William C. Whitford, "The Rule of Law," 2000 *Wisconsin Law Review* 723 (2000); Richard H. Fallon, Jr., " 'The Rule of Law' as a Concept in Constitutional Discourse," 97 *Columbia Law Review* 1 (1997); Francis J. Mootz, "Is the Rule of Law Possible in a Postmodern World?" 68 *Washington Law Review* 249 (1993); Robert S. Summers, "A Formal Theory of the Rule of Law," 6 *Ratio Juris* 127 (1993); Margaret Jane Radin, "Reconsidering the Rule of Law," 60 *Boston University Law Review* 781 (1989); Joseph Raz, "The Rule of Law and Its Virtue," in *The Authority of Law: Essays on Law and Morality* (New York: Oxford University Press, 1979), at 210.

2. *United States v. Nixon,* 418 U.S. 683 (1974) (President must comply with subpoena issued in a criminal investigation) (Justice Rehnquist did not participate in the decision). The subpoena in question was for audiotapes that President Nixon made and maintained of conversations within the Oval Office. On August 9, 1974, four days after release of transcripts of the tapes and sixteen days after the decision of the Court, President Nixon resigned.

3. My research assistant queried the term "rule of law" in Westlaw as a self-contained phrase, excluding serendipitous conjunctions of the words, in the Clinton Impeachment Transcripts database. The term was counted when referenced in the verbatim transcripts of the House of Representatives Judiciary Committee Hearing, the House Floor Debate, and the Senate Impeachment Hearings, and not in any other materials. Clinton Impeachment Transcripts, www.westlaw.com.

4. U.S. Representative Henry Hyde (R-Illinois) Holds Hearings on Articles of Impeachment of President Clinton, Hearing Before the House Comm. On the Judiciary, 105th Cong. (1998) (opening statement of Stephen E. Buyer (R-Indiana)).

5. House Floor Debate on the Four Articles of Impeachment Against President Clinton, 105th Cong. (1998) (statement of Representative Henry Hyde (R-Illinois)); U.S. Senate Holds the Impeachment Trial of President Clinton, 105th Cong. (1999) (statement of Representative Henry Hyde (R-Illinois)).

6. U.S. Senate Impeachment Trial of President Clinton, 105th Cong. (1999) (statement of Gregory B. Craig, Office of the White House Counsel).

7. U.S. Senate Impeachment Trial of President Clinton, 105th Cong. (1999)

(statement of Charles F. C. Ruff, Office of the White House Counsel); see also U.S. Senate Impeachment Trial of President Clinton, 105th Cong. (1999) (statement of David E. Kendall, Attorney for President Clinton): "The rule of law is more than rhetoric. It means that in proceedings like these, where important rights are being adjudicated, that evidence matters. Fairness matters. Rules of procedural regularity matter. The presumption of innocence matters. And proportionality matters."

8. Thomas Carothers, "The Rule of Law Revival," *Foreign Affairs,* March–April 1988, at 95.

9. Id. at 99.

10. Rosa Ehrenreich Brooks, "The New Imperialism: Violence, Norms, and the 'Rule of Law'," 101 *Michigan Law Review* 2275, 2280 (2003): "In an increasing number of places, promoting the rule of law has become a fundamentally imperialist enterprise. . . ."

11. The State Department Web site features a publication in seven languages called "Principles of Democracy;" among the fourteen principles described is the Rule of Law, which means, in part, that "no individual, president or private citizen, stands above the law." Http://usinfo.state.gov/products/pubs/principles/law.htm, visited September 28, 2004. On September 15, 2004, former Deputy Secretary of State Richard Armitage told a gathering of Iraqi judges that "democracy, justice, and the rule of law demand our fullest efforts. And I can promise you with a 100-percent certainty that President Bush is not going to rest until this job [is] done. He is not going to rest until the Iraqi judges are seated on the bench, making just and wise decisions for Iraqi people." Http://usinfo.state.gov/mena/Archive/2004/Sep/15-65729.html, visited September 28, 2004. Fostering the rule of law is officially part of the war on terror. National Strategy for Combating Terrorism, February 2003, at 20, 23, http://www.whitehouse.gov/news/releases/2003/02/counter_terrorism/counter_terrorism_strategy.pdf, visited September 28, 2004.

12. The White House, Humane Treatment of al Qaeda and Taliban Detainees, February 7, 2002, http://usinfo.state.gov/xarchives/display.html?p=washfile-english&y=2004&m=June&x=20040623203050cpataruko.1224024&t=livefeeds/wf-latest.html, visited September 28, 2004.

13. Article 15-6 Investigation of the 800th Military Police Brigade, March 2002, available at www.npr.org/iraq/2004/prison_abuse_report.pdf. The prison abuse scandal is widening. As of fall 2004, there had been eight official reports; forty-three congressional briefings or hearings; and forty-five individuals had been referred for courts-martial. However, the Department of Defense continued to deny that any of its officials authorized or condoned the abuses. Department of State, Defense Dept. Report, September 13: Prison Abuse Investigations, September 13, 2004, available at http://usinfo.state.gov/xarchives/display.html?p=washfile-english&y=2004&m=September, visited September 28, 2004.

14. Alberto R. Gonzales (now Attorney General of the United States), Decision re Application of the Geneva Convention on Prisoners of War to the Conflict with Al Qaeda and the Taliban, January 25, 2002, available at http://msnbc.msn.com/id/4999148/site/newsweek, visited September 28, 2004 (memorandum from White House Counsel urging the President to abide by his preliminary decision not to apply the Geneva Conventions because it is "difficult to predict with confidence" what actions could be prosecuted as war crimes under those conventions).

15. Investigative reporter Seymour Hersh uncovered much of the information about the prison abuses and the intense discussion in 2002 among the White House, Department of State, and Department of Defense about the limits of legal restraint upon the war on terror. Seymour M. Hersh, "Torture at Abu Ghraib," *New Yorker,* May 10, 2004, at 42. In a recent book, Hersh claims that high officers in the executive branch knew in January of 2004 of specific prison abuses, and that a secret intelligence unit had participated in the abusive interrogations. Seymour M. Hersh, *Chain of Command: The Road from 9/11 to Abu Ghraib* (New York: Harper Collins, 2004).

16. Judith N. Shklar, "Political Theory and the Rule of Law," in Hutchinson and Monahan, note 1 at 1.

17. *United States v. Nixon,* 418 U.S. at 708. Consider also the possible superfluity of words in the decision of the California Supreme Court, holding that the Mayor of San Francisco did not have the power to grant marriage licenses to same-sex couples in the spring of 2004. "[T]he legal question at issue—the scope of the authority entrusted to our public officials—involves the determination of a fundamental question that lies at the heart of our political system: the role of the rule of law in a society that justly prides itself on being a 'government of laws, and not of men' (or women)." *Lockyer v. City and County of San Francisco,* 95 P. 3d 459, 463 (Cal. 2004) (citation omitted).

18. In response to a general desegregation order, *Clark v. Thompson,* 206 F. Supp. 539 (S.D. Miss. 1962), the city of Jackson desegregated its public parks, auditoriums, golf courses, and zoo but decided to close its five public swimming pools rather than desegregate them. Eventually, the United States Supreme Court upheld that decision because there is no duty for a municipality to have any swimming pools, and there was no state action involved in subsequent private operation of those same pools. *Palmer v. Thompson,* 403 U.S. 217 (1971).

19. See Ann Scales, "Surviving Legal De-Education: An Outsider's Guide," 15 *Vermont Law Review* 139 (1990).

20. Ann Scales, "Midnight Train to Us," 75 *Cornell Law Review* 710 (1990).

21. This is not a point that I am actually willing to concede. Ann Scales, "Soft on Defense: The Failure to Confront Militarism," 20 *Berkeley Journal of Gender, Law and Justice* 369 (2005).

22. Family violence is a context in flux. Limited corporeal punishment of

children is still practiced with social approval in private, though it is no longer thought appropriate in schools. Deana A. Pollard, "Banning Corporal Punishment: A Constitutional Analysis," 52 *American University Law Review* 447, 453 (2002). The use of force to control adult women in the domestic context is nominally prohibited. For a provocative critique of law's responses to woman battering, see G. Kristian Miccio, "A House Divided: Mandatory Arrest, Domestic Violence, and the Conservatization of the Battered Women's Movement," 42 *Houston Law Review* 237 (2005).

23. Andrea Dworkin—always suspicious of law and lawyers—once asked me why I had gone over. I told her that my heart needed for the world to change in more immediate and more enforceable ways than observable from nonlegal political activism. I told her that since my sophomore year in college, I had been taken with Rousseau's question about whether anyone could "force them to be free." At this point, Andrea burst out: "See! Books *do* ruin girls!"

24. Consider the contrasting views of scientific progress held by Karl Popper and Thomas Kuhn. Both were operating in a postfoundationalist world (see chapter 2). Both accepted that even if the truth is out there, we will never have a way of knowing whether we know it. Popper, however, described a relatively smooth progression in science: what is called "objectivity" emerges from testing ideas through intersubjective critique. Popper's wisdom is often encapsulated in the admonition that we don't have to die with our ideas. We have to be able to amend or let go of ideas that don't cut the critical mustard. Karl R. Popper, *The Logic of Scientific Discovery* (New York: Basic Books, 1959). Kuhn had a more staccato view of progress. Scientists operate within the paradigm of knowledge in which they were trained. "Normal science" proceeds by solving puzzles identified by that paradigm as worthy and capable of investigation. Anomalies pile up, however, and when the pile gets big enough, the paradigm itself comes into question. In this period of "incommensurability," competing paradigms can be simultaneously operable and productive. The prior paradigm will yield whatever it can until it peters out. During all this, however, the adherents to competing paradigms have no way of talking to one another. One can't see what another sees, much less be available to persuasion. The old way of knowing dies when its proponents die. Thomas S. Kuhn, *The Structure of Scientific Revolutions* (Chicago: University of Chicago Press, 1962).

25. Judith Shklar, *Legalism: Law, Morals and Political Trials,* quoting R. Lewis and A. Maude, *Professional People* (1952), at 208 (Cambridge: Harvard University Press, 1964), at 14.

26. John Austin, *The Province of Jurisprudence Determined* (1832) (Noonday Press: New York, 1954), at 184.

27. *Worcester v. Georgia,* 31 U.S. 515 (1832), discussed in Stephen Breyer, "The Cherokees, The Supreme Court, and the Early History of American Conscience," *New Republic* (August 7, 2000), at 32.

28. *Cooper v. Aaron,* 358 U.S. 1 (1958), discussed in Stephen Breyer, "Centennial Address," 46 *Syracuse Law Review* 1179, 1182 (1996).

29. *Bush v. Gore,* 531 U.S. 98 (2000) (*per curiam*) (procedures ordered by Florida court to govern partial recount of presidential election ballots violate Equal Protection clause), discussed in Stephen Breyer, "Commencement Remarks," University of Pennsylvania Law School, May 19, 2003, www.supreme courtus.gov/publicinfo/speeches/sp_05-19-03.html, visited September 1, 2004.

30. Breyer, "The Cherokees," note 27 at 39. In his dissent in *Bush v. Gore,* Breyer called that case a "self-inflicted wound[ing]" of public confidence in the Court, that "public treasure" which is a "vitally necessary ingredient of . . . the rule of law itself." 531 U.S. 98, 157–58 (Breyer, J., dissenting). In his dissent, Breyer refers to the Cherokee episode, adding that in spite of the harm done by the majority opinion in *Bush v. Gore,* we have "no risk of returning to the days" when Presidents would ignore orders of the Court. Id. at 158. Any conscientious citizen should wonder, I believe, about whether that is because Presidents have (or any particular President has) allegiance to the rule of law or because the rule of law serves as cover for the excessive exercise of executive power.

31. Duncan Kennedy, *A Critique of Adjudication {fin de siècle}* (Cambridge: Harvard University Press, 1997), at 14.

32. Id. at 237. See also Morton J. Horwitz, "The Rule of Law: An Unqualified Human Good?" 86 *Yale Law Journal* 561 (1977). As Professor David Kairys argues, courts have more often been a barrier to human rights than a means for their realization. Kairys, note 1 at 307, 323–24 (2003).

33. A. V. Dicey, *Introduction to the Study of the Law of the Constitution* (1885) (8th ed., London: Macmillan, 1924).

34. Fallon, note 1, at 9 (the law must have guidance capability, efficacy, stability, supremacy, and instrumentalities of impartial dispute resolution).

35. Kairys, note 1, at 12–14. In surveying a vast rule of law literature, Professor Kairys identified fourteen overlapping themes: certain relationships should be governed by rules; rules should be accessible; rules should be generally applicable; rules laid down should be followed; procedures for administration of law should be fair; rules should be enacted by established processes; processes should be democratic; some concept of justice should be at play; there should be certain basic rules or "rights;" rules should limit government as well as individuals; decision making by judges should be publicly available; there should be judicial review of actions of other branches of government; there should be reasons for judicial decisions; and, the rule of law is part of a larger political and social system.

36. The question of what the law could have done to prevent or defuse the Third Reich was the topic of the most famous academic exchange to date in

U.S. legal history: the Hart-Fuller debate. H. L. A. Hart, "Positivism and the Separation of Law and Morals," 71 *Harvard Law Review* 593 (1958); Lon L. Fuller, "Positivism and Fidelity to Law: A Reply to Professor Hart," 71 *Harvard Law Review* 630 (1958).

37. Lon L. Fuller, *The Morality of Law* (New Haven: Yale University Press, 1964).

38. David Kairys notes that rule of law scholars, including Fuller, do not ordinarily even mention the importance of corporate/commercial accountability to law. Our national political consciousness seems at once to embrace the idea of restraints on government, while simultaneously accepting the systematic removal of legal restraints on corporations and businesses. Kairys, note 1 at 313. Concern about state institutions (such as law) as cover for capitalist hegemony is a main theme of Michael Hardt and Antonio Negri, *Empire* (Cambridge: Harvard University Press, 2000). Whereas the Clintonian mantra was that the era of big government is over, the empire theorists say that the era of *any* government is over. The logic of state sovereignty maintains its hold by playing on the anxieties of the people but is ultimately a smokescreen for boundary-blurring imperial private capital. Id. at 74. Postmodern and postcolonial theories are in a sense the supporting doctrines of imperial capitalism, which was already doing away with modern forms of sovereignty and "setting differences to play across boundaries." Id. at 142, 150.

39. In a devastating example of the evil of retroactivity, Fuller refers to Hitler's "Roehm Purge" of 1934. Having ordered the killing of more than one hundred political enemies, Hitler subsequently arranged for the passage of a statute declaring those to have been lawful criminal executions. Fuller, *Morality of Law,* note 37 at 54.

40. Id. at 65–66.

41. Id. at 82–91.

42. Fuller noted that "due process" captures what he called his "procedural version of natural law." Id. at 103.

43. L. L. Fuller and William R. Perdue, Jr., "The Reliance Interest in Contract Damages: 1," 46 *Yale Law Journal* 52 (1936–37) (emphasis in original).

44. Fuller, *Morality of Law,* note 37 at 4.

45. 530 U.S. 703 (2000), reviewing Colorado Revised Statute § 18-9-122 (2002), which forbids a person to "knowingly approach another person within eight feet of such person, unless such other person consents, for the purpose of passing a leaflet or handbill to, displaying a sign to, or engaging in oral protest, education, or counseling with such other person in the public way or sidewalk area within a radius of one hundred feet from any entrance door to a health care facility."

46. 530 U.S. at 723.

47. Alan K. Chen, "Statutory Speech Bubbles, First Amendment Overbreadth, and Improper Legislative Purpose," 38 *Harvard Civil Rights–Civil Liberties Law Review* 31, 50–53 (2003) (analyzing state legislative record).

48. Criticism from the civil libertarian side includes William E. Lee, "The Unwilling Listener: *Hill v. Colorado*'s Chilling Effect on Unorthodox Speech," 35 *University of California at Davis Law Review* 387 (2002); Kathleen M. Sullivan, "Sex, Money, and Groups: Free Speech and Association Decisions in the October 1999 Term," 28 *Pepperdine Law Review* 723 (2001); Colloquium, Professor Michael W. McConnell's Response, 28 *Pepperdine Law Review* 747, 750 (2001) (quoting Professor Laurence Tribe as calling *Hill* "slam dunk simple and slam dunk wrong"). From the right wing, the most virulent criticism is from a Canadian lawyer. Charles Lugosi, "The Law of the Sacred Cow: Sacrificing the First Amendment to Defend Abortion on Demand," 79 *Denver University Law Review* 91, 93, 123 (2001) (referring to bubble laws as "a new form of Iron Curtain" and blaming feminists).

49. 530 U.S. at 741.

50. The leading Canadian case is from the Supreme Court of British Columbia. *R. v. Lewis,* 24 B.C.L.R. (3d) 247, [1997] 1 W.W.R. 496, 39 C.R.R. (2d) 26, 130 D.L.R. (4th) 480. The court took to heart evidence of how antiabortion organizations have succeeded through violence and intimidation to make abortion unavailable or to discourage women in need from seeking it. Id. at ¶¶ 44–46, 84, 97–98.

NOTES TO CHAPTER 2

1. *Lochner v. New York,* 198 U.S. 45, 75–76 (1905) (Holmes, J. dissenting).

2. *Atkins v. Virginia,* 536 U.S. 304 (2002), overruling *Penry v. Lynaugh,* 492 U.S. 302 (1989).

3. 536 U.S. at 338, 348.

4. *Roper v. Simmons,* 125 S. Ct. 1183 (2005), abrogating *Stanford v. Kentucky,* 492 U.S. 361 (1989).

5. 125 S. Ct. at 1217. In *Roper* as in other cases, Justice Scalia is critical of the majority's reliance on authorities from other countries.

6. 125 S. Ct. at 1229–30 (emphasis in original).

7. Robin West, "Re-Imagining Justice," 14 *Yale Journal of Law and Feminism* 333 (2002).

8. "We remain participants in a familiar morality play in which the question is whether the judges' personal ideology or 'partisan politics' will overcome their oaths to interpret the law rather than overthrow it." Duncan Kennedy, *A Critique of Adjudication {fin de siècle}* (Cambridge: Harvard University Press, 1997), at 81.

9. A fabulous articulation of the strategy of making one's opponents feel stu-

pid and crazy is Andrea Dworkin, "The Politics of Intelligence," in *Right-Wing Women* (New York: Perigee Books, 1983), at 37–69.

10. 389 U.S. 347 (1967).

11. Id. at 364.

12. Id. at 373.

13. John W. Wright, ed., *The New York Times Almanac* (New York: Penguin Books, 2004), at 757–58. In addition to protons, neutrons, and electrons, my roller skates are comprised of muons, pions, neutrinos, quarks (six different kinds of these), gluons, J/psi particles, W and Z particles, strange particles, and antiatoms. The list sounds like the creation of Jorge Luis Borges, made most famous by Foucault: "This passage quotes a 'certain Chinese encyclopedia' in which it is written that 'animals are divided into: (a) belonging to the Emperor, (b) embalmed, (c) tame, (d) suckling pigs, (e) sirens, (f) fabulous, (g) stray dogs, (h) included in the present classification, (i) frenzied, (j) innumerable, (k) drawn with a very fine camelhair brush, (l) et cetera, (m) having just broken the water pitcher, (n) that from a long way off look like flies.' " Michel Foucault, *The Order of Things XV* (New York: Pantheon Books, 1971).

14. W. B. Gallie, "Essentially Contested Concepts," *Aristotelian Society Proceedings, n.s 56* (1955–56), 167, 169.

15. Of course there already are such sports, such as boxing and figure skating, where those in control of the sport have superimposed systems of "scoring" upon what are otherwise often nonquantitative judgments about the quality of play. For my expanded take on the role of sports metaphors in law, see Ann Scales, "Surviving Legal De-Education: An Outsiders' Guide," 15 *Vermont Law Review* 139 (1990).

16. Gallie, note 14, at 170–71 (emphasis in original).

17. "[T]he notion of possible ultimate universal agreement is a highly sophisticated one and does not figure among the familiarly recognized criteria for rational justification." Id. at 188–89.

18. Id. at 193.

19. This part of the story is fascinating to me. As a student, when reading the work of some philosophers, I found myself wondering, if he's right, why bother writing it down? If this account is necessarily the way the world is or necessarily the way history will play out, why the need to memorialize it or persuade anybody? Of course, there could be millions of Pyrrhos in world history: brilliant thinkers or shamans who really did have "the answer" and didn't write it down or even drop a hint to anyone. Just as likely, of course, is that there have been millions of brilliant thinkers who had a lot to contribute but were voiceless by virtue of their social position. See Virginia Woolf, *A Room of One's Own* (New York: Harcourt, Brace and World, 1929), at 43–53 (hypothesizing Shakespeare's sister and her struggles).

20. Myles F. Burnyeat, "Can the Skeptic Live His Skepticism?" in Myles F.

Burnyeat, ed., *The Skeptical Tradition* (Berkeley: University of California Press, 1983), at 140.

21. In light of the variousness of postmodernist thought, it is difficult to define it or to point the reader to concise expositions of it. Among the best is Jean-François Lyotard, *The Postmodern Condition: A Report on Knowledge,* Geoff Bennington and Brian Massumi, trans. (Minneapolis: University of Minnesota Press, 1984), at xxiv ("I define postmodernism as incredulity toward metanarratives.").

22. For example, in the case that invalidated the Indianapolis version of the MacKinnon-Dworkin pornography civil rights ordinance, Judge Easterbrook stated: "This is thought control. It establishes an 'approved' view of women, of how they may react to sexual encounters, of how the sexes may relate to each other. Those who espouse the approved view may use sexual images; those who do not, may not." *American Booksellers Association, Inc. v. Hudnut,* 771 F.2d 323, 328 (7th Cir. 1985), *aff'd without opinion,* 475 U.S. 1001 (1986).

23. See Manfred Frank, *What Is Neostructuralism?,* Sabine Wilke and Richard Gray, trans. (Minneapolis: University of Minnesota Press, 1989).

24. Professor MacKinnon has described postmodernism as "familiar if fancier reasons for doing nothing." Catharine A. MacKinnon, "Points Against Postmodernism," 75 *Chicago-Kent Law Review* 687, 710 (2000). She recalls the epigraph of this chapter, id. at 704, quoting Gertrude Stein, *Brewsie and Willie* (New York: Random House, 1946), at 30, for the proposition that many of the insights of postmodernism are old stuff. It is unsurprising to find MacKinnon on that side of the debate, as one salient dispute among postmodern and non-postmodern feminists has been pornography. Antipornography feminists such as MacKinnon believe that pornography can be defined and resisted, but only if understood as deeply gendered and an arm of gender oppression. Postmodernist feminists believe that the notion of gender itself emerges from the order of discourse, so that it is regressive to participate in the modernist projection of gender of which pornography is an expression. Rather, our aim should be to subvert every expression of gender by "safeguard[ing] the uncontrollability of the signified." Judith Butler, "The Force of Fantasy: Feminism, Mapplethorpe, and Discursive Excess," reprinted in Drucilla Cornell, ed., *Feminism and Pornography* (Oxford: Oxford University Press, 2000), at 504. Perhaps that means that pro-sex women should become creators of sexually explicit imagery ourselves and therefore somehow displace or undermine the power of pornographers to construct women, sexuality, and gender. I'm not sure what it means the law should do, if anything.

25. Thus, I believe Duncan Kennedy overstates the case when he describes "the birth of the virus" of skepticism in law. Kennedy, note 8 at 81. It is an interesting metaphor because bodies do fight viruses, and it is true that doubt can be debilitating in excess. However, I am of the opinion that all good-faith

discourse involves constant recalibration of the tension between certainty and doubt, and that lawyers, in particular, are obligated to be aware of that process. To me, that is what distinguishes the good-faith actors from the bad-faith actors.

26. The most influential work is H. L. A. Hart, *The Concept of Law* (New York: Oxford University Press, 1961).

27. H. L. A. Hart, "Positivism and the Separation of Law and Morals," 71 *Harvard Law Review* 593, 596 (1958).

28. Kennedy, note 8 at 97.

29. Ronald Dworkin, *Taking Rights Seriously* (Cambridge: Harvard University Press, 1977).

30. Many fine pieces are collected in Michael Brint and William Weaver, eds., *Pragmatism in Law and Society* (Boulder: Westview Press, 1991).

31. The author of modern skepticism, David Hume, was firm in his belief that skepticism could not form the basis of daily life:

> When [the skeptic] awakes from his dream, he will be the first to join in the laugh against himself, and to confess, that all his objections are mere amusement, and can have no other tendency than to show the whimsical condition of mankind, who must act and reason and believe; though they are not able, by their most diligent enquiry, to satisfy themselves concerning the foundation of these operations, or to remove the objections, which may be raised against them.

David Hume, *An Enquiry Concerning Human Understanding* (1748) (Chicago: Open Court Publishers, 1927), at 170–71.

32. Richard Rorty, *Philosophy and Social Hope* (New York: Penguin Books, 1999), at 18.

33. Id. at xxix.

34. Richard Rorty, *Contingency, Irony, and Solidarity* (New York: Cambridge University Press, 1989).

35. Note 19.

36. See Christine Swanton, *Virtue Ethics: A Pluralistic View* (New York: Oxford University Press, 2003); Rosalind Hursthouse, *On Virtue Ethics* (Oxford: Oxford University Press, 1999); Roger Crisp and Michael Slote, eds., *Virtue Ethics* (New York: Oxford University Press, 1997).

NOTES TO CHAPTER 3

1. 486 F. 2d 1139 (D.C. Cir. 1973) (en banc), cert. denied 414 U.S. 980 (1973). For an intellectual history of the assumption of freedom in law, see Ronald J. Rychlak and Joseph F. Rychlak, "Mental Health Experts on Trial: Free Will and Determinism in the Courtroom," 100 *West Virginia Law Review* 193 (1997).

2. In the juvenile death penalty case, *amici* submitted new scientific evidence about the neurological immaturity of teenage brains and the probable connections among those characteristics and poor decision making. See *Brief Amicus Curiae of the American Medical Association, et al.*, 2004 WL 1633549 (2004). In vacating the death sentence, the Court relied on that evidence to some extent. *Roper v. Simmons,* 125 S. Ct.1183, 1195 (2005). Unsurprisingly—at least as of now—neither the scientists nor the Court postulated any precise connections between that evidence and the moral culpability of the teenage defendants.

3. See Matthew Jones, "Overcoming the Myth of Free Will in Criminal Law: The True Impact of the Genetic Revolution," 52 *Duke Law Journal* 1031 (2003).

4. One author estimates that 60 percent of child custody determinations, for example, violate the First Amendment in the ways that they take or do not take a prospective custodial parent's religion into account. Jennifer Ann Drobac, "For the Sake of the Children: Court Consideration of Religion in Child Custody Cases," 50 *Stanford Law Review* 1609 (1988).

5. *McCreary County, Kentucky v. American Civil Liberties Union of Kentucky,* 125 S. Ct. 2722 (2005).

6. *Van Orden v. Perry,* 125 S. Ct. 2854 (2005). Only four Justices agreed on the reasoning for allowing Texas the monument. Justice Stephen Breyer merely agreed with the result in the Texas case. Indeed, Breyer's was the deciding vote in both cases. For him, the dispositive different fact seemed to be public acquiescence. In Kentucky, the counties kept changing the format for the religious display, which had been hanging on the walls for "roughly nine months." 125 S. Ct. at 2758. In the Texas case, the monolith had been on the capital grounds for forty years before anyone objected. 125 S. Ct. at 2870.

7. *Zorach v. Clauson,* 343 U.S. 306, 313 (1952) (permitting students to leave public school for purpose of religious education), repeated with approval in *Van Orden v. Perry,* 125 S. Ct. at 2859, n. 2; *Lynch v. Donnelly,* 465 U.S. 668, 675 (1984) (upholding a public Christmas display including a crèche); *Marsh v. Chambers,* 463 U.S. 783, 792 (1983) (upholding prayer in a state legislature); *School District of Abingdon Township v. Schempp,* 374 U.S. 203, 213 (1963) (invalidating Bible reading and recitation of Lord's Prayer in public schools); *McCreary County v. A.C.L.U.,* 125 S. Ct. at 2750 (Scalia, dissenting).

8. *Van Orden v. Perry,* 125 S. Ct. at 2869 (Breyer, concurring).

9. Scalia says 97.7 percent of the U.S. faithful are monotheists. *McCreary County,* 125 S. Ct. at 2753 (Scalia, dissenting). While arguing that such numbers are entirely irrelevant to the meaning of the Establishment Clause, Stevens notes that of that 97.7 percent, 95.5 percent are Christian. The number of Buddhists (whom Stevens describes as nontheistic) in the United States is nearly equal to the number of Muslims. *Van Orden,* 125 S. Ct. at 2881, n. 18 (Stevens, dissenting).

10. Many of the founding fathers (including Benjamin Franklin, George Washington, Thomas Jefferson, Thomas Paine, and James Madison) followed the theology of Deism. Eighteenth-century Deists believed in divine reason—which some termed "God"—as the ultimate cause of the universe. Deists rejected most tenets of Christianity, including the notion that God intervened in history, and some Deists regarded monotheistic divinities as myths. See Peter Occhiogrosso, *The Joy of Sects: A Spirited Guide to the World's Religious Traditions* (New York: Doubleday, 1996).

11. The government has a hard time making this distinction, and generally a hard time distinguishing the Iraq and Afghanistan wars from the Crusades. The task is not made easier by loose cannons. As disclosed in the fall of 2003, Army Lt. General William Boykin attended at least twenty-three church meetings and prayer breakfasts—usually wearing his uniform—where he portrayed U.S. battles with Muslim radicals as a fight against "Satan." He stated that militant Islamists sought to destroy the United States "because we're a Christian nation." In a classic among Freudian outbursts, General Boykin referred to a Muslim fighter in Somalia, stating, "[M]y God was bigger than his. I knew that my God was a real God, and his was an idol." Reuters, "Rumsfeld Praises Army General Who Ridicules Islam as 'Satan'," *New York Times,* October 17, 2003, at A7. Though the Inspector General of the Department of Defense recommended in August 2004 that the Army "take appropriate corrective action" with respect to General Boykin, he continues in his post as Deputy Under Secretary of Defense for Intelligence. Editorial, "Words of War," *Boston Globe,* July 24, 2005, at D10.

12. *Ballard v. United States,* 322 U.S. 78, 95 (1944) (Jackson, dissenting) (case regarding mail fraud allegedly committed by founders of "I Am" movement).

13. *United States v. Seeger,* 380 U.S. 163,176 (1965). This rule takes a contestable point of view about the grand design of the universe. Though the rule exempts some pacifists who are not identified with any "organized religion," it may not exempt nonviolent postmodernists, or others who reject "logocentrism" in spiritual matters.

14. Dalia Martinez, "Say Amen, Boss!" *Newsweek,* August 25, 3003, commenting on the Employment Equality (Religion or Belief) Regulations, adopted in 2003 to give effect to the European Community Equal Treatment Framework Directive (No. 2000/78).

15. Eve Kosofsky Sedgwick, *Epistemology of the Closet* (Berkeley: University of California Press, 1990), at 4.

16. Rachel Carson was one of the first to explain the cumulative nature of the thousands of toxic exposures that we absorb every day: "Like the constant dripping of water that in turn wears away the hardest stone, this birth-to-death contact with dangerous chemicals may in the end prove disastrous." Rachel Carson, *Silent Spring* (Boston: Houghton Mifflin, 1962), at 173–174.

17. Only eleven days after the attacks, Congress passed the Victims Compensation Act, a scheme to benefit the persons and the families of persons on the ground at the attack sites, or in the planes used as weapons. The Air Transportation Safety and System Stabilization Act, 49 U.S.C. §40101, Title IV Victim Compensation, § 408(b)(3), Pub. L. No. 107-71, §201, 115 Stat. 230, 40 (September 22, 2001), as amended by Pub. L. No. 107-71, § 201, 115 Stat. 597, 645 (November 19, 2001). However, the Victims Compensation Act did not cover property owners, those physically injured but not "on site," and, perhaps most interestingly, the "mere exposure" claimants. That is, although thousands of people were killed or physically injured on September 11, there are possibly hundreds of thousands of others who may not yet know of their injuries due to the unprecedented mixture and intensity of toxins released that day. See Robert L. Radin, "Indeterminate Future Harm in the Context of September 11," 88 *Virginia Law Review* 1831, 1843 (2002).

18. Mario Bunge, *Causality and Modern Science* (New York: Dover Publications, 3rd ed. 1959), at xviii (describing difference between epistemological and ontological aspects of causal problems in scientific research). Specifically regarding the confusion of ontology and epistemology in toxic tort cases, see Danielle Conway-Jones, "Factual Causation in Toxic Tort Litigation: A Philosophical View of Proof and Uncertainty in Uncertain Disciplines," 35 *University of Richmond Law Review* 875 (2002).

19. Most toxic tort claims end up in federal court because of the "diversity of citizenship" of injured plaintiffs and corporate defendants, and in the federal courts, the federal rules of evidence apply regardless of the substantive law governing the underlying claims.

20. *Daubert v. Merrell Dow Pharmaceuticals, Inc.*, 509 U.S. 579, 590–91 (1993) (emphasis added). There are many excellent commentaries on the effects of the *Daubert* ruling. Among my favorites is Lucinda M. Finley, "Guarding the Gate to the Courthouse: How Trial Judges Are Using Their Evidentiary Screening Role to Remake Tort Causation Rules," 49 *DePaul Law Review* 335 (1999). *Daubert* itself involved Bendectin, an anti-morning-sickness medication taken by thirty million pregnant women over the course of twenty-seven years. Bendectin has been associated with various severe birth defects. In the post-*Daubert* regime, none of the jury verdicts in plaintiffs' favor have been left standing. Compare Joseph Sanders, "The Bendectin Litigation: A Case Study in the Life Cycle of Mass Torts," 43 *Hastings Law Journal* 301, 355–62, nn. 227–232 (1992) with *Raynor v. Merrell Pharmaceuticals, Inc.*, 104 F.3d 1371 (D.C. Cir. 1997) (affirming judgment for defendant nothwithstanding the jury's verdict in favor of plaintiff); *Merrell Dow Pharmaceuticals, Inc. v. Havner*, 706 S.W. 2d 706 (Tex. 1997) (vacating jury verdict); and *Oxendine v. Merrell Dow Pharamaceuticals, Inc.*, 1996 WL 680992 (D.C. Super. 1996). The last of these

provided relief to Merrell, after four appeals, from the jury verdict rendered against it thirteen years earlier.

21. Among federal courts adhering to the rigid causal regime, see *Cano v. Everest Minerals Corp.*, 362 F.Supp. 2d 814, 824 (W.D. Tex. 2005) (victims of various cancers allegedly caused by uranium tailings must show sufficient epidemiological connection on issue of specific causation); *Saldo v. Sandoz Pharmaceuticals Corp.*, 244 F. Supp. 2d 434 (W.D. Pa. 2003) (insufficient epidemiological evidence to connect antilactation drug Parlodel to stroke); *Hollander v. Sandoz Pharmaceutical Corp.*, 95 F. Supp. 2d 1230 (W.D. Okla. 2000) (same); *Blanchard v. Eli Lilly & Co.*, 207 F. Supp. 2d 308 (D. Vt. 2002) (insufficient epidemiological connection between antidepressant Prozac and risk of murder/ suicide); *Forsyth v. Eli Lilly Co.*, No. 95-00185, 1998 U.S. Dist. Lexis 541 (D. Haw. 1998) (Prozac and risk of suicide); *Miller v. Pfizer Inc.*, 196 F. Supp. 2d 1095 (D. Kan. 2002) (insufficient epidemiological evidence regarding antidepressant Zoloft and risk of suicide); *In re Breast Implant Litigation,* 11 F. Supp. 2d 1217 (D. Colo. 1998) (no further scientific evidence admissible, given epidemiological study indicating relative risk between silicone implants and associated autoimmune diseases of "1.24"); *Schudel v. General Electric,* 120 F. 3d. 991 (9th Cir. 1997) (insufficient epidemiological evidence to connect industrial solvents trichoroethane [TCA] and percholoroehylene [perc] to neurological and respiratory illnesses); *In re Agent Orange Product Liability Litigation,* 611 F. Supp. 1223 (E.D.N.Y. 1985) (granting summary judgment to defendants in claims of opt-out veterans), *aff'd* 818 F.2d 187 (2d Cir. 1987).

The few exceptions among federal courts, those rejecting the rigid epidemiological scheme, are *In re Hanford Nuclear Reservation Litigation,* 292 F.3d 1124 (9th Cir. 2002); *In re Silicone Breast Implants Products Liability Litigation,* 318 F. Supp. 2d 879 (C.D. Cal. 2004) (relative risk must be greater than "1" for "general causation"; must be greater than "2" for "specific causation"); *Benedi v. McNeil-P.P.C., Inc.,* 66 F.3d 1378 (4th Cir. 1995) (no epidemiological evidence required where there is other expert testimony on the relationship between acetaminophen and liver disease); *Smith v. Wyeth-Ayerst Laboratories Co.,* 278 F.Supp. 2d 684 (W.D.N.C. 2003) (in case involving primary pulmonary hypertension caused by diet drug Fen-Phen, epidemiological evidence required only because other experts relied on it in arriving at "differential diagnosis").

Some state courts have taken flexible approaches similar to that taken by the Ninth and Fourth Circuits. *Vassallo v. Baxter Healthcare Corp.,* 696 N.E. 2d 909 (Mass. Sup. Ct. 1998); *Jennings v. Baxter Healthcare Corp.,* 954 P.2d 829 (Or. App. 1998); *Bloomquist v. Wapello County,* 500 N.W. 2d 1 (Iowa 1993); *Landrigan v. Celotex Corp.,* 605 A. 2d 1079 (N.J. 1992).

22. David Hume, *An Enquiry Concerning Human Understanding* (1748) (Chicago: Open Court Publishers, 1927).

23. Tim Folger, "Nailing Down Gravity: New Ideas About the Most Mysterious Power in the Universe," *Discover,* October 2003, at 34 (describing anomalies presently explained by hypothetical "dark matter").

24. *Cay v. State of Louisiana Dept. of Transportation and Development,* 631 So. 2d 393 (La. 1994) (affirming bench trial judgment for plaintiffs but reapportioning only 10 percent of responsibility to the Department of Transportation and 90 percent to the decedent). If one needed confirmation of the law's facility (not usually acknowledged) with causal slippage, one need only look at the degree to which law allows comparative fault schemes to fudge the questions, without precisely identifying what questions are being fudged.

25. In many respects, this proof pattern was invented by Judge Jack Weinstein, in his handling of the original Agent Orange cases in the 1980s. Though he had approved a settlement between the class of Vietnam veterans and the manufacturers of Agent Orange, *In re Agent Orange Product Liability Litigation,* 597 F. Supp. 740 (E.D.N.Y. 1984), Weinstein disallowed individual Vietnam veteran plaintiffs from presenting any proof of what actually happened to them, based in large part on an epidemiological study published by the Air Force in 1984 that showed that there was no connection between Agent Orange and the vast range of diseases suffered by exposed veterans. *In re Agent Orange Product Liability Litigation,* 611 F. Supp. 1223 (E.D.N.Y. 1985) (granting summary judgment to defendants in cases of "opt-out" veterans), *aff'd* 818 F.2d 187 (2d Cir.1985) (on basis of government contractor defense). Judge Weinstein may not have intended for his privileging of epidemiological proof to be so influential, but it has been. See Jack B. Weinstein, *Individual Justice in Mass Tort Litigation* (Evanston: Northwestern University Press, 1995).

26. The "signature disease" is a useful legal fiction. It is not true, for example, that clear cell adenocarcinoma (CCA) occurs only in premenopausal women exposed to DES. The fact that DES daughters are forty times more likely than others to develop CCA, however, is enough for scientists presumptively to discount other causes. See "Known Health Effects for DES Daughters," Centers for Disease Control, http://www.cdc.gov/DES/consumers/about/effects_daughters.html, visited November 3, 2003.

27. For a judicial explanation of the results of epidemiological studies, see *DeLuca v. Merrell Dow Pharmaceuticals, Inc.,* 911 F.2d 941, 945–48 (3rd Cir. 1990).

28. See www.cancerprev.org/Journal/Issues/22/101/22/2627 (relative risk of "4" for breast cancer); http://cnts.wpi.edu/rRSH/Data_docs/1/2/1/1/12115ber5.html (relative risk of "2.09" for stomach cancer); http://cnts.wpi.edu/rsh/docs/MinelR10-JpSurvMort.pdf (other cancers widely known to have been caused by the bombs show relative risk of less than "2"), sites visited October 18, 2004.

29. Reliable evidence of increased risk is admissible on the element of causation. See *Reynolds v. The Texas and Pacific Railway Company,* 37 La. Ann.

694, 1885 WL 6364 (La. 1885) (judgment for plaintiff who fell down unlighted staircase affirmed where defendant's negligence increased the chances of accident).

30. *In re Breast Implant Litigation,* 11 F. Supp. 2d 1217, 1225–26 (D. Colo. 1998).

31. Sander Greenland, "The Need for Critical Appraisal of Expert Witnesses in Epidemiology and Statistics," 39 *Wake Forest Law Review* 291, 304 (2004).

32. David Egilman, M.D., M.P.H., Joyce Kim, and Molly Biklen, "Proving Causation: The Use and Abuse of Medical and Scientific Evidence Inside the Courtroom—An Epidemiologist's Critique of the Judicial Interpretation of the Daubert Ruling," 58 *Food and Drug Law Journal* 223, 227 (2003).

33. Marcia Angell, *Science on Trial: The Clash of Medical Evidence and the Law in the Breast Implant Case* (New York: W. W. Norton, 1996), at 196 (quoted in *In re Breast Implant Litigation,* 11 F. Supp. 2d at 1226). The study at issue was Charles H. Hennekens et al., "Self-reported Breast Implants and Connective-Tissue Diseases in Female Health Professionals," 275 *Journal of the American Medical Association* 616, 618 (1996). Dr. Angell's interpretation and the misjudgment by the Colorado federal court are discussed in Finley, note 20 at 359–60.

34. This is true even when there is not any epidemiology on a toxin, or where the epidemiology is very preliminary. *Sutera v. Perrier Group of America, Inc.,* 986 F.Supp. 655 (D. Mass. 1997)(expert testimony disallowed where there had been no epidemiologic study addressing association of benzene with acute promyelocytic leukemia at plaintiff's dose); Finley, note 19 at 352.

35. Finley, note 20 at 364–65; Sanders, note 20 at 343. Epidemiologist Sander Greenland calls this "privileging the null hypothesis." Greenland, note 31 at 296. Professor Greenland opines that this position, clinging to the presumption of "no association," is discredited in philosophy, health sciences, and statistics. Moreover, he says, when experts present a court with that position, they encourage multiple distortions in both science and social policy. Id.

36. Bert Black and David L. Lilienfeld, "Epidemiologic Proof in Toxic Tort Litigation," 52 *Fordham Law Review* 732 (1984).

37. Among the best-known of these works are H. L. A. Hart and Tony Honoré, *Causation in the Law* (1959) (Oxford: Clarendon Press, 2d ed. 1985); Richard W. Wright, "Causation, Responsibility, Risk, Probability, Naked Statistics, and Proof: Pruning the Bramble Bush by Clarifying the Concepts," 73 *Iowa Law Review* 1001 (1988); Mark Kelman, "The Necessary Myth of Objective Causation Judgments in Liberal Political Theory," 63 *Chicago-Kent Law Review* 579 (1987); Richard W. Wright, "Causation in Tort Law," 73 *California Law Review* 1735 (1985); John Borgo, "Causal Paradigms in Tort Law," 8 *Journal of Legal Studies* 419 (1979).

38. Austin Bradford Hill, "The Environment and Disease: Association or

Causation?" 58 *Proceedings of the Royal Society of Medicine* 295 (1965). Professor Bradford Hill's article is a salient example of the influence of Bayesian epistemology on twentieth-century science. Named for an eighteenth-century cleric, Thomas Bayes, the central insight of the Bayesian analysis is that a hypothesis tends to be confirmed by *any* body of data that renders its truth probable. See Rudolf Carnap, *Logical Foundations of Probability* (Chicago: University of Chicago Press, 1962).

39. After a study by Merck showed an association between its blockbuster arthritis drug Vioxx and heart attack and stroke, the company withdrew the drug from the market. The president of Merck Research Labs said, "We certainly don't understand the cause of this effect, but it is statistically significant and it indicated there is an issue." Gina Kolata, "A Widely Used Arthritis Drug is Withdrawn," *New York Times,* October 1, 2004.

40. Sanders, note 20 at 330; Margaret A. Berger, "Eliminating General Causation: Notes Toward a New Theory of Justice and Toxic Torts," 97 *Columbia Law Review* 2117 (1997).

41. Bradford Hill, note 38, at 299.

42. The defense bar has done this in two ways. First, instead of being overlapping considerations, the points of view have become "criteria," a nine-part test for causation. Second, they have been added to the silly epidemiological test (rather than displacing it), something the plaintiffs' experts must explain after epidemiological evidence showing a relative risk of at least "2" has been found admissible. Thus, in cases where courts are willing to consider the Bradford Hill points of view, they don't really need to because they've already been persuaded by epidemiological evidence. See *In re Phenylpropanolamine (PPA) Product Liability Litigation,* 289 F.Supp. 2d 1230, 1243 n. 13 (W.D. Wash. 2003) (finding discussion of Bradford Hill criteria neither "necessary or helpful" where epidemiology had shown relative risk of hemorrhagic stroke from over-the-counter diet drug and cough/cold ingredient PPA to be 16.58); *Smith v. Wyeth-Ayerst Laboratories Co.,* 278 F. Supp. 2d 684, 691, 693–94 (W.D.N.C. 2003) (regarding relationship between diet drug Fen-Phen and primary pulmonary hypertension, epidemiology showing increased risk of 630 percent is consistent with Bradford Hill factors).

43. *Dunn v. Sandoz Pharmaceuticals Corp.,* 275 F. Supp. 2d 672, 678 (M.D.N.C. 2003).

44. Id. at 679–80. The district court was attempting to conform with the somewhat less strenuous causal regime in the Fourth Circuit, mentioned in note 20, but succeeded primarily in showing the emptiness of the familiar incantation that plaintiffs are not *required* to produce epidemiological evidence.

45. The Victims Compensation Act for those injured on September 11, 2001, is only one example of congressional action to supplant common law tort remedies for mass injuries, and each effort has had its own features, more or

less suited to the situations at hand. See, for example, Black Lung Benefits Act of 1969, 30 U.S.C. §§901–45, providing benefits for coal miners affected by pneumoconiosis and limiting liability of mining companies; National Vaccine Injury Compensation Program of 1986, 42 U.S.C. §§300aa1-034; National Swine Flu Immunization Program of 1976, 42 U.S.C. §247(j)–(k); Price-Anderson Act of 1957, 42 U.S.C. §2210, providing immunity for actions arising from nuclear energy accidents while providing health benefits for nuclear workers; Comprehensive Environmental Response, Compensation, and Liability Act of 1980, 42 U.S.C. §§9601–75, as amended, providing limited compensation for "downwinders," persons affected by above-ground nuclear testing in Nevada; and the Veterans Administration, 5 U.S.C. §2108, which has existed in some form since colonial times to provide health benefits to military veterans based on service relatedness of health conditions.

46. Testing delays entry into the market; testing is expensive; in most situations manufacturers need not worry about it because subsequently injured consumers in the United States will almost certainly not be able to meet the burden on causation.

47. Most famous among the studies in the legal literature is Thomas Koenig and Michael Rustad, "His and Her Tort Reform: Gender Injustice in Disguise," 70 *Washington Law Review* 1 (1995).

48. Among the notable feminist contributions to tort literature, see Leslie Bender, "A Lawyer's Primer on Feminist Theory and Tort," 38 *Journal of Legal Education* 3 (1988); Lucinda M. Finley, "A Break in the Silence: Including Women's Issues in a Torts Course," 1 *Yale Journal of Law and Feminism* 41 (1989); Martha Chamallas and Linda K. Kerber, "Women, Mothers, and the Law of Fright: A History," 88 *Michigan Law Review* 814 (1990); and Leslie Bender, "An Overview of Feminist Torts Scholarship," 78 *Cornell Law Review* 575 (1993). Soon to be classics, I believe, are Martha Chamallas, "The Architecture of Bias: Deep Structures in Tort Law," 146 *University of Pennsylvania Law Review* 463 (1998); Lucinda M. Finley, "The Hidden Victims of Tort Reform: Women, Children, and the Elderly," 53 *Emory Law Journal* 1263 (2004); and even perhaps Ann Scales, "Nooky Nation: On Tort Law and Other Arguments from Nature," in Catharine A. MacKinnon and Reva B. Siegel, *Directions in Sexual Harassment Law* (New Haven: Yale University Press, 2004), at 307.

49. Investigation of toxic effects of drugs on pregnant women and their children is both ethically and legally complex. That is not always an answer, however, to recognition of the facts that women are encouraged to have children, are encouraged to medicalize their pregnancies, and have been relatively powerless against the campaigns of the pharmaceutical and medical industries who have given them so many insufficiently tested and devastating drugs. See R. Alta Charo, "Protecting Us to Death: Women, Pregnancy, and Clinical Research Trials," 38 *Saint Louis University Law Review* 135 (1993).

50. William M. Landes and Richard A. Posner, "Causation in Tort Law: An Economic Approach," 12 *Journal of Legal Studies* 109, 131 (1983). Judge Guido Calabresi endorsed the same obfuscation in a slightly different way: "*in law* the term 'cause' is used in different guises but always to identify those pressure points that are most amenable to the social goals we wish to accomplish. . . . [U]se of such concepts has great advantages over explicit identification and separation of the goals. Terms with an historical, common law gloss [like 'cause'] permit us to consider goals (like spreading) that we do not want to spell out or too obviously assign to judicial institutions." Guido Calabresi, "Concerning Cause and the Law of Torts: An Essay for Harry Kalven, Jr.," 43 *University of Chicago Law Review* 69, 106–07 (1975) (emphasis in original).

NOTES TO CHAPTER 4

1. John Locke, *Second Treatise of Government* (1690).
2. My attorney, J. Michele Guttmann, put her finger on this. Check it out: particularly if English is your first language, you probably already know all of *Hamlet,* but just don't know the lines in the right order.
3. An unsurprising juxtaposition in the Federalist Papers is the need of a central government to protect against domestic strife, see *Federalist No. 9* (1787), and the efficacy of the limitations on that government, such as separation of powers, checks and balances, and a bicameral legislature. See *Federalist Nos. 49, 51* (1788).
4. Gary Peller, "The Metaphysics of American Law," 73 *California Law Review* 1151 (1985).
5. *Brown v. Board of Education,* 349 U.S. 294 (1954). In Professor Archibald Cox's famous words, "Once loosed, the idea of Equality is not easily cabined." Archibald Cox, "Forward: Constitutional Adjudication and the Promotion of Human Rights," 80 *Harvard Law Review* 91 (1966).
6. *San Antonio Independent School District v. Rodriguez,* 411 U.S. 1 (1973) (poverty is not a suspect basis for legislative action; Equal Protection clause does not guarantee proportionately equal funding for public schools). By contrast, Canadian courts have held that poverty and dependence on public assistance are prohibited grounds of discrimination under Canadian constitutional equality provisions. *Dartmouth/Halifax County Regional Housing Authority v. Sparks* (1993), 101 D.L.R. (4th) 224 (N.S.C.A.), at 233; *Falkner v. Ontario* (2002), 56 O.R. (3d) 481 (C.A.), at ¶84.
7. Catharine A. MacKinnon, "Playboy's Money," in *Feminism Unmodified* (Cambridge: Harvard University Press, 1986), at 134–145.
8. *Hymowitz v. Eli Lilly and Company,* 541 N.Y.S.2d 941 (1989) (drug companies held proportionately liable based upon their market share), reprinted

in Arthur Best and Jake Barnes, *Basic Tort Law: Cases, Statutes, and Problems* (New York: Aspen Publishers, 2003), at 198.

9. *Strauss v. Cilek,* 418 N.W.2d 378 (Iowa Ct. App. 1987) (disallowing this plaintiff's claim but allowing that some extramarital conduct could give rise to legal claims); reprinted in Best and Barnes, note 8 at 76.

10. *Eisel v. Board of Education of Montgomery County,* 597 A.2d 447 (Md. 1991) (action may proceed where school had specific information about young woman's intentions); reprinted in Best and Barnes, note 8 at 229.

11. *Brower v. Ackerley,* 943 P.2d 1141 (Wash. Ct. App. 1997) (words alone do not constitute assault); reprinted in Best and Barnes, note 8 at 41.

12. *Lundy v. Adamar of New Jersey, Inc.,* 34 F.3d 1173 (3d Cir. 1994) (in light of "Good Samaritan Rule"—that you don't have to be one—casino had no obligation to aid patron in need); reprinted in Best and Barnes, note 8 at 506; see also *Yania v. Bigan,* 155 A.2d 343 (Pa. 1959) (specifically noting a moral obligation to aid another in peril but denying any legal obligation), noted in Best and Barnes, note 8 at 510.

13. These phrases were used in a public relations campaign undertaken in 1983 by the American Society of Plastic and Reconstructive Surgeons, quoted in Rebecca Weisman, "Reforms in Medical Device Regulation: An Examination of the Silicone Gel Breast Implants Debacle," 23 *Golden Gate University Law Review* 973, 990 and n. 138 (1993). "Micromastia" is defined as "a failure of the breast to respond to hormonal stimulation during the normal maturation phase." William C. Grabb and James W. Smith, eds., *Plastic Surgery, A Concise Guide to Clinical Practices* (Boston: Little Brown, 2nd ed., 1973), at 987.

14. Julie M. Spanbauer, "Breast Implants as Beauty Ritual: Woman's Scepter and Prison," 9 *Yale Journal of Law and Feminism* 152, 164 (1997). Professor Spanbauer recounts the history from foot-binding, ceruse abuse (a lead-based white paint used to lighten the complexion), corseting, breast augmentation (by means including the surgical implantation of glass balls and direct injection of silicone), to a huge range of treatments for weight loss.

15. Dr. Marcia Angell, Executive Editor of the *New England Journal of Medicine,* derided the 1992 decision of then-F.D.A. Commissioner Dr. David Kessler restricting implant availability as unjustified paternalism. Marcia Angell, *Science on Trial: The Clash of Medical Evidence and the Law in the Breast Implant Case* (New York: W. W. Norton, 1996), at 63.

16. "[T]he metaphysical assumption of human beings as individual atoms which in principle are separable from social molecules does discourage liberals from conceiving of rationality as constituted by or defined by group norms, let alone being a property of social structures." Alison M. Jaggar, *Feminist Politics and Human Nature* (Totowa, New Jersey: Rowman & Allanheld, 1983), at 29.

17. I've earlier mentioned the centrality to liberalism of the public/private

distinction. The golf club's right to exclude women is part of decision making in the sacred private realm. The problem is that this glorified right to privacy usually obscures underlying equality problems. People who are socially unequal usually have no privacy to protect: think of the homeless, indigent families forced to live in a single room, and critics of the government under surveillance. Think of almost all children. Think of almost all women. As many feminist lawyers have argued, the privacy principle actually isolates women from one another and from public recourse for harms done to them. The destructive effects of the public/private distinction are among the reasons that feminists insist that "the personal is political."

18. This organization is taken from Charles Frankel, "Equality of Opportunity," 81 *Ethics* 191 (1971).

19. The article that made me start thinking seriously about equality theory when I was just a legal tot, and that is still an excellent exposition of these conceptual issues, is Richard A. Wasserstrom, "Racism, Sexism, and Preferential Treatment: An Approach to the Topics," 24 *U.C.L.A. Law Review* 582 (1977).

20. The most depressing liberal version of equality is the specter of eradication of individualism and the excellence that only individualism allegedly can produce. In one of his early short stories, Kurt Vonnegut described a society where, pursuant to the 211th, 212th, and 213th Amendments to the Constitution, everyone was equally stupid, equally lazy, and equally ugly. Kurt Vonnegut, "Harrison Bergeron," in *Welcome to the Monkey House* (New York: Delacorte Press, 1968), at 7.

21. Thanks to Anne Hunter, of the Massachusetts Institute of Technology, for this example.

22. *Foley v. Connelie,* 435 U.S. 291, 296 (1978) (a state may assume that citizen-officers will be more "familiar with and sympathetic to American traditions"). Exclusion of resident aliens from governmental involvement does have limits. Compare *Ambach v. Norwick,* 441 U.S. 68 (1979) (state may preclude aliens from employment as public school teachers) with *Bernal v. Fainter,* 467 U.S. 216 (1984) (commission of notaries public may not be limited to citizens).

23. Typical of these few cases are *Smith v. Olin Chemical Corp.,* 555 F. 2d 1283 (5th Cir. 1977) (discharge of employee because of his sickle cell anemia could demonstrate race discrimination prohibited by Title VII, but facts not shown in the case) and *Peoples v. City of Salina,* 1990 U.S. Dist. LEXIS 4070 (active sickle cell anemia symptoms could disqualify plaintiff from firefighter job). Sickle-cell anemia was a prominent analogy in the pregnancy disability cases of the 1970s. See *General Electric Company v. Gilbert,* 429 U.S. 125, 153 (1977) (Brennan, J., dissenting).

24. Again, Charles Frankel 1971's article, note 18, was the model here.

25. *Garrett v. Board of Education of the School District of the City of Detroit,*

775 F. Supp. 1004 (E.D. Mich. 1991) (important purpose for which all-male academies came into being not enough to overcome sex discrimination charge).

26. Erin A. McGrath, "The Young Women's Leadership School: A Viable Alternative to Traditional Coeducational Public Schools," 4 *Cardozo Women's Law Journal* 455 (1998).

27. A three-judge panel upheld Texas' mid-decade redistricting plan, *Session v. Perry,* 298 F. Supp. 2d 451 (E.D. Tex. 2004), but the United States Supreme Court has ordered the lower court to reconsider in light of the recent "political gerrymandering" case from Pennsylvania noted below. *Jackson v. Perry,* 543 U.S. 351 (2004).

28. *Vieth v. Jubelirer,* 541 U.S. 267 (2004)(pursuant to political question doctrine, there are no judicially discernible and manageable standards to determine whether the Pennsylvania redistricting scheme, a political gerrymander that will increase Republican representation in the federal House, violates the "one person, one vote" requirement). *Vieth* was a close and inconclusive decision. See Mitchell N. Berman, "Managing Gerrymandering," 83 *Texas Law Review* 781 (2005). We shall see whether the Supreme Court's order requiring reconsideration of the Texas reapportionment scheme, 543 U.S. 351, will shed any further light on the subject of political gerrymandering.

29. See *Georgia v. Ashcroft,* 539 U.S. 461 (2003) (Georgia plan to increase minority "influence districts" does not meet requirements of Voting Rights Act; purpose of act is "to foster transformation to a society that is no longer fixated on race").

30. See for example, *Egan v. Canada* [1995] 2 S.C.R. 513; *Vriend v. Alberta* [1998] 1 S.C.R. 493.

31. The allusion is to *Williamson v. Lee Optical of Oklahoma, Inc.,* 348 U.S. 483 (1955). The Supreme Court held against claims brought by opticians challenging a state law that prohibited opticians from fitting or duplicating lenses without a prescription. In deciding that the law did not unconstitutionally discriminate between opticians on one hand and ophthalmologists and optometrists on the other, the Court famously indulged in a speculative account of why the Oklahoma legislature might have enacted such a law. *Id.* at 489. A court could less fancifully conclude that this was not the sort of problem that constitutional equality provisions were intended to address.

32. Compare *Law v. Canada* [1999] 1 S.C.R. 497 with *Williamson v. Lee Optical,* 348 U.S. 483 (1955).

33. Professor Martha Minnow has written insightfully of how powerful entities, such as corporations, have appropriated the places and expressions of injured parties in their various campaigns for more power, including in the tort reform movements. Martha Minnow, "Surviving Victim Talk," 40 *U.C.L.A. Law Review* 1411 (1993).

34. The Constitution Act, Part I, Canadian Charter of Rights and Freedoms, § 15(2) (1982).

35. The Constitution Act, Part I, Canadian Charter of Rights and Freedoms, § 1 (1982). In any section 1 analysis, however, the government bears a heavy burden of proof, very close to what American lawyers would recognize as "strict scrutiny."

36. See for example, Donald L. Beschle, "Clearly Canadian? *Hill v. Colorado* and Free Speech Balancing in the United States and Canada," 28 *Hastings Constitutional Law Quarterly* 187 (2001).

37. *Andrews v. Law Society of British Columbia* [1989] 1 S.C.R. 143.

38. Compare *Geduldig v. Aiello,* 417 U.S. 484 (1974) with *Brooks v. Canada Safeway Limited* [1989] 1 S.C.R. 1219.

39. *Vriend v. Alberta* (1998), 156 D.L.R. (4th) 385 (S.C.C.), at 131, 134–36.

40. Id.(holding that the Alberta legislature must include sexual orientation as a protected ground in that province's human rights legislation).

41. *Ontario Human Rights Commission and O'Malley v. Simpsons-Sears, Limited* [1985] 2 S.C.R. 536.

42. *Washington v. Davis,* 426 U.S. 229, 248 (1976).

43. In the gender realm, Professor MacKinnon has put this most pithily:

> [E]very quality that distinguishes men from women is already affirmatively compensated in society's organization and values, so that it implicitly defines the standards that it neutrally applies. Men's physiology defines most sports, their health needs largely define insurance coverage, their socially designed biographies defined workplace expectations and successful career patterns, their perspectives and concerns define quality in scholarship, their experiences and obsessions define merit, their military service defines citizenship, their presence defines family, their inability to get along with each other—their wars and rulerships—defines history, their image defines god, and their genitals define sex. These are the standards that are presented as gender neutral. For each of men's differences from women, what amounts to an affirmative action plan is in effect, otherwise known as the male-dominant structure and values of American society.

Catharine A. MacKinnon, *Toward a Feminist Theory of the State* (Cambridge: Harvard University Press, 1989), at 224.

44. See Martha Albertson Fineman, *The Autonomy Myth* (New York: Free Press, 2004); Patricia J. Williams, "Gilded Lilies and Liberal Guilt," in *The Alchemy of Race and Rights* (Cambridge: Harvard University Press, 1991), at 15–43; Robin West, "The Difference in Women's Hedonic Lives: A Phenomenological Critique of Feminist Legal Theory," 3 *Wisconsin Women's Law Journal* 81 (1987).

45. As an example of the convolutions of "choice," consider the matter of

Kirk v. Washington State University, 746 P.2d 285 (Wash. 1987) (en banc). The university moved cheerleading practice from a padded gymnastics facility to an artificial turf surface, without warning the cheerleaders of the increased dangers of practicing on that new surface. In 1978, while practicing shoulder stands, a maneuver where the female cheerleaders had to stand on the shoulders of male cheerleaders, a female fell, permanently injured her elbow, and suffered depression. The university argued that the plaintiff should not recover damages because she voluntarily assumed the risk of injury, and that her damages should be reduced in accordance with preexisting depression that the university claimed was a result of her having had abortions. The result was that the damages were reduced based on plaintiff's participation in the maneuver, but not based on the abortions because the evidence of having had abortions was "prejudicial." Beyond the holding of the case, however, I have some questions about choices. In the year of the injury, before Title IX had much changed college athletics, might we want to know more about the plaintiff's "choice" to become a cheerleader, especially when they had unsafe practice premises? Might we ask about the female cheerleaders' "choice" to be the ones thrown around in the air? What sorts of "choices" about their sexuality lead young women to "choose" to have abortions? How many times in one case can a plaintiff be punished for having anything that even looks like a choice?

46. The Supreme Court of Canada has explicitly rejected the idealism of U.S. First Amendment law. In a case upholding the Canadian criminal prohibition on racial and religious hate speech, that Court stated:

> [W]e are less confident in the 20th century that the critical faculties of individuals will be brought to bear on the speech and writing which is directed at them. . . . While holding that over the long run, the human mind is repelled by blatant falsehood and seeks the good, it is too often true, in the short run, that emotion displaces reason and individuals perversely reject the demonstrations of truth put before them and forsake the good they know. The successes of modern advertising, the triumphs of impudent propaganda such as Hitler's, have qualified sharply our belief in the rationality of man.

R. v. Keegstra [1990] 3 S.C.R. 697, ¶66 (quoting Special Committee on Hate Propaganda in Canada [Cohen Committee], 1966).

47. See Jacques Lacan, *Écrits: A Selection* (New York: Norton Books, A. Sheridan trans. 1977)(describing fear of contingency and attempts to suppress it by imposition of a "phallocentric" order on the world).

48. Virginia Woolf speaks of the fear of unimportance in a typically disarming way:

> Life for both sexes—and I looked at them, shouldering their way along the pavement—is arduous, difficult, a perpetual struggle. It calls for gigantic courage and strength. More than anything, perhaps, creatures of

> illusion as we are, it calls for confidence in oneself. . . . And how can we generate this imponderable quality, which is yet so invaluable, most quickly? By thinking that other people are inferior to oneself. . . . Women have served all these centuries as looking-glasses possessing the magic and delicious power of reflecting the figure of man at twice its natural size. Without that power probably the earth would still be swamp and jungle.

Virginia Woolf, *A Room of One's Own* (1929) (New York: Harcourt, Brace and World, 1957), at 35.

49. For the legal repercussions of a psychology of dependency (as opposed to a psychology of individualism and aggression), see J. C. Smith, "The Sword and Shield of Perseus: Some Mythological Dimensions of the Law," 6 *Journal of Law and Psychiatry* 235, 241–42 (1983).

50.

> Creative mythology . . . springs not, like theology, from the dicta of authority, but from the insights, sentiments, thoughts, and vision of an adequate individual. . . . Renewing the act of experience itself, it restores to existence the quality of adventure, at once shattering and reintegrating the fixed, already known, in the sacrificial creative fire of the becoming thing that is no thing at all but life, not as it will be, or as it should be, as it was or as it never will be, but as it is, in depth, in process, here and now, inside and out.

Joseph Campbell, *The Masks of God: Creative Mythology* (New York: Viking Press, 1968), at 8.

51. Andrea Dworkin, *Right-Wing Women* (New York: Perigee Books, 1983), at 221.

NOTES TO CHAPTER 5

1. It is not always easy to locate that membership. Increasingly, there are ragged boundaries demarcating the formerly dualistic biological grouping of the sexes. See Anne Fausto-Sterling, *Sexing the Body: Gender Politics and the Construction of Sexuality* (New York: Basic Books, 2000).

2. See Grant Gilmore, *The Ages of American Law* (New Haven: Yale University Press, 1977), at 87 (the Realist "revolution may have been merely a palace revolution, not much more than a changing of the guard."); Robert Stevens, *Law School: Legal Education in America from the 1950s to the 1980s* (Chapel Hill: University of North Carolina Press, 1983), at 156 ("The effect of the Realists was much like the role that Carlyle pronounced for Matthew Arnold: 'He led them into the wilderness and left them there.' ").

3. See Ann Scales, "Towards a Feminist Jurisprudence," 56 *Indiana Law Journal* 375 (1981).

4. A mere "rational basis" test applied in sex discrimination cases until

1976, when the U.S. Supreme Court elevated the standard for measuring sex discrimination to "intermediate scrutiny." *Craig v. Boren,* 429 U.S. 190 (1976) (requiring that the state has the burden of showing both that its action serves an important governmental objective and that the means chosen to achieve that objective are substantially related to it).

5. Catharine A. MacKinnon, *Sexual Harassment of Working Women* (New Haven: Yale University Press, 1979), at 101–41.

6. Aristotle, *Nichomachean Ethics V(3),* David Ross, trans. (Oxford: Oxford University Press, 1972) (1925), at 112–14.

7. *Reed v. Reed,* 404 U.S. 71 (1971).

8. *Geduldig v. Aiello,* 417 U.S. 484 (1974) (exclusion of pregnancy from risks covered by state employees' insurance plan does not constitute sex discrimination under the Equal Protection clause); *Dothard v. Rawlinson,* 433 U.S. 321 (1977) (refusal to hire female prison guards authorized by Title VII of the Civil Rights Act of 1964); *Rostker v. Goldberg,* 453 U.S. 57 (1981) (upholding constitutionality of exclusion of women from draft registration). For the other side of that familiar coin, see *Personnel Administrator v. Feeney,* 442 U.S. 256 (1979) (upholding Massachusetts veterans' preference for civil service positions); *Nguyen v. Immigration and Naturalization Service,* 533 U.S. 53 (2001) (upholding immigration provision forcing male citizens, but not female citizens, to prove parentage of children born abroad who wish to acquire citizenship).

9. In U.S. legal theory, the canonical text on the need for transcendence of results in constitutional adjudication is Herbert Wechsler, "Toward Neutral Principles of Constitutional Law," 73 *Harvard Law Review* 1 (1959).

10. Carol C. Gould, "The Woman Question: Philosophy of Liberation and the Liberation of Philosophy," in Carol C. Gould and Marx W. Wartofsky, eds., *Women and Philosophy: Toward a Theory of Liberation* (New York: Putnam, 1976), at 5–13.

11. Underlying this approach is the "correspondence theory of truth" and "reference theory of meaning," associated with the Rationalist tradition in philosophy described in chapter 2. Pursuant to the correspondence theory, there is an "objective" reality "out there" and the truth value of our knowledge or statements about the world is a function of how closely they correspond to that reality. As applied to law, judgments are valid only when they reflect objective facts. For a fuller explanation of correspondence theory, see Bertrand Russell, *The Problems of Philosophy* (New York: Oxford University Press, 1980) (1912), at 126–130. For a detailed account of why correspondence theory doesn't work in law, see chapter 3.

12. Gould, note 10, at 20.

13. Id. at 21.

14. Catharine A. MacKinnon, *Toward a Feminist Theory of the State* (Cambridge: Harvard University Press, 1989), at 116–17. For an analysis of how

rationality came to be defined as maleness and vice versa, see Sandra Harding, "Is Gender a Variable in Conceptions of Reality? A Survey of Issues," in Carol C. Gould, ed., *Beyond Domination: New Perspectives on Women and Philosophy* (Totowa, N.J.: Rowman and Allenheld 1984), at 52.

15. Ann Scales, "The Emergence of Feminist Jurisprudence," 95 *Yale Law Journal* 1373, 1378 (1986).

16. Daniel Farber and Suzanna Sherry, *Beyond All Reason: The Radical Assault on Truth in American Law* (New York: Oxford University Press, 1997), at 26, 101 (presenting my work as ridiculous on its face); Walter Olson, "The Law On Trial," *Wall Street Journal,* October 14, 1997 (quoting my description of objective reality as a myth, and referring to me as a "radical multiculturalist").

17. At least in the classical world, myth was "the exemplary model for all significant human activities." Rex Warner, "Foreword," *Encyclopedia of World Mythology* (New York: Galahad Books, 1975), at 11. Contemporary feminist authors regard myth as a connection to transformational ideational energy. Jane Caputi, *Goddesses and Monsters: Women, Myth, Power, and Popular Culture* (Madison: University of Wisconsin/Popular Press, 2004), at 291–93.

18. Most famous among judicial expressions of the notion is Justice Bradley's concurrence in *Bradwell v. Illinois,* 83 U.S. (16 Wall.) 130, 14–42 (1872) (holding 14th Amendment's privileges and immunities clause did not entitle Myra Bradwell to bar membership):

> [T]he civil law, as well as nature herself, has always recognized a wide difference in the respective spheres and destinies of man and woman. Man is, or should be, a woman's protector and defender. The natural and proper timidity and delicacy which belongs to the female sex evidently unfits it for many of the occupations of civil life. The constitution of the family organization, which is founded in the divine ordinance, as well as in the nature of things, indicates the domestic sphere as that which properly belongs to the domain and functions of womanhood. . . . The paramount destiny and mission of woman are to fulfill the noble and benign offices of wife and mother. This is the law of the Creator. And the rules of civil society must be adapted to the general constitution of things. . . .

19. For a helpful synopsis of early theories about the "nature of woman," see Caroline Whitbeck, "Theories of Sex Difference," in *Women and Philosophy: Toward a Theory of Liberation,* note 10, at 54.

20. *Palsgraf v. Long Island Railway,* 248 N.Y. 339, 162 N.E. 99 (1928).

21. Heisenberg formulated the uncertainty principle in 1926; see Stephen W. Hawking, *A Brief History of Time: From the Big Bang to Black Holes* (New York: Bantam Books, 1988), at 54–55, and later included it as part of his quantum theory. Werner Heisenberg, *The Physical Principles of the Quantum Theory,* Carl Eckart and Frank C. Hoyt, trans. (New York: Dover Publications, 1930), at 4, 20, 62–65. In 1982, Professor Morton Horwitz noted the simul-

taneity between the displacement of strict causality in the natural sciences and the development of pro-capitalist "proximate cause" doctrines in the common law. Morton J. Horwitz, "The Doctrine of Objective Causation," in David Kairys, ed., *The Politics of Law: A Progressive Critique* (New York: Pantheon Books, 1982), at 212–13, note 10.

22. See Laurence H. Tribe, "The Curvature of Constitutional Space: What Lawyers Can Learn from Modern Physics," 103 *Harvard Law Review* 1 (1989) (at the least, the metaphors of physics have heuristic ramifications for constitutional law).

23. These ideas were first articulated in a feminist context in Simone de Beauvoir, *The Second Sex*, H. Parshley, trans. (New York: Vintage Books, 1974) (1952).

24. For examples of such an approach in science and psychology, see Evelyn Fox Keller, *Reflections on Gender and Science* (New Haven: Yale University Press, 1985), at 178 ("A healthy science is one that allows for the productive survival of diverse conceptions of mind and nature, and of correspondingly diverse strategies. In my vision of science, it is not the taming of nature that is sought, but the taming of hegemony."); and Gilbert Ryle, *The Concept of Mind* (New York: Barnes and Noble, 1949), at 28–29:

> The well-regulated clock keeps good time and the well-drilled circus seal performs its tricks flawlessly, yet we do not call them "intelligent." We reserve this title for the persons responsible for their performances. To be intelligent is not merely to satisfy criteria, but to apply them; to regulate one's actions and not merely to be well-regulated. . . . [A person] applies criteria in performing critically, that is, in trying to get things right.

25. Ludwig Wittgenstein, *Philosophical Investigations,* G. E. M. Anscombe, trans. (Oxford: Blackwell, 1968) (1958), at ¶¶ 66–78, at 31–36. I do not mean to imply that I think of the process of legal justification as a game. On the contrary, it is misleading when legal philosophers do; see, e.g., John Rawls, "Two Concepts of Rules," 64 *Philosophical Review* 3, 24–27 (1955) (comparing adjudication to baseball), because legal proceedings often require us to question the rules themselves as well as what the rules mean. Wittgenstein's point is that when we use even a very familiar concept (like "games"), we are making a complex but reliable judgment by means of criteria we cannot even articulate.

26. Wittgenstein, note 25 at ¶ 67, at 32. I relish the fact that, in this example and the next, Wittgenstein talks about activities that are traditionally relegated to women: spinning thread and child tending.

27. Id. at 33 (paragraph without number).

28. Id. ¶ 415, at 125.

29. Gould, note 10, at 27.

30. Wittgenstein, note 25, ¶ 88, at 41.

31. Id. ¶ 71, at 34.

32. See Thomas S. Kuhn, *The Structure of Scientific Revolutions* (Chicago: University of Chicago Press, 2d ed. 1970) (1962), at 108 (abandonment by eighteenth-century scientists of attempt to explain gravity reflected "neither a decline nor a raising of standards, but . . . the adoption of a new paradigm").

33. One of the favorite targets of Wittgenstein's assault on philosophical muddles was metaphysical solipsism, which maintains that the self of the thinker is the whole of reality; the external world and other persons have no independent existence. This argument asserts that I cannot be certain of your existence because I cannot experience your sensations; I cannot, for example, "know" your "pain." Beginning from the perspective of how people actually use language, Wittgenstein demonstrated that such an assertion merely evinces confusion about the grammar of the word "know" (Wittgenstein, note 25, ¶ 246, at 89) and of the word "pain" (id. ¶¶ 293, 303, 384, at 100, 102, 118). Thus, it makes sense to say "I feel my pain," or "I know your pain" (id. ¶ 246, at 89), but to maintain that I know my pain and don't know yours makes no more sense than to say, "Someone is in pain—I don't know who!" (id. ¶¶ 407–408, at 123).

34. Id. ¶ 67, at 32.

35.

> No systematic thought has made progress apart from some adequately general working hypothesis, adapted to its special topic. Such an hypothesis directs observation, and decides upon the mutual relevance of various types of evidence. In short, it prescribes method. To venture upon productive thought without such an explicit theory is to abandon oneself to the doctrines derived from one's grandfather.

Alfred North Whitehead, *Adventures of Ideas* (New York: Macmillan, 1933), at 286.

36. MacKinnon, *Sexual Harassment of Working Women,* note 5, at 117. The critical word in the standard is not "gender." I believe that similar standards could be developed to apply in cases regarding various socially mistreated groups—including those intersectionally situated—because the standard *is* the legalized expression of the general principle of "antisubordination." Among the critical features of that expression are the absence of a requirement to show intention on the part of discriminators, the necessity of thorough contextualization to identify "integral" contributions to social hierarchy, and the condemnation of disadvantage based on "status" rather than on identity or the fact of classification itself.

37. There are a number of versions of the standard to choose among. Professor Robert Post, for example, has recently proposed something much like the MacKinnon standard, calling it the "sociological account." Robert C. Post, "Prejudicial Appearances: The Logic of American Antidiscrimination Law," in Robert C. Post with K. Anthony Appiah, Judith Butler, Thomas C. Grey, and

Reva B. Siegel, *Prejudicial Appearances* (Durham: Duke University Press, 2001), at 21–22, 40–52.

38. See, for example, my description of Canadian equality principles in chapter 4. A burgeoning comparative law literature describes Canadian jurisprudence as "dialogic," engaging openly with other countries in order to "identify the normative and factual assumptions underlying [its] own constitutional jurisprudence." Sujit Choundhry, "Globalization in Search of Justification: Toward a Theory of Comparative Constitutional Interpretation," 74 *Indiana Law Journal* 819, 825 (1999). By contrast, the United States Supreme Court in particular remains focused on a "heroic view" of its own constitutional work (David Strauss, "The New Textualism in Constitutional Law," 66 *George Washington Law Review* 1153, 1154 (1998)), which leads it to positions that are isolationist and perhaps paranoid; that are aggressively and undemocratically authoritative; that reject "the existence and even the possibility of ambiguity"; and that risk underenforcement of constitutional rights. Sarah K. Harding, "Comparative Reasoning and Judicial Review," 28 *Yale Journal of International Law* 409, 446–48, 443, 435 (2003).

39. Regarding different kinds of stereotypes, see K. Anthony Appiah, "Stereotypes and the Shaping of Identity," in *Prejudicial Appearances*, note 37, at 55.

40. Id. at 64–65.

41. See *Nguyen v. Immigration and Naturalization Service*, 533 U.S. 53 (2001) (upholding requirement that fathers of children born abroad undergo more administrative steps than mothers to secure child's citizenship); *Michael M. v. Sonoma County Superior Court*, 450 U.S. 464, 476 (1981) (upholding statutory rape law that presumes male is culpable aggressor because "consequences of sexual intercourse and pregnancy fall more heavily on the female than on the male"); *Geduldig v. Aiello*, 417 U.S. 484, 496 n. 20 (1974) (disability insurance system did not "exclude anyone from benefit eligibility because of gender but merely removes one physical condition—pregnancy—from the list of compensable disabilities").

42. MacKinnon, *Sexual Harassment of Working Women*, note 5 at 118.

43. Id. at 117.

44. Ratification of the Nineteenth Amendment, for example, which in 1920 guaranteed women the right to vote, required seventy-five years of ceaseless struggle from its female proponents but could not finally have been accomplished without the action of surrogates.

45. Thus, I believe the inequality approach would oppose the result in *Michael M. v. Sonoma County Superior Court*, 453 U.S. 57 (1981), the case that upheld a version of the California statutory rape law for which only males could be prosecuted. Such a provision is not intended to remedy disadvantages suffered by women. Rather, such provisions were designed, first, to render females incapable of consent (thereby institutionalizing their nonpersonhood),

and second, to preserve the chastity of females (thereby preventing property damage). In 1993, California changed its statutory rape law to make it gender neutral. Cal. Penal Code § 261.5 (West 2000).

46. There is so much backlash that backlash results from the mention of backlash. For example, the Eighth Circuit reversed summary judgment for the defendant in a hostile-environment sexual harassment case, where, among other things, during a conversation among coworkers about Susan Faludi, *Backlash: The Undeclared War Against American Women* (New York: Crown, 1991), a male employee called the plaintiff a "bitch," and the district manager "became 'very angry' and 'exploded' stating: 'You women, since when are women always right and men are always wrong? If your women's movement had its way, every woman would be working and our children would be being raised in communes.'" *Hocevar v. Purdue Frederick Co.,* 223 F.3d 721, 725 (8th Cir. 2000). This sort of episode informs the song lyric that is the epigraph to this chapter, "People sure get nervous when a woman's free." Michael Henderson, "The Restless Kind" (Colgems-EM Music, Inc., 1981), as sung by Trisha Yearwood on the album *Thinkin' About You* (Nashville: MCA, 1995).

47. Meika Schmidt-Gleim and Mieke Verloo, "One More Feminist Manifesto of the Political," *IWM Working Paper No. 2/2003,* Vienna 2003, at 4, available at http://www.iwm.at/publ-wp/wp-03-02.pdf (visited August 3, 2005).

48. Id. at 10–14.

49. Professor Owen Fiss found the path from the singular focus on individual opportunity to the "group-disadvantaging principle." Owen M. Fiss, "Groups and the Equal Protection Clause," 5 *Philosophy and Public Affairs* 107 (1976). It was Professor MacKinnon, however, who in 1979 provided the name as well as the outlines of antisubordination theory. MacKinnon, *Sexual Harassment of Working Women,* note 5.

50. See for example, John O. Calmore, "Social Justice Advocacy in the Third Dimension: Addressing the Problem of 'Preservation-Through-Transformation'," 16 *Florida Journal of International Law* 615 (2004); Laura Rovner, "Disability, Equality, and Identity," 55 *Alabama Law Review* 1043 (2004); Pamela S. Karlan, "Foreword: Loving *Lawrence,*" 102 *Michigan Law Review* 1447 (2004).

51. Among the most useful papers on the topic of the relationships among systems of subordination is Nancy Ehrenreich, "Subordination and Symbiosis: Mechanisms of Mutual Support Between Subordinating Systems," 71 *University of Missouri—Kansas City Law Review* 251 (2002).

52. Postmodernist theorists argue, for example, that feminists must get over the binary categories of gender, and indeed the category of gender itself, because every time we use those categories, we "limit and constrain in advance the very cultural possibilities that feminism is supposed to open up." Judith Butler, *Gen-*

der Trouble: Feminism and the Subversion of Identity (New York: Routledge, 1990), at 146.

53. Aldous Huxley, *The Perennial Philosophy* (New York: Harper and Brothers, 1945), at 93.

54. Id. at 135.

55. In the emerging literature of "virtue ethics," for example, Professor Rosalind Hursthouse argues that racism results from miseducation in virtue, those aspects of human flourishing described by Aristotle—wisdom, courage, generosity, and honesty—the learning of which are a life's work. Rosalind Hursthouse, *On Virtue Ethics* (New York: Oxford University Press, 1999), at 108–20.

56. It must be that there is or has been something fun and sexy about hurting other people in ways that track existing maps of subordination. Consider this remark from the highly decorated Marine Corps Lieutenant-General James Mattis:

> You go into Afghanistan, you got guys who slap women around for five years because they didn't wear a veil. You know, guys like that ain't got no manhood left anyway. So it's a hell of a lot of fun to shoot them.

Reported in John J. Lumpkin, "Shooting Some People Is A 'Hoot,' General Said," *Chicago Sun Times,* February 4, 2005, at 5. General Mattis was "counseled" to use his words more carefully. Id. This outburst about the pleasure derived from intersectional racialized and gendered violence resonates with the insights of progressive theorists. For example, bell hooks describes sexualized aspects in the historical appropriation of black bodies and black culture. bell hooks, *Black Looks: Race and Representation* (Boston: South End Press, 1992); Anthony Farley argues that race is experienced as a form of bodily pleasure. Anthony Paul Farley, "The Poetics of Colorlined Space," in Francisco Valdes, Jerome McCristal Culp, and Angela P. Harris, eds., *Crossroads, Directions, and a New Critical Race Theory* (Philadelphia: Temple University Press, 2002), at 97.

57. Speaking of the mess between the 2004 invasion of Falluja and the elections in Iraq, a retired general said, "[Y]ou've got to go with what you've got. I mean, you have to make the best of a broken play." General Montgomery Meigs (Ret.), Former Commander, NATO Stabilization Force, *Meet The Press* (NBC), December 12, 2004, transcript available at http://msnbc.msn.com/id/6702005/. I believe that General Meigs was talking about football; earlier in the broadcast he had spoken of the relative lack of preparation of troops from the National Guard. "It's not that anyone is discriminating against the Guard. You've trying to make the scrimmage as tough as the game."

58. de Beauvoir, note 23.

59. Dorothy Dinnerstein, *The Mermaid and the Minotaur: Sexual Arrangements and Human Malaise* (New York: Harper, 1977), at 214–24.

60. *Rostker v. Goldberg,* 453 U.S. 57 (1981) (in spite of evidence that regis-

tration of women would increase military readiness, Equal Protection clause did not preclude male-only draft registration). For further discussion of *Rostker,* see Ann Scales, "Militarism, Male Dominance, and the Law: Feminist Jurisprudence as Oxymoron?" 12 *Harvard Women's Law Journal* 25 (1989).

61. Damien Cave, "Army Recruiters Say They Feel Pressure to Bend Rules," *New York Times,* May 3, 2005, at A23.

62. Michael Janofsky and Adam Nagourney, "Governors Concerned Over National Guard Deployments in Iraq," *New York Times,* July 17, 2005, at 122.

63. Although the rate of discharge of gay and lesbian soldiers has dropped by half since September 1, 2001, the Pentagon has spent more than $200 million to recruit and train personnel to replace those discharged pursuant to the "don't ask, don't tell" policy in the past decade. Interestingly, the United Kingdom, the closest ally of the United States in the Iraqi war, has completely changed its tune on gay and lesbian soldiers. Five years after lifting its ban on gays in the military, and less than a year after the beginning of the Iraqi war, the Royal Navy began actively to recruit gays and lesbians. John Files, "Rules on Gays Exact A Cost In Recruiting, A Study Finds," *New York Times,* February 24, 2005, at A21.

64. Damien Cave, "Pentagon May Consider Older Recruits," *New York Times,* July 22, 2005, at A11 (Pentagon asks Congress to increase maximum recruiting age from 39 to 42); Alan Cooperman, "Peace Corps Option for Military Recruits Sparks Concerns," *Washington Post,* August 2, 2005, at A11 (law that allows recruits to meet part of military obligation by serving in Peace Corps may endanger reputation and safety of Peace Corps volunteers); Cave, "Pressure to Bend Rules," note 61 (improprieties in recruiting practices).

65. Damien Cave, "For Recruiters, A Hard Toll From a Hard Sell," *New York Times,* March 27, 2005, at 11. See also James Dao, "The Draft Card: The Option Nobody's Pushing Yet," *New York Times,* October 3, 2004, at 41 (Pentagon took position that draft could be avoided only if recruiting numbers stayed high; recruiting numbers have fallen dramatically short). Under the present regime, men ages 18 to 25 must register for Selective Service. Should a draft be reinstated, the first to be called would be men whose twentieth birthday fell during the year the lottery was held. As needed, the number would rise, 21-year-olds next, and so forth. The Pentagon suggests that 18- and 19-year-olds would not be drafted. Jane Gordon, "Men 18 to 25 Must Still Register," *New York Times,* October 31, 2004.

66. David M. Kennedy, "The Best Army We Can Buy," *New York Times,* July 25, 2005, at A19.

67. The policy since 1994 is that women may not serve in ground-combat units smaller than brigades, on the theory that larger units have less contact with the enemy. Direct-combat units include infantry, armor, Special Forces, field artillery, and combat engineers. Women are allowed, however, to fly attack

aircraft and to serve in "forward support companies" and transportation companies that regularly come under fire in Iraq. Thom Shanker, "House Bill Would Preserve, and Limit, the Role of Women in Combat Zones," *New York Times,* May 20, 2005, at A20.

68. Nick Papps, "Should Women Soldiers Be Dying in Iraq?" *Sunday Telegraph* (Sydney), July 10, 2005, at 44. As of 2004, women made up about 10 percent of the number of U.S. soldiers serving in Iraq but only 3 percent of the deaths. Monica Davey, "The Conflict in Iraq: For 1,000 Troops, There Is No Going Home," *New York Times,* September 9, 2004, at A1.

69. "House Passes Defense Authorization Bill," *Army,* July 1, 2005, at 10.

70. Scales, Militarism, note 60, at 40–42 (quoting a marine quoted by Cynthia Enloe, *Does Khaki Become You? The Militarization of Women's Lives* (Boston: South End Press, 1983), at 212).

71. For a fuller account of why this is so, see Ann Scales, "Soft on Defense: The Failure to Confront Militarism," 20 *Berkeley Journal of Gender, Law and Justice* 369 (2005).

72. Why so much brouhaha, for example, over the story of six-time murderer Aileen Wuornos, wrenchingly portrayed in the award-winning film *Monster* (Patty Jenkins, Dir., 2003)? Other serial killers—almost always men—get lots of attention, even adoration, but it is not quite the same. Wuornos was the first iconic *female* serial killer. Her story was compelling because (at least she said in some interviews) that she killed the men because they were men, for what men did to women. It is socially acceptable to notice the gendered nature of *her* violence, I believe, because her story can be used to argue that sexualized violence is an equal opportunity debacle. See sources collected in Caputi, note 17, at 187, 410–11.

73. Women are overwhelmingly the victims of "intimate" violence, and men are overwhelmingly the perpetrators. According to the United States Department of Justice, in 1998, for example, females were the victims in 72 percent of intimate murders and the victims of about 85 percent of nonlethal intimate violence. http://www.ojp.usdoj.gov/bjs/cvict_c.htm#relate (visited May 29, 2005). Ninety-three percent of adult women and 86 percent of adult men who are raped or physically assaulted are raped or physically assaulted by male perpetrators. http://www.ncjrs.org/pdffiles/172837.pdf (visited August 3, 2005). The fact that the epidemic of intimate violence is discussed in gender-neutral terms speaks volumes about the psychological stakes of preventing discussion in gendered terms.

NOTES TO CHAPTER 6

1. Adrienne Rich, "A Vision (Thinking of Simone Weil)," in *A Wild Patience Has Taken Me This Far* (New York: W. W. Norton, 1981), at 50.

2. I do not wish to understate the nature of the Bush agenda. If it finally succeeds, it will undermine not just political liberalism but philosophical liberalism. It will transform the liberal individual into a manufactured citizen. A useful way of identifying the threat is to recall the difference between George Orwell's *1984* (New York: Harcourt Brace, 1949) and Aldous Huxley's *Brave New World* (New York: Harper, 1950), as explained by Professor Neil Postman:

> Huxley and Orwell did not prophesy the same thing. Orwell warns that we will be overcome by an externally imposed oppression. But in Huxley's vision . . . people will come to love their oppression, to adore the technologies that undo their capacities to think. . . . What Orwell feared were those who would ban books. What Huxley feared was that there would be no reason to ban a book, for there would be no one who wanted to read one. Orwell feared those who would deprive us of information. Huxley feared those who would give us so much that we would be reduced to passivity and egoism. Orwell feared that the truth would be concealed from us. Huxley feared the truth would be drowned in a sea of irrelevance.

Neil Postman, *Amusing Ourselves to Death: Public Discourse in the Age of Show Business* (New York: Penguin Books, 1985), at vii.

3. Although Mr. Meese did not actually participate, the Justice Department at the time empaneled a commission to study pornography, which found that there is a connection between pornography exposure and sexual violence. Of course, antipornography feminists had been making that connection for a long time. The alleged alignment was said to be the kiss of death because of conflicting interests in similar legislation: the feminist interest in pornography regulation is to provide civil remedies for pervasive practices that harm women; the right-wing women's interest is supposedly in the perpetration of their own ideas of virtue, both feminine and masculine. Pornography regulation is to them a vehicle for imposing their narrow morality on everyone else. For a great synopsis of the Meese Commission controversy, see Robin West, "The Feminist-Conservative Anti-Pornography Alliance and the 1986 Attorney General's Commission on Pornography Report," 1987 *American Bar Foundation Research Journal* 681 (1987).

4. See Janet Halley, "Sexuality Harassment," in Catharine A. MacKinnon and Reva B. Siegel, eds., *Directions in Sexual Harassment Law* (New Haven: Yale University Press, 2003), at 182.

5. Margaret Talbot, "Men Behaving Badly," *New York Times,* October 13, 2002, (Magazine), at 52, 84.

6. Andrea Dworkin, *Right-Wing Women* (New York: Perigee Books, 1983), at 13–25.

7. Lon L. Fuller, "Positivism and Fidelity to Law—A Reply to Professor Hart," 71 *Harvard Law Review* 630, 632 (1958).

8. *Rabidue v. Osceola Refining Company,* 805 F.2d 611 (6th Cir. 1986), cert. denied, 481 U.S. 1041 (1987). Contrary to the Sixth Circuit view, at least one court has recognized that workplace saturation by pornography can give rise to a hostile environment claim. *Robinson v. Jacksonville Shipyards, Inc.,* 760 F. Supp. 1486 (M.D. Fla. 1991).

9. "The sexually oriented poster displays had a *de minimis* effect on the plaintiff's work environment when considered in the context of a society that condones and publicly features and commercially exploits open displays of written and pictorial erotica at the newsstands, on prime-time television, at the cinema, and in other public places." 805 F. 2d at 622.

10. Chapter 5, note 19.

11. The first United States Supreme Court case to accept sexual harassment doctrine involved a plaintiff who had had a prior relationship with her harasser. The Court held that the lower court had erroneously focused on the voluntariness of that conduct. *Meritor Savings Bank v. Vinson,* 477 U.S. 57, 68 (1986).

12. *Kahn v. Objective Solutions, Intl.,* 86 F. Supp. 2d 377, 382 (S.D.N.Y. 2000).

13. *Lipphardt v. Durango Steakhouse of Brandon, Inc.,* 267 F.3d 1183, 1188 (11th Cir. 2001).

14. Andrea Dworkin, "Against the Male Flood: Censorship, Pornography, and Equality," in *Letters from a War Zone* (New York: E. P. Dutton, 1988), at 253.

15. *Texas Beef Group v. Winfrey,* 11 F. Supp. 2d 858 (N.D. Tex. 1998), *aff'd* 201 F. 3d 680 (5th Cir. 2000). Thirteen states have "food defamation" laws, and other states are considering them. Margot S. Fell, "Agricultural Disparagement Statutes: Tainted Beef, Tainted Speech, and Tainted Law," 9 *Fordham Intellectual Property, Media and Entertainment Law Journal* 981 (1999).

16. Al Franken, *Lies and the Lying Liars Who Tell Them: A Fair and Balanced Look at the Right* (New York: Penguin, 2003).

17. *Fox News Network, LLC. v. Penguin Group,* 03 Civ. 6162 (RLC) (DC) (S.D.N.Y. 2003).

18. "Fox News Drops Franken Lawsuit," *CBSNews.com,* August 25, 2003.

19. Maria Newman, "CBS Pulls Miniseries on Reagans," *International Herald Tribune,* November 5, 2003 (describing efforts of Republican National Committee and right-wing groups). CBS sold the miniseries to Showtime, which meant that the program went to 14 million homes instead of 180 million homes. Both CBS and Showtime are owned by Viacom. Bill Carter, "Shifting 'Reagans' To Cable Has CBS Facing New Critics," *New York Times,* November 5, 2003.

20. Frederick Schauer, "Slippery Slopes," 99 *Harvard Law Review* 361, 368–69, 373–76 (1985). It is easy to confuse the slippery slope argument with the argument concerning overbreadth. The slippery slope argument refers to the

scenario where a narrowly drawn rule may be susceptible to illegitimate expansion later. In contrast, overbreadth presupposes the linguistic possibility of currently narrowing a rule in order to eliminate any "danger cases." Id. at 366–67.

21. Jeffrey Toobin, "The Trouble With Sex," *New Yorker,* February 9, 1998, at 48, 55.

22. Schauer, note 20 at 365.

23. *Disclosure,* Barry Levinson, dir. (1994).

24. Oliver Wendell Holmes, Jr., *The Common Law* (Boston: Little Brown, 1923) (1881), at 125 (discussing the necessity of continually conforming legal standards to experience).

25. Catharine A. MacKinnon, *Toward a Feminist Theory of the State* (Cambridge: Harvard University Press, 1989), at 183.

26. Id. at 181–82.

27. Evelyn Fox Keller, *Reflections on Gender and Science* (New Haven: Yale University Press, 1985), at 163.

28. Richard Rorty, *Objectivity, Relativism, and Truth* (New York: Cambridge University Press, 1991), at 109.

29. Mari J. Matsuda, "Looking to the Bottom: Critical Legal Studies and Reparations," 22 *Harvard Civil Rights–Civil Liberties Law Review* 323, 324 (1987).

30. It is not possible for this or any other purpose simply to make a list of actionable versions of oppression, particularly in this "nation of minorities," *Regents of the University of California v. Bakke,* 438 U.S. 265, 292 (1987), where different groups enjoy greater or lesser societal opprobrium at different times, and where one's own group memberships are neither singular nor static. Nonetheless, "[t]o conceptualize a condition called subordination is a legitimate alternative to denying that such a condition exists." Mari J. Matsuda, "Public Response to Racist Speech: Considering the Victim's Story," 87 *University of Michigan Law Review* 2320, 2362 (1989). Of course, there are hard cases—from assimilated, affluent members of otherwise subjugated groups to scapegoated white males—that will especially require the painstaking consideration described in the text. But there are also millions of paradigmatic cases in which we all know exactly who we're talking about. This is simply a call for taking history and its group-based harms seriously; this is a call for an end to the "unknowing." Id. at 2362–74.

31. *Degraffenreid v. General Motors Assembly Division,* 413 F. Supp. 142, 143 (E.D. Mo. 1976), *aff'd in part, rev'd in part,* 558 F. 2d 480 (8th Cir. 1977).

32. *Judge v. Marsh,* 649 F. Supp. 770, 780 (D.D.C. 1986) (allowing plaintiff to raise claim as a black woman but limiting theory by prohibiting plaintiffs from relying on more than two subclasses protected by law, e.g., disallowing women of color who are also disabled or members of religious minorities from suing on all those grounds).

33. 833 F.2d 1406 (10th Cir. 1987). Outside the sexual harassment context, it appears that the first court to recognize the discrimination claim of women of color qua women of color was the Fifth Circuit. *Jefferies v. Harris County Community Action Association,* 615 F.2d 1025 (5th Cir. 1980).

34. Commentators generally have two criticisms of *Hicks* and the line of cases of which it is part. First, in merely allowing evidence of racialized harassment to be aggregated with other evidence to prove hostile-work-environment sexual harassment, the Tenth Circuit did not actually recognize or honor the experience of black women. Second, *Hicks* and related cases did not sufficiently contextualize the needs of women of color, so took tiny steps that appear *ad hoc,* and failed to build a reliable platform for women of color in litigation. Cathy Scarborough, "Conceptualizing Black Women's Employment Experiences," 98 *Yale Law Journal* 1457, 1470–71 n. 100 (1989); Kathryn Abrams, "Title VII and the Complex Female Subject," 92 *Michigan Law Review* 2479 (1994); Carole H. Hofstein, "African American Women and the Limits of Law and Society," 1 *Cardozo Women's Law Journal* 373, 391–92 and n. 110 (1994); Andrea L. Dennis, "Because I Am Black, Because I Am a Woman: Remedying the Sexual Harassment Experience of Black Women," 1996 *Annual Survey of American Law* 555, 573–77 (1996); Pamela J. Smith, "Part II—Romantic Paternalism—The Ties That Bind: Hierarchies of Economic Oppression That Reveal Judicial Disaffinity for Black Women and Men," 3 *Journal of Gender, Race and Justice* 181, 212–24 (1999).

35. 40 F. 3d 1551, 1562 (9th Cir. 1994) (citations omitted). At footnote 20 on page 1562, the court cites Kimberlé Crenshaw, "Demarginalizing the Intersection of Race and Sex: A Black Feminist Critique of Antidiscriminatory Doctrine, Feminist Theory and Antiracist Politics," 1989 *University of Chicago Legal Forum* 139, and Judith A. Winston, "Mirror, Mirror on the Wall: Title VII, Section 1981 and the Intersection of Race and Gender in the Civil Rights Act of 1990," 79 *California Law Review* 775 (1991).

36. *Hicks v. Gates Rubber Company,* 928 F. 2d 966, 972–73 (10th Cir. 1991) (discussing plaintiff's failure to mention specific evidence in EEOC filing, describing supervisor's conduct as "boorish, belligerent and uncalled for," and describing supervisor's comments as "a few isolated incidents of racial enmity").

37. For example, some time ago Professor Charles Lawrence exposed the stereotypes implicit—and the harms unrecognized—in the exception to First Amendment coverage that was judicially manufactured for "fighting words." Charles R. Lawrence III, "If He Hollars Let Him Go: Regulating Racist Speech on Campus," 1990 *Duke Law Journal* 431, 449–57 (1990).

38. I date the present storm to the case brought in Hawaii. Though the Supreme Court of that state held that its Equal Rights Amendment required same-sex marriage, *Baehr v. Lewin,* 852 P.2d 44 (Haw. 1993), the people of

Hawaii amended their own Constitution to prohibit it. Nonetheless, the Hawaii case led very quickly to the federal Defense of Marriage Act, note 39, infra.

39. The U.S. Senate defeated the Employment Non-Discrimination Act, S. 2056, 104th Cong. (1996), which would have prohibited employment discrimination on the basis of sexual orientation, by a vote of 49-50. 142 Cong. Rec. S10,129 (daily ed. Sept. 10, 1996). The federal Defense of Marriage Act (DOMA) passed the Senate on the same day by a vote of 85-14. 142 Cong. Rec. S10, 138–39 (daily ed. Sept. 10, 1996). DOMA had previously passed the House of Representatives by a vote of 342-67. 142 Cong. Rec. H7505 (daily ed. July 12, 1996). DOMA defines marriage for federal law purposes as the union of one man and one woman, and allows the states to refuse recognition of same-sex marriages celebrated in other states. 1 U.S.C. §7 (2000); 28 U.S.C. §1738C (2000).

40. See *Hicks,* 928 F. 2d at 173. Also, the outrages that gave rise to the University of Michigan racial hate speech regulation were referred to as "isolated and purposeless acts." *Doe v. University of Michigan,* 721 F. Supp. 852, 854 (E.D. Mich. 1989). Similarly, after the massacre of fourteen women at the Ecole Polytechnique in Montreal on December 6, 1989, the mainstream press consistently portrayed it as a an anomalous and meaningless act, in spite of the facts that the killer asked men to leave the room before shooting and left a letter expressing his rage at feminists, listing the names of eighteen specific targets. See Louise Malette and Marie Calouh, eds., *The Montreal Massacre,* Marlene Wildeman, trans. (Charlottetown, P.E.I.: Gynergy Press, 1991).

41. The "pornography civil rights ordinance" is that authored by Andrea Dworkin and Catharine MacKinnon, passed in three U.S. cities but halted in its progress by the decision of the Seventh Circuit in *American Booksellers Association v. Hudnut,* 771 F. 2d 323 (7th Cir. 1985), *aff'd mem.,* 475 U.S. 1001 (1986).

42. For my analysis of how this syndrome demoralizes lawyers to keep them out of the arena of progressive politics, see Ann Scales, "Midnight Train to Us," 75 *Cornell Law Review* 710 (1990).

43. Though abortion is still a legal right, fewer and fewer women have actual access to the procedure. See Ann Scales with Wendy Chavkin, M.D., "Abortion, Law and Public Health," in Kary L. Moss, ed., *Man-Made Medicine: Women's Health, Public Policy, and Reform* (Durham: Duke University Press, 1996).

44. See Karen Barth Menzies, "A Cure Worse Than The Disease," 41 *Trial* 20 (March 2005).

45. See for example *Miller v. Pfizer Inc.,* 196 F. Supp. 2d 1095 (D. Kan. 2002) (in addition to other failures of causal proof, plaintiff failed to present sufficient epidemiological evidence).

46. In the case thought to have inaugurated the regime of strict liability for

injuries caused by faulty products, Justice Roger Traynor of the California Supreme Court stated:

> As handicrafts have been replaced by mass production with its great markets and transportation facilities, the close relationship between the producer and the consumer of a product has been altered. Manufacturing processes, frequently valuable secrets, are ordinarily either inaccessible to or beyond the ken of the general public. The consumer no longer has means or skill enough to investigate for himself the soundness of a product, even when it is not contained in a sealed package, and his erstwhile vigilance has been lulled by the steady efforts of manufacturers to build up consumer confidence by advertising and marketing devices such as trade-marks. . . .

Escola v. Coca Cola Bottling Co. of Fresno, 150 P. 2d 436, 467 (Traynor, J. concurring).

47. On the issue of legal cause, the most familiar burden-shifting occasions are those regarding "alternative liability," as exemplified by *Summers v. Tice,* 199 P.2d 1 (Cal. 1948),and "market share liability" as exemplified by *Sindell v. Abbott Laboratories,* 607 P.2d 924 (Cal. 1980). In torts, the doctrines of *negligence per se* and *res ipsa loquitur* shift the burden in slightly different ways than the explicit causal burden-shifting doctrines do. In any case, all of these judge-created doctrines have worked pretty well; I see nothing to prevent courts from developing other burden-shifting doctrines in order in order more fairly to configure the causal problem in toxic torts cases.

48. There is disagreement about whether the common law can compensate in situations where the "but for" test of causation is not technically satisfied. One problem is that of future harms, involving whether plaintiffs can at present recover anything, sometimes including damages for the fear of disease, for damages that they believe they will suffer because of a toxic exposure. Ordinarily, plaintiffs cannot recover for the fear alone, *Good Fund, Ltd.-1972 v. Church,* 540 F. Supp. 510 (D.Colo. 1982), *rev'd in part* 703 F.2d 464 (10th Cir. 1982), but a number of courts have begun to allow plaintiffs the costs of medical monitoring in order to discover the onset of any eventual disease. See *In Re Paoli R. Yard PCB Litigation,* 916 F.2d 829 (3d Cir. 1990). The other problem area is the "lost chance" doctrine, usually malpractice cases where a misdiagnosis reduced the chance of an already slim chance of recovery. See *Lord v. Lovett,* 770 A. 2d 1103 (N.H. 2001). In such cases, the emerging norm is "odds-based partial recovery." That was the remedy in the DES cases, as well, where the problem of the impossibility of causal proof—proof that tied any given manufacturer to any given plaintiff's damages—was solved by allowing a given plaintiff to recover from each named defendant the percentage of that plaintiff's damages attributable to the share of a given defendant's share of the relevant market at the relevant time. That doctrine of "market share liability" has been

applied by only a few courts and to only a few other products: mineral spirits, the gasoline additive MTBE, diphtheria-pertussis-tetanus (DPT) vaccine, blood clotting proteins, lead paint, and asbestos brake pads. For an argument that proportional liability should be expanded to include many other products, see Allen Rostron, "Beyond Market Share Liability: A Theory of Proportional Share Liability for Nonfungible Products," 52 *U.C.L.A. Law Review* 151 (2004).

49. Among articles proposing burden-shifting rules or the creation of presumptions based upon failures to test or insufficient testing, see Margaret A. Berger, "Eliminating General Causation: Notes Toward a New Theory of Justice and Toxic Torts," 97 *Columbia Law Review* 2117 (1997); Wendy E. Wagner, "Choosing Ignorance in the Manufacture of Toxic Products," 82 *Cornell Law Review* 773 (1997); Rebecca S. Dresser, Wendy E. Wagner, and Paul C. Giannelli, "Breast Implants Revisited: Beyond Science on Trial," 1997 *Wisconsin Law Review* 705 (1997).

50. Joseph Sanders, "The Bendectin Litigation: A Case Study in the Life Cycle of Mass Torts," 43 *Hastings Law Journal* 301 (1992).

NOTES TO CHAPTER 7

1. *Daily Mirror* (London), November 4, 2004, MGN, Ltd. (emphasis in original), http://www.mirror.co.uk/news/allnews/page.cfm?objectid=14835905&method=full&siteid=50143.

2. Randal C. Archibold, "Shift Toward Skepticism for Civil Rights Panel," *New York Times,* December 10, 2004, quoting Gerald A. Reynolds, named by President George W. Bush as Chairman of the United States Civil Rights Commission.

3. Joan Williams, "From Difference to Dominance to Domesticity: Care as Work, Gender as Tradition," 76 *Chicago-Kent Law Review* 1441, 1470–71 (2001). I do not mean unfairly to single out Professor Williams. The voluntarism she assumes, though I regard it as naïve, enjoys a long and distinguished history in U.S. thought. See Aileen S. Kraditor, *The Radical Persuasion, 1890–1917: Aspects of the Intellectual History and the Historiography of Three American Radical Organizations* (Baton Rouge: Louisiana State University Press, 1981), at 66–71, 88–90 (rejecting notion of false consciousness, stressing segmented nature of American society).

4. "For all of his quite moving anecdotalizing about his own history, Thomas . . . effectively supplants a larger common history with individualized hypotheses about free choice, in which each self chooses her destiny even if it is destitution." Patricia J. Williams, "Clarence X," in *The Rooster's Egg: On the Persistence of Prejudice* (Cambridge: Harvard University Press, 1995), at 131.

5. Kate Millett, *Sexual Politics* (Garden City, New York: Doubleday Books,

1970), at 26: "Hannah Arendt observed that government is upheld by power support whether through consent or imposed through violence; conditioning to an ideology amounts to the former. Sexual politics obtains consent through the 'socialization' of both sexes to basic patriarchal polities with regard to temperament, role, and status."

6. Among other defects in the liberal view is the assumption that equality among individuals already exists, so that choice is equally a possibility for everybody. The other major flaw is that we are "rational" in our choices. "Rational choice theory" is the name by which law and economics scholars explain way too much. It is a model that takes the market as an aspect of nature, and that does not imagine the currents of self-doubt, ambivalence, oppression, confusion, and psychic need that batter us against the rocks of life. Rational choice theory is not a particularly good account of the behavior of either individuals or most groups. "Even granting a measure of rationality, what looks like the pursuit of self-interest may only make a virtue of necessity." T. J. Jackson Lears, "The Concept of Cultural Hegemony: Problems and Possibilities," *American Historical Review*, vol. 90, Is. 3 (June 1985), 567, at 580.

7. See Erika Sussman, "Contending with Culture: An Analysis of the Female Genital Mutilation Act of 1996," 31 *Cornell International Law Journal* 193, 212 n. 127 (1998): "[R]adical feminist scholars such as Catharine MacKinnon argue that subjugated women's failure to recognize their oppression is merely a function of their own ignorance."

8. Catharine A. MacKinnon, *Toward a Feminist Theory of the State* (Cambridge: Harvard University Press, 1989), at 115–17.

9. Friedrich Engels, Letter to Franz Mehring, July 14, 1893, in Robert C. Tucker, *The Marx-Engels Reader* (New York: Harper, 1972), at 648–50: "Ideology is a process accomplished by the so-called thinker, but with a false consciousness. The real motive forces impelling him remain unknown to him; otherwise it simply would not be an ideological process."

10. Clinton Rossiter and James Lare, eds., *The Essential Lippmann: A Political Philosophy for Liberal Democracy* (Cambridge: Harvard University Press, 1982) (1963); Edward L. Bernays, ed., *The Engineering of Consent* (Norman: University of Oklahoma Press, 1955); Harold D. Lasswell, *The Analysis of Political Behaviour* (Hamden, Conn.: Archon Books, 1966).

11. Thomas Frank, *What's the Matter with Kansas? How Conservatives Won the Heart of America* (New York: Metropolitan Books, 2004), at 1–2: "This species of derangement is the bedrock of our civic order; it is the foundation on which all else rests."

12. It does work. John T. Jost, "Negative Illusions: Conceptual Clarification and Psychological Evidence Concerning False Consciousness," *Political Psychology*, vol. 16, no. 2, 1995, at 397.

13. In disciplines from Marxism to postcolonial theory, the mechanisms of

ideology consistently are described as including false belief in the naturalness (versus social construction) of the social order, the necessity (as opposed to contingency) of the social order, the universality (as opposed to partiality) of the social order, and the superiority of the values embraced by the social order, including beliefs on the part of the oppressed that they deserve to be oppressed.

14. Habermas stressed the failure of particular widely held beliefs to withstand intense "intersubjective" discussion. Jürgen Habermas, *Knowledge and Human Interests,* Jeremy J. Shapiro, trans. (Boston: Beacon Press, 1971).

15. Gramsci went on to say that "this consent is 'historically' caused by the prestige (and consequent confidence) which the dominant group enjoys because of its position and function in the world of production." Antonio Gramsci, *Selections from the Prison Notebooks,* Quentin Hoare and Geoffrey Nowell Smith, eds. and trans. (New York: International Publishers, 1971), at 12.

16. The person in the mass has a contradictory consciousness, one that unites him with his fellows in interest, and another that he has inherited from his past and that he uncritically absorbs. Neither is necessarily conscious, but the contradiction tends a person to political passivity. Lears, note 6, at 570.

17. Michael Hardt and Antonio Negri, *Empire* (Cambridge: Harvard University Press, 2000), at 33.

18. Noam Chomsky, "The Manufacture of Consent" (1984), in *The Chomsky Reader,* James Peck, ed. (New York: Pantheon Books, 1987), at 132.

19. Hardt and Negri, note 17, at 16–17. An excellent recent analysis by a legal scholar of the role of exceptionalism in legal justification is Kim Lane Sheppele, "Law in a Time of Emergency: States of Exception and the Temptations of 9/11," 6 *University of Pennsylvania Journal of Constitutional Law* 1001 (2004).

20. Hardt and Negri, note 17, at 189.

21. Chomsky, note 18, at 126.

22. Adrienne Rich, "Forward: On History, Illiteracy, Passivity, Violence, and Women's Culture," in *On Lies, Secrets and Silence: Selected Prose, 1966–1978* (New York: W. W. Norton, 1979), at 11.

23. Denise Myerson, *False Consciousness* (New York: Oxford University Press, 1991), at 34.

24. *Pretty Woman,* Garry Marshall, dir. (1990). Jane Caputi's analysis of that movie compares it with Julia Roberts's next movie, wherein she was stalked by her battering husband. See Jane Caputi, "Sleeping with the Enemy as Pretty Woman Part II?" in *Goddess and Monsters: Women, Myth, Power and Popular Culture* (Madison: University of Wisconsin/Popular Press, 2004), at 37 (describing the two films as portraits of successive phases in the same abusive relationship).

25. Lears, note 6, at 573.

26. MacKinnon, *Toward a Feminist Theory of the State,* note 8, at 115.

27. Postmodern philosophy expands upon this critique of ideology by "problematizing" the subject, that is, by emphasizing the fluidity (if not incoherence) of the notion of a self that can have any interests, true or false. In addition, the postmodern critique—particularly in the work of Foucault—emphasizes the spiraling relationship between truth and power. They produce and sustain each other, so that questions of truth are always political questions and vice versa. Michel Foucault, *Power/Knowledge: Selected Interviews and Other Writings, 1972–1977,* Colin Gordon, ed. and trans. (New York: Pantheon Books, 1980), at 85.

28. David Brooks, "The Triumph of Hope Over Self-Interest," *New York Times,* January 12, 2003.

29. Indeed, there is a residue of Cold War mentality infusing debates about false consciousness, particularly because the notion emerged from classical Marxism. A critique of the objective point of view implicit in the false consciousness charge is even easier to sustain against the determinism of Marxist thought. That is, Marx and those strictly in the Marxist tradition, such as Antonio Gramsci, believed in materialism as the basis of society, and believed that history was inexorably moving toward the workers' revolution.

30. Herbert Marcuse, *One-Dimensional Man: Studies in the Ideology of Advanced Industrial Society* (Boston: Beacon Press, 1966) (1964), at 5–6.

31. J. C. Smith and Carla Ferstman, *The Castration of Oedipus: Feminism, Psychoanalysis, and the Will to Power* (New York: New York University Press, 1996).

32. For Marx, while the oppressed workers were caught up in the illusions of a certain stage of capitalism, their self-consciousness could not fully develop. Thus, only when capitalism had reached a certain stage of contradiction, only when conditions were ripe, could the people break free. In any case, the proletariat had to change itself and its circumstances rather than being changed by hierarchical leadership. See *The Marx-Engels Reader,* note 9, at 108. Among the conundrums of the Russian Revolution was that Russian capitalism was underdeveloped from a Marxist point of view. The Russian proletariat was just emerging, and ostensibly required leadership to develop its consciousness.

33. According to Sandra Lee Bartky, the "achievement" of femininity is to "inferiorize" oneself in various ways, including to mark one's own body as something to be looked at by men, and to embrace one side of a polarity knowing that it is the devalued side. Sandra Lee Bartky, *Femininity and Domination: Studies in the Phenomenology of Oppression* (New York: Routledge, 1990).

34. "From this identification [with their men] follows the belief of women born of, or married (legally or not) to bourgeois men that they are themselves 'bourgeois.' This is false consciousness. They do not participate in the privileges of their men's class, whatever they may think." Christine Delphy, *Close to*

Home: A Materialist Analysis of Women's Oppression, Diana Leonard, ed. and trans. (London: Hutchinson/Explorations in Feminism Collective, 1984), at 129–130.

35. Liz Stanley and Sue Wise, *Breaking Out: Feminist Consciousness and Feminist Research* (London, Boston: Routledge and K. Paul, 1983), at 119–20.

36. See Williams, note 3, at 1470–71 (citation omitted):

> [G]ender is not just a power differential between men and women. In fact, gender plays diverse roles in creating meaning in people's lives. . . . Gender provides rich cultural imagery most people find a convenient metaphoric. Gender is one of the 'metaphors we live by'; it can carry so many loads of cultural meaning that the prospect of persuading people to abandon it seems slim indeed. . . . Gender is unbending not only because of its infinite availability as a metaphor but because it intertwines gender roles with attractive ideals, as when domesticity links the economic and social marginalization of mothers with mothers' dreams for their children.

37. Chomsky, note 18, at 136. See also Hardt and Negri, note 17, at 156: "Truth will not make us free, but taking control of the production of truth will."

38. Alice Walker, *Possessing the Secret of Joy* (New York: Pocket Books, 1992), at 279.

NOTES TO CHAPTER 8

1. The Citadel, a military institution in South Carolina akin to the Virginia Military Institute, was also judicially compelled to admit female cadets. *Faulker v. Jones,* 51 F. 3d 440 (4th Cir.), cert. denied, 516 U.S. 938 (1995). Professor Valorie Vojdik, who was counsel to Ms. Faulkner in the Citadel litigation, thoroughly describes the brutal yet shrill masculinity at work in the military school controversies. Valorie J. Vojdik, "Gender Outlaws: Challenging Masculinity in Traditionally Male Institutions," 17 *Berkeley Women's Law Journal* 68 (2002); "At War: Narrative Tactics in the Citadel and VMI Litigation," 19 *Harvard Women's Law Journal* 1 (1996). In a scathing account of the culture of the Citadel, Susan Faludi describes "a submerged gender battle, a bitter but definitely fixed context between the sexes, concealed from view by the fact that men played both parts." Susan Faludi, "The Naked Citadel," *New Yorker* (September 5, 1994), at 70. Pat Conroy wrote an absorbing fictionalized account of his Citadel education. In one passage, he said:

> The entire design of our education . . . demanded a limitless conformity from its sons, and we concurred blindly. We spent our four years as passionate true believers, catechists of our harsh and spiritually arctic milieu, studying, drilling, arguing in the barracks, cleaning our rooms, shining our shoes, writing on the latrine walls, writing papers, breaking down our

> rifles, and missing the point. The Institute was making us stupid; irretrievably, tragically, and infinitely stupid.

Pat Conroy, *The Lords of Discipline* (Boston: Houghton Mifflin, 1980) (Bantam ed., 1982), at 80–81. This quote speaks to me not only of the depleting effects of militarism but of popular culture and most educational systems.

2. *United States v. Virginia,* 518 U.S. 515 (1996) (Virginia Military Institute ordered to admit females as cadets).

3. *J.E.B. v. Alabama ex rel. T.B.,* 511 U.S. 127 (1994) (exclusion of jurors on basis of sex violates Equal Protection clause). *J.E.B.* cited *Batson v. Kentucky,* 476 U.S. 79 (1986), the case in which an African-American defendant charged with burglary and receipt of stolen goods successfully challenged the peremptory exclusion of all African-Americans from the jury.

4. 511 U.S. at 149 (O'Connor, concurring).

5. The phrase is the title of the generative work on this issue. Judith Butler, *Gender Trouble: Feminism and the Subversion of Identity* (New York: Routledge, 1990).

6. Id. at 3.

7. 523 U.S. 75 (1998) (allowing same-sex sexual harassment claim to proceed).

8. For one of the published versions of this argument, see Janet Halley, "Sexuality Harassment," in Catharine A. MacKinnon and Reva B. Siegel, eds., *Directions in Sexual Harassment Law* (New Haven: Yale University Press, 2004), at 183.

9. A gem in this genre is the case in which a child's father who claimed that the mother had practiced contraceptive fraud brought a claim against her for, among other things, conversion of his sperm. *Wallis v. Smith,* 22 P. 3d, 683, 683 (N.M. App. 2001) (dismissing all of the father's claims).

10. Marc Spindelman, "Sex Equality Panic," 13 *Columbia Journal of Gender and Law* 1 (2004).

11. Referring specifically to how she imagines "cultural feminism" would respond to a specific vignette in the Hill-Thomas hearings, Professor Halley states: "It thinks that a man who would joke to a female subordinate at work about pubic hairs appearing on his Coke can has shown himself unfit for high office. It's easily offended; it is schoolmarmish, judgmental, self-righteous." Janet Halley, "Sexuality Harassment," in Wendy Brown and Janet Halley, eds., *Left Legalism and Left Critique* (Durham: Duke University Press, 2002), at 89.

12.

> Halley's normative enthusiasm for the pleasures of sexual hierarchy risks making it seem that the sexual subordination forced upon members of these groups is the product of our own unwillingness to pursue the hierarchical pleasures we should. From this it's a small step to claiming that our social subordination is a matter of our own choosing.

Marc Spindelman, "Discriminating Pleasures," in *Directions in Sexual Harassment Law,* note 8 at 211.

13. Ms. Jespersen said that wearing the makeup made her feel "sick, degraded, exposed and violated." She said that the casino was forcing her to be feminine, and to become a sexual object, and that this interfered with her job performance. As a bartender, she said, she had to deal with unruly, intoxicated guests, and the makeup "took away [her] credibility as an individual and as a person." *Jespersen v. Harrah's Operating Company, Inc.,* 392 F.3d 1076, 1077 (9th Cir. 2004), rehearing en banc granted, 409 F.3d 1061 (9th Cir. 2005).

14. 392 F.3d at 1077 (emphasis added).

15. *Rene v. MGM Grand Hotel, Inc.,* 305 F.3d 1061 (9th Cir. 2002) (en banc); *Nicholas v. Azteca Restaurant Entertainment, Inc.,* 256 F.3d 864 (9th Cir. 2001).

16. 490 U.S. 228 (1989).

17. Whereas it is difficult for judges to imagine how it could be unlawful for men to dictate how *women* look, the same judges understand the injury in the *Rene* and *Nichols* cases. Consider this thought experiment: if all members of Congress had to conform for a day with the standards Harrah's imposed on male servers—short haircuts, trimmed fingernails, no makeup, and no colored nail polish—I suspect Hillary Clinton and Cynthia McKinney and company could hang with it. However, never in my lifetime would every member of Congress (publicly) wear stockings, mascara, blush, and colored lipstick (though many already wear their hair "teased, curled, or styled"). The male members just don't want other people to perceive them as girls. Hence, the epigraph from Professor Rorty at the beginning of this chapter. Richard Rorty, "Feminism and Pragmatism," 30 *Michigan Quarterly Review* 231, 234 (1992).

18. 392 F. 3d at 1086.

19. The problem of grooming doctrine is illustrated by the panel's reasoning in *Jespersen.* The majority upheld the trial court's grant of summary judgment to Harrah's on the grounds that Ms. Jespersen had not shown that the Personal Best brand standard either discriminated against her on the basis of "immutable characteristics" associated with her sex or that the Personal Best brand standard had imposed unequal burdens on men and women in Harrah's employ. On the first ground, the majority opinion capitulates to an unexamined notion of equality, that equality means only freedom from disadvantage based upon immutable characteristics. Thus, while one's biological sex is *prima facie* immutable, how one wears one's hair or paints one's face is always subject to change, hence, not part of what Congress was getting at in prohibiting employment discrimination "because of sex." On the second ground, the court indicated that the plaintiff might have gotten to trial had she produced evidence of a sufficient differential cost of makeup for females, as opposed to neat haircuts for males. 392 F. 3d at 1081. The grooming cases and the nest of related issues—stereotyping, identity

politics, subordination, and self-determination—are usefully treated in a collection of essays by Robert C. Post, with K. Anthony Appiah, Judith Butler, Thomas C. Grey, and Reva B. Siegel, *Prejudicial Appearances: The Logic of American Antidiscrimination Law* (Durham: Duke University Press, 2001).

20. Professor MacKinnon made this point in various ways in her *amicus* brief in *Oncale,* published at 8 *U.C.L.A. Women's Law Journal* 9 (1997), a text I often assign my students as an exemplar of how theory meets practice. The Court's opinion in *Oncale* was actually pretty low-key and authored by noted homophobe Justice Scalia. Perhaps the closest the Court came to embracing MacKinnon's position was in stating:

> [H]arassing conduct need not be motivated by sexual desire to support an inference of discrimination on the basis of sex. A trier of fact might reasonably find such discrimination, for example, if a female victim is harassed in such sex-specific and derogatory terms by another woman as to make it clear that the harasser is motivated by general hostility to the presence of women in the workplace.

523 U.S. at 80. I believe this is much like saying, Title VII is violated when anyone in the workplace interferes with other workers by attempting to enforce gender hegemony, a result I think most queer theorists would applaud.

21. Butler, *Gender Trouble,* note 5 at viii.

22. N.M.S.A. 1978, § 28-1-2 (Q). Concomitantly, " 'sexual orientation' means heterosexuality, homosexuality or bisexuality, whether actual or perceived." N.M.S.A. 1978, § 28-1-2 (P). New Mexico became the fourteenth state to prohibit sexual orientation discrimination in housing, employment, credit, etc., and only the third state to prohibit gender identity discrimination in the same contexts.

23. That is, some legislators asked why they shouldn't just rewrite the human rights law to say "you can't unfairly discriminate"? I viewed this question as a manifestation of privileged ignorance. Each of the categories in antidiscrimination laws, including New Mexico's, refers to a demonstrable history of mistreatment of people based upon their membership in one or more of the enumerated groups. Addressing the history is more important than the fact that the groups can't always be precisely defined. On the other hand, particularly here in the United States, we are dreadfully hung up on the list of categories. But that needn't be so, as demonstrated, for example, in Canadian law. As explained in chapter 4, Canadian law enumerates the predictable historical categories, but explicitly recognizes that those group categorizations are not all there is to unfair discrimination. And Canada does this in a way that engages in the interplay of legal fixity and cultural fluidity. Particularly in comparison with U.S. judges, the Canadian judges seem fearless. See Sarah K. Harding, "Comparative Reasoning and Judicial Review," 28 *Yale Journal of International Law* 409 (2003).

24. Though there is no record of these conversations with legislators, they were reminiscent of some "hypothetical" questions raised by a doctor in Louisville, Kentucky, who brought a declaratory judgment action on many constitutional grounds in a losing effort to preclude enforcement of that city's and county's similarly worded prohibitions on "gender identity" discrimination: "What is meant by 'manifesting,' 'identity' 'traditionally associated,' and 'biological maleness or femaleness,' is simply impossible to tell from the face of either Ordinance. Does manifesting mean pretending? Does identity mean an identity at any time, a permanent identity, or a temporary identity?" Plaintiff's Motion for Summary Judgment in *Hyman v. City of Louisville,* 132 F. Supp. 2d 528, 546 (W.D. Ky. 2001).

25. *Hispanic AIDS Forum v. Estate of Bruno,* 792 N.Y.S.2d 43, 47 (App. Div. 2005) (interpreting New York City Human Rights Law that included in definition of "gender" a person's behavior whether or not consistent with birth sex); see also *Goins v. West Group,* 635 N.W.2d 717 (Minn. 2001) (same result under state prohibition); but see *Kastl v. Maricopa County Community College District,* 2004 WL 2008954 (D. Ariz. 2004) (federal sex discrimination claim stated against a policy requiring transsexual to prove completion of sex reassignment surgery before allowing her to use women's restroom).

26. *Kastl,* 2004 WL 2008954, at 3.

27. To date, most transgender and intersex cases have been disability cases. These are matters involving medical funding for the costs of Gender Identity Disorder and/or for the costs of transition from male-to-female or vice versa. Another class of cases is about the protection of the confidentiality of transsexuals. An example of the latter class of cases is *Powell v. Schriver,* 175 F.3d 107, 111–12 (2d Cir. 1999) (citations omitted), a case upholding the right of a male-to-female transsexual, incarcerated in a women's prison, not to have her transsexual status disclosed. As the court stated:

> Individuals who have chosen to abandon one gender in favor of another understandably might desire to conduct their affairs as if such a transition was never necessary. . . . The excrutiatingly private and intimate nature of transsexualism, for persons who wish to preserve privacy in the matter, is really beyond debate. . . . [Another case describes] transsexualism as "a gender identity disorder, the sufferers of which believe that they are 'cruelly imprisoned within a body incompatible with their real gender identity,' " and noting that "[t]he disorder is commonly accompanied by a desire to change one's anatomic sexual features to conform physically with one's perception of self. . . ." It is similarly obvious that an individual who reveals that she is a transsexual "potentially exposes herself . . . to discrimination and intolerance."

The question for queer politics/law is how to reconcile what the court calls the "excruciatingly private" nature of transsexualism with the injunction toward a political program of repetitive and public subversion, "proliferating gender configurations [and] destabilizing substantive identity," demonstrating that gender is "open to splittings, self-parody, self-criticism, and those hyperbolic exhibitions of 'the natural' that, in their very exaggeration, reveal its fundamentally phantasmatic status." Butler, *Gender Trouble,* note 5 at 146.

28. *Geduldig v. Aiello,* 417 U.S. 484 (1974) (state workers' disability program that excluded coverage for pregnancy did not constitute sex discrimination). Professor Wendy Williams was counsel for the plaintiffs in this historic case.

29. Butler, *Gender Trouble,* note 5 at 148 (emphasis added).

30. Judith Butler, "The Force of Fantasy: Feminism, Mapplethorpe, and Discursive Excess," in Drucilla Cornell, ed., *Feminism and Pornography* (New York: Oxford University Press, 2000), at 504.

31. *See* comment of Professor Vicki Schultz in Karen Engle, Elizabeth M. Schneider, Vicki Schultz, Nathaniel Berman, Adrienne Davis, and Janet Halley, "Round Table Discussion: Subversive Legal Moments?" 12 *Texas Journal of Women and Law* 197, 203 (2003):

> [T]he formal law itself, in the sense of a Supreme Court decision, cannot be 'subversive.' Law in this sense cannot be anything, really, on its own. But law is an important arena of struggle in our society, one in which the social movements of the twentieth century have invested a great deal of energy.

32. Although most lawyers wouldn't use Judith Butler's language, many would agree with her assertion that "the constitutive identifications of an autobiographical narrative are always already partially fabricated in the telling." Butler, *Gender Trouble,* note 5 at 67.

33. Id. at 47.

34.

> The assimilation/resistance opposition is often critiqued as overly simplistic, a criticism applicable to most dichotomies. . . . When the issue is simply stated, it often involves pie: whether the object of our struggles is obtaining a (bigger) piece of the pie or whether we are challenging the way the pie is cut, who has the power to cut it, or even the entire notion of "pie."

Ruthann Robson, "Introduction: Assimilation and/or Resistance?" 1 *Seattle Journal for Social Justice* 631 (2003) (citation omitted).

35. Angela P. Harris, "Race and Essentialism in Feminist Theory," 42 *Stanford Law Review* 581 (1990).

36. Id. at 582.

37. Id. at 581, quoting Jorge Luis Borges, "Funes the Memorious," in *Labyrinths: Selected Stories and Other Writings* (Daniel A. Yates and James E. Irby, eds.) (New York: Modern Library, 1983) (1964), at 59.

38. See, for example, Cass R. Sunstein and Martha C. Nussbaum, eds., *Animal Rights: Current Debates and New Directions* (New York: Oxford University Press, 2004).

39. Judith Butler, *Undoing Gender* (New York: Routledge, 2004), at 8–16 (endorsing the pursuit of equality in "livable lives"). Some poststructuralist theorists seem to incorporate philosopher Friedrich Nietzsche's conclusion that altruism is a self-delusory and/or self-aggrandizing affliction. See Professor Halley's remarks in *Round Table Discussion,* note 31, at 225–28, 242 (invoking feminism's "will to power").

40. See remarks of Professor Halley, id. at 225.

41. See for example, Ruthann Robson, *Lesbian (Out)Law: Surviving Under the Rule of Law* (Ithaca: Firebrand Books, 1992); Ruthann Robson, "Assimilation, Marriage, and Lesbian Liberation," 75 *Temple Law Review* 709 (2002).

42. *Maher v. Roe,* 432 U.S. 464, 479 n. 11 (1977) (upholding restrictions on use of public funds for nontherapeutic abortions). See also *Harris v. McRae,* 448 U.S. 297 (upholding restrictions on use of public funds even for therapeutic abortions).

43. The Defense of Marriage Act "is rationally related to the legitimate government interest of encouraging procreation, or of encouraging the creation of stable relationships that facilitate rearing children by both biological parents. . . . Because procreation is necessary to perpetuate humankind, encouraging the optimal union for procreation is a legitimate government interest." *Smelt v. County of Orange,* 374 F. Supp. 2d 861, 879 (C.D. Cal. 2005) (citations omitted) (abstaining from question of constitutionality of state one man/one woman marriage statute, but upholding constitutionality of federal one man/one woman definition of marriage).

44. In the case that upheld the Florida statute that prohibits adoption by homosexuals, the United States Court of Appeals for the Eleventh Circuit relied not only on the rationale that stability for children can be best provided by an opposite-sex couple but also on the "vital role that dual-gender parenting plays in shaping sexual and gender identity and in providing heterosexual role modeling." *Lofton v. Sec. of Dep't of Children & Family Services,* 358 F. 3d 804, 818–19 (11th Cir. 2004), rehearing en banc denied, 377 F. 3d 1275 (11th Cir. 2004), cert. denied 125 S. Ct. 869 (2005).

45. *Lawrence v. Texas,* 539 U.S. 558 (2003) (right of privacy extends to private consensual homosexual activity), overruling *Bowers v. Hardwick,* 478 U.S. 186, 194 (1986) (claim of constitutional right to engage in homosexual sex is "at best, facetious").

46. Lynn Barnhill, "Gentlemen Prefer Fetuses," final paper in Feminist Jurisprudence seminar, University of New Mexico Law School, 1991.

47. See *Stenberg v. Carhart,* 530 U.S. 914 (2000) (invalidating state prohibi-

tion on specific abortion practices due to lack of exception for saving life of the mother).

48. *Webster v. Reproductive Health Services,* 492 U.S. 490, 560 (1989) (Blackmun, J., concurring in part and dissenting in part).

49. Linda Greenhouse, *Becoming Justice Blackmun: Harry Blackmun's Supreme Court Journey* (New York: Times Books, 2005), at 207.

50. Id. at 209.

51. Id. at 221–25.

52. Rorty, "Feminism and Pragmatism," note 17 at 237, n. 17.

Index

About the Author

Ann Scales is a lawyer, teacher, and feminist activist. Having taught law for twenty-five years, she is at present an associate professor at the University of Denver College of Law. She is a founding contributor to the field known as feminist jurisprudence.